Health Tourism

Also by David Reisman

Adam Smith's Sociological Economics
Alfred Marshall: Progress and Politics
Alfred Marshall's Mission
Anthony Crosland: The Mixed Economy
Conservative Capitalism: The Social Economy
Crosland's Future: Opportunity and Outcome
Democracy and Exchange: Schumpeter, Galbraith, T.H. Marshall, Titmuss and
    Adam Smith
The Economics of Alfred Marshall
Galbraith and Market Capitalism
Health Care and Public Policy
The Institutional Economy: Demand and Supply
Market and Health
The Political Economy of Health Care
The Political Economy of James Buchanan
Richard Titmuss: Welfare and Society
Schumpeter's Market: Enterprise and Evolution
Social Policy in an Ageing Society: Age and Health in Singapore
State and Welfare: Tawney, Galbraith and Adam Smith
Theories of Collective Action: Downs, Olson and Hirsch

Health Tourism
Social Welfare through International Trade

David Reisman

Edward Elgar
Cheltenham, UK • Northampton, MA, USA

Published by
Edward Elgar Publishing Limited
The Lypiatts
15 Lansdown Road
Cheltenham
Glos GL50 2JA
UK

Edward Elgar Publishing, Inc.
William Pratt House
9 Dewey Court
Northampton
Massachusetts 01060
USA

A catalogue record for this book
is available from the British Library

Library of Congress Control Number: 2009940748

Mixed Sources
Product group from well-managed
forests and other controlled sources
www.fsc.org Cert no. SA-COC-1565
© 1996 Forest Stewardship Council

FSC

ISBN 978 1 84844 892 6

Printed and bound by MPG Books Group, UK

Contents

1. Introduction

Health tourism is old. Just as people have always wanted to travel to visit the wonders of the world, so people have long wanted to take the waters at a spa, be seen by a Harley Street specialist, go as a pilgrim to a holy place because the spirits there could soothe and heal. Even the ancient Greeks went to Epidauria because of the health-giving god Asklepios. Even the ancient Romans went to thermal baths because warm water is good for the joints. What is new is not the phenomenon but the magnitude. It is not just the elite but the middle classes who are actively involved in the international trade of a service that can make them feel well. Minority health tourism is old. Mass health tourism is, however, the creature of modernity and *embourgeoisement*.

The convention is to say health tourism. It would be better to say something else. Health is not the same as medicine: what most patients are going abroad to consume is not organic vegetables or an hour in the gym but the attention of skilled doctors and nurses. Tourism is not the same as travel: the patient who buys hernia repair in the open market is not shopping for a pleasurable holiday in the sun. It would be better to say treatment abroad, medical travel, global health care or international patient business rather than health tourism which is emotive and journalistic. Yet the phrase is there. The websites, the search engines, the travel agents and the media all recognise health tourism. They are less receptive to a term like global medical care. Global medical care is the same thing but packaged in grey.

This book is about cross-border care. It is concerned with the improvement in felt well-being that results when the consumers and the producers take advantage of the world economy to demand and supply not just medical equipment but medical attention as well. Britain and Portugal were exchanging wine for textiles even before the classical free marketeers informed a post-mercantilist world that it would be a waste of scarce resources to grow grapes in Scotland or produce decent woollens in the Algarve. This book shows that even intangible personal services like rhinoplasties and hernia repairs are susceptible to the same gains from trade that the economists have validated and found to be good.

The book is divided into ten chapters. Chapter 2, 'A taxonomy of trade',

defines the nature of transnational treatment. It explains the four key
modes in which the service is delivered. Chapter 3, 'Price', shows that elective care abroad will often be cheaper than the same medical intervention
if consumed at home. Chapter 4, 'Quality', argues that the standard of
service can be the same or even higher abroad and that the medical experience can be a satisfactory one. Chapter 5, 'Differentiation', demonstrates
that foreign treatment need not be a cut-price replica of a standard size.
Foreigners eat garlic. Garlic is only one of the many ways in which Over
There is different from Us.

Chapters 3, 4 and 5 are about the individual. Chapters 6, 7 and 8 are
about the nation. Chapter 6, 'Health tourism: the benefits', shows that
both the importing and the exporting countries are better off in the hard
currency of services, jobs and growth. Chapter 7, 'Health tourism: the
costs', concedes that both the importing and the exporting countries can
lose out where a deficiency shunted abroad is never corrected or where the
villages are drained of doctors because the real money is in the lucrative
top end. Chapters 6 and 7 do not give a clean bill of health. That is why
they look forward to Chapter 8. Chapter 8, 'Health tourism and public
policy', says that the State should correct a market failure. It does not say
that the State should kill the golden goose.

Chapters 9 and 10 discuss the real-world experience of countries such
as Singapore, Dubai, India, Malaysia and Thailand. The case-studies
show what can be done. They confirm the intuition that the world is flat.
Nigerians spend over US$1 billion on medical attention outside their own
country. Latin Americans spend US$6 billion. Tiny Costa Rica receives
150,000 medical tourists a year. About 90 per cent of its cosmetic procedures are performed on foreigners (Bookman and Bookman, 2008: 5).
Britons in 2007 are thought to have spent £135 million on medical treatments abroad. About 100,000 Britons in 2007 went out of country for
medical care. As many as 1.29 million are thought to have had dental treatment abroad (Deloitte Center for Health Solutions, 2009: 5). At the same
time one fifth of the hospital beds in London were occupied by foreigners.

More than 400,000 non-residents are believed to have come to the
United States for medical attention in 2008. Mainly from the Middle
East, South America and Canada, they accounted for 2 per cent of
hospital throughput and brought in US$5 billion (Deloitte Center for
Health Solutions, 2008: 19). In the same year between 500,000 to 750,000
Americans are believed to have sought treatment abroad. It is estimated
that Americans spend about US$2 billion a year on health tourism. It is
a small fraction of the US$1.5 trillion (Bies and Zacharia, 2007: 1145)
to US$2 trillion (Grail Research, 2009: 3) that they spend every year on
health care as a whole. Things will change. The rising cost and the limited

availability of care in the United States are central to the issue of health tourism.

The figure of 400,000 could be as high as 800,000 by 2017. The figure of 750,000 could be 15.7 million (Deloitte Center for Health Solutions, 2008: 4). The headcount is growing exponentially. Exports of health services worldwide doubled between 1997 and 2003. They increased worldwide ten times faster than foreign earnings from tourism and five times faster than global exports of services. Health services in 2003 accounted for 0.73 per cent of world trade. The figure had been 0.38 per cent in 1997. The market share of the developing countries in 2003 was 40 per cent (Lautier, 2008: 104).

There are approximately 4 million international patients each year. The worldwide market is worth between US$20 billion and US$40 billion (Smith et al., 2009: 595). It may be worth as much as US$60 billion. About US$7 billion of that business goes to Asia. It is believed that medical tourism already accounts for 5 per cent of total tourism worldwide. All in all, the market is huge: 'It's a $60 Billion Global Business that's growing at 20 per cent a year. . . . Whatever [you] call it, it's economics applied to healthcare for the first time in 50 years' (Bina, 2007: 48).

2. A taxonomy of trade

The World Trade Organization, created in 1994, is one of many international bodies that are favourable to barrier-free international trade. The WTO continues the work of the General Agreement on Trade and Tariffs that goes back to 1948. The WTO in its time had wrestled with the definition and status of services. A tangible consequence was the General Agreement on Trade in Services (http://gats-info.eu.int). Negotiated by 120 countries throughout the world, it was adopted by the WTO in the course of its Uruguay Round and came into force in 1995.

The GATS has provided a template (Blouin, 2006: 171–4). It has suggested that cross-border trade on invisible account can usefully be categorised into four modes or dimensions: services, patients, capital and labour. These four modes will be examined in the first four sections of this chapter. The fifth section will suggest that the first four sections only repeat what has long been known. Unrestricted multilateral exchange, sensibly managed, can result in greater efficiency, faster growth and higher living standards. It can greatly expand the freedom to choose.

In spite of that less than 40 per cent of WTO members as of 2009 had voluntarily committed themselves to opening up their health care sectors. The figure for finance, tourism and telecommunications is over 90 per cent (Smith et al., 2009: 593). Countries can liberalise without doing so under GATS. GATS affects health sovereignty since it sets down rules of its own on market access and national treatment. GATS, moreover, is legally binding and effectively irreversible. Countries, clearly, will want to be certain before they sign up to GATS. Meanwhile, there are bilateral free trade agreements (often with the United States). There are also multilateral attempts at liberalisation within the framework of regional groupings such as the EU and ASEAN. Trade in services for such groupings cannot be separated from other provisions on the movement of capital and labour.

2.1 MODE 1: DISTANCE CARE

In the case of Mode 1, the parties to the contract are situated in different countries. The service crosses the border. The patient or the provider does not.

Historically, the position was that manufactures could be shipped but that services had to be consumed face to face. The electronic revolution has necessitated a major reappraisal of the time-bound distinction between tradables and non-tradables. Information technology has radically altered the way in which the producer/exporter and the consumer/importer interact with one another across the frontiers. Communication transcends distance. Microelectronics makes the international market as local as the shop next door:

> The old assumption that if you cannot put it in a box, you cannot trade it is thus hopelessly obsolete. Because packets of digitized information play the role that boxes used to play, many more services are now tradable and many more will surely become so. In the future, and to a great extent already, the key distinction will no longer be between things that can be put in a box and things that cannot. Rather, it will be between services that can be delivered electronically and those that cannot (Blinder, 2006).

Taxi drivers and office cleaners, airplane pilots and street policemen are unlikely to be outsourced over a broadband link. Uneducated chicken-rice men and highly-trained physiotherapists both enjoy non-tariff protection against a virtual challenge. Well educated security consultants and less educated call-centre operators are more exposed. It is no longer a distinction between blue-collar and white: 'The dividing line between the jobs that produce services that are suitable for electronic delivery (and are thus threatened by offshoring) and those that do not does not correspond to traditional distinctions between high-end and low-end work' (Blinder, 2006).

The jobs migrate from high-wage to low-wage countries with little or no degradation in quality. The workers do not. Over a million service-sector jobs have been lost to outsourcing in the United States. Improvements in global communications (together with a higher level of general education in exporting countries such as India and China) suggest that it is only the start: 'We have so far barely seen the tip of the offshoring iceberg, the eventual dimensions of which may be staggering' (Blinder, 2006). The world as a whole will grow richer as a result of the new division of labour. People and countries that lose jobs will, however, have to adapt.

Outsourcing is not a synonym for offshoring. Outsourcing is happening within countries as well as between countries. 'Physical presence' (Blinder, 2006) is no longer the decisive characteristic in every case. About 60 per cent of total employment in the United States consists of jobs that must be performed near to the consumer. They are non-tradable. Yet 40 per cent are tradable, and of these more are in services than in manufacturing: 'This suggests that the current dominance of world trade by manufactures. . . . may be only temporary. In the long run, trade in serv-ices, delivered electronically, may become the most important component of world trade' (Krugman and Obstfeld, 2009: 23). Hartford, Connecticut, specialises in insurance. New York has Wall Street. It is a reminder that some regions within a country will experience more job losses than others.

Personal contact is not needed for share-dealing effected online. Offshoring and outsourcing are all around. Jensen and Kletzer, writing about the United States, calculate that 'there are more workers in tradable professional and business service industries than in tradable manufactur-ing industries' (Jensen and Kletzer, 2005: 3). They also identify the service occupations which have the largest shares of employment that may be classified as tradable. These include architecture and engineering (63 per cent), business and financial operations (68 per cent), legal services (96 per cent) and computer and mathematical occupations (100 per cent).

Occupations that are largely non-tradable, they say, are education and library services (99 per cent) and food preparation (96 per cent). Medical care, they say, is non-tradable as well. The non-tradable element in the services of health care practitioners is 86 per cent. In health care support services it is 97 per cent (ibid: 11). Face-to-face contact is the *sine qua non* for a medical examination or for residential nursing in a ward. Every building labourer knows that: 'You can't hammer a nail over the Internet' (Blinder, 2006).

One point of view is that it cannot be done. A different point of view is that it can. It is clear enough that Mode 1 would not be feasible for filling a tooth, for delivering a baby or for changing a dressing. Audio and visual excludes tactile. You can't fix up a blood transfusion on the phone. Other aspects of the medical experience are, however, more amenable to an entrepreneurial use of the information divide.

Thus credit-card bookings can be made by email. Tax returns can be processed abroad. Medical advice can be given on the telephone. On-call prescriptions can be transmitted electronically. Drugs can be shipped from a mail-order pharmacy. Rx.com and TelaDoc are in a position to trade across time and space: 'Entrepreneurs can solve many of the health care problems that critics condemn. Public policy should encourage, not discourage, these efforts' (Herrick, 2008: 2). Face-to-face is not the whole of the medical encounter.

Distance trading breaks through the checkpoints. E-databases such as Medline, Health InterNetwork and Planet Medica already pinpoint focused books, relevant papers and current statistics at low or zero cost. Hospitals create websites. Governments post advice. E-education means that a specialist lecture can be heard and a surgical technique demonstrated in a global classroom. Medical trials, success indicators and evidence-based medicine become a common possession. One consequence of diffusion and communication might be an international convergence in standards and treatments. Distance learning and sharing of know-how in that way reduce the dispersion of professional practice which is so often the cause of unnecessary expense and even death.

Mode 1 can also take the form of paperwork sent abroad. Satellite communication means that an architect can transfer plans easily and economically. The same is the case with back-office support in forms such as online ordering, online searches and online billing. The finance, accounting and human resources departments of a large hospital can be based abroad. Data entry, data storage, data analysis, transcription of histories and medical claims-processing can be farmed out to a country where labour costs less. Electronic record-keeping makes it possible to transfer files in real time. Customer inquiries can be answered by Philippine medical graduates working part-time. They will have online access to the patient's notes. They will make use of software algorithms that spotlight contraindicated drugs. Geographical location in the era of remote control is not the barrier that it was.

Mode 1, finally, can relate to the medical experience, narrowly defined. Samples can be sent abroad for telepathology. Medication can be monitored digitally through telediagnostics. Laboratory tests can be conducted far away. X-rays, CAT scans and MRI scans can be interpreted by senior professionals in different time zones across the globe. Second opinions can be sought border-free through teleconferencing or fax. Interactive audiovisuals obviate the need for time-consuming travel.

Computers facilitate the task of cost-effective surveillance. Rapid reaction can save the patient's life. Apollo Gleneagles in Kolkata provides telepathology and teleradiology to Bhutan and Nepal. It has a subsidiary centre in Kazakhstan to service the northern part of the region. Teleradiology Solutions, based in Bangalore, interprets imaging from 35 hospitals in the United States. In Latin America, based in Cuba, there is the Telemedicine Network.

Technology can bring medical services into remote and under-doctored areas. It can also diagnose and contain an infectious disease before it has had time to spread. Improvements in equipment and communications will open ever more new doors. Surgery can already be performed by remote control along a fibre-optic cable. A doctor in South India can, directing a robotic arm, already remove the gall bladder of a patient in Bulawayo. Online monitoring allows the surgeon to follow up the recovery of the patient.

Service industries tend to be labour-intensive. Productivity rises more slowly in one-to-one talking therapies and lifestyle counselling than it does in manufactures where mass production is possible: 'The theory goes a long way toward explaining why the prices of health care and college tuition have risen faster than the consumer price index for decades' (Blinder, 2006). That is the great advantage of Mode 1. Tutorial teaching, like the call centres, is already available from India. If one-to-one instruction can be outsourced to a country where the human input costs less, then the price can remain affordable, and larger groups need not crowd out smaller ones. A physics lesson with 40 children does not deliver the same learning outcomes as a physics class with 10. Centripetal outsourcing protects the quality of the service. The worldwide sub-divisions and synergies keep the cost of production down.

Mode 1 has great attractions. Yet there are real limitations as well. One of these is the nature of the interaction. Not everyone feels comfortable with psychotherapy on the screen. Not everyone is confident that a doctor abroad will pick up the cultural nuances encoded in the expression of symptoms. While cholesterol crosses the codes, sterility or abortion might not. The reply would be that consumers who prefer the in-country alternative must retain the right to choose. Some students will want to be taught by the millions in the University of the Air. Other students will prefer to be taught eyeball-to-eyeball in Brasenose or Christ Church. The productivity per hour will be higher in the former educational system than in the latter. The fees and the charges will be in the inverse proportion. People who do not like Mode 1 must retain the right to fashion their payment to the delivery system that best satisfies their needs and preferences.

There is a further difficulty. Mode 1 presupposes critical mass. The network effect is moving towards universal access. Even so, the virtual community is still deficient in crucial links. The high-speed telecommunications infrastructure is not always in place. Less-developed regions are often lacking in computers and peripherals. Sometimes the more isolated do not have a reliable supply of electricity. It is a social failing. In Africa the cost of Internet access is five times that in the OECD countries. Hardware-intensive connectivity can be an expensive luxury: 'In this sense, globalization could extend the development gap, as the comparative advantage in e-health, as a capital- rather than labour-intensive industry, is unlikely to lie with developing countries' (Smith, 2006: 169).

E-commerce presupposes e-payment. The link is always a problem. Insurance companies might not reimburse for microelectronic consultations. Quality might be difficult to certify. Licences and standards might be disputed. Electronic banking might compromise security. Telehealth disclosure might compromise confidentiality. Credit cards might not be accepted. There might be exchange controls. It might be difficult to establish where liability for malpractice lies. It might be impossible to secure redress of grievances. The most that can be said is that with time many of the shortcomings associated with Mode 1 will be overcome through technological improvements.

The breaking up of the production process is a characteristic of the globalised economy. It is common in manufacturing for assembly to be situated in one country, production of components in another, research and development in a third, the head office in a fourth. Multinationals cross borders. Downsized organisations subcontract. What is true of microelectronics can be true of medical services as well.

Information is anecdotal and incomplete. Estimates of global e-health range from US$1 billion to US$1 trillion. Yet some things are known. In India, for example, Mode 1 created 30,551 jobs in all sectors of the economy in 2000. It created 242,500 jobs in 2005. Revenue rose from US$264 million to US$4072 million in the same period (Smith et al., 2009: 594).

2.2 MODE 2: PATIENTS

The second mode involves the cross-national movement of consumers. The client moves. The supplier stays at home. Importers cannot import their visits save by exporting themselves. They must uproot themselves to the producer's territory. Tourists who want to see the Great Wall must go to China. Patients who want a hip replacement must go to Chennai.

The international movement of patients is, of course, only an extension of the intra-national movement that has long taken the unwell from one part of a single country to another. Intrabound flows are least likely where a national health system promises a uniform standard of service. Intrabound flows are more likely where the country is federal and each province is in a position to differentiate its product. Intrabound flows are more likely as well where there are domestic centres of excellence such as the Great Ormond Street Hospital for Children in London or the Philippine Heart Center in Manila to which the residents of the same country will be drawn for care.

Intra-national medical tourism is a growth area in the United States. Since plastic surgery is twice as expensive in New York or California as it is in Knoxville, Tennessee, it is rational for American consumers to keep their eyes open for bargains and discounts. Medical travel agents like Healthplace America make it their business to attract non-local customers through packages that leverage upon geographical variations. It is in the financial interest of group plans and insurance companies to encourage their members to take a train or a plane for a lower price. Sometimes US employers offer to pay the cost-share or to reimburse the travel.

Some successes have been reported. A heart bypass officially priced at US$100,000 was on offer in 2008 through the Healthbase agency for US$15,000 (*International Medical Travel Journal*, 2008b). This is not very different from the cost of the same treatment delivered abroad. Domestic suppliers were in effect matching the foreigners in order to attract patients who were prepared to be mobile. Hospitals are posting information online about survival rates and medical complications. They know that patients travel not just for a lower price but for a better outcome.

It is easier to travel domestically than to go abroad. Visas and languages aside, legal liability is easier to assign. Tourist destinations match the museums and the beaches abroad. Jacksonville, Florida, boasts not just the Mayo Clinic but a short hop to Disneyworld plus all the attractions of a holiday resort. In the first half of 2006 12 per cent of the inpatients treated in North Florida were out-of-region. At the Mayo Clinic the figures could be a third or more. The intra-national movement of patients shows what can be done. The international movement of patients is more of the same.

Both the domestic and the cross-border flows are difficult to quantify. Reliable statistics are not collected on patients who move about. A traveller entering a country will often say that he or she is there for a break. Immigration cards do not always include a medical option. The statistic would in any case be impure if general tourism and health tourism were regarded by the traveller as joint products that make up a single choice. Many travellers combine an operation with a holiday. Whichever box they tick is going to illuminate only a part of the whole.

Foreign students are not called education tourists. Everyone assumes that they have a single academic objective in mind. Foreign students may or may not be single-minded. What is clear is that foreign patients are heterogeneous and diversified. The broad category must be divided up into its component species. It is a statistician's nightmare but that is the way it is. Good evidence is hard to find:

> Last year, one tourism body for a Middle Eastern state repeatedly claimed a figure for probable inbound medical tourists by 2012 that was so high it was twice the current estimated world total. The scarcity of believable figures means that people can make up their own in the knowledge that there are rarely actual figures to contradict them (Yeoman, 2009).

Concentrating on major non-cosmetic elective procedures such as joint replacement, back problems, coronary artery bypass, new or repaired heart valves, even an informed guess might not mean very much

(Comarow, 2008). Estimates of Americans seeking medical treatment abroad range from 5000 to 500,000 or more a year: 'All these estimates are as scientific as a fortune teller. . . . The truthful answer? Nobody knows!' (Yeoman, 2009). No reliable statistics are collected centrally. One reason is a reluctance in liberal democracies like America to pry into the private lives of its people going abroad. Another reason is that there is no practical way of actually collecting the data.

Sample surveys fill the statistical vacuum. One such study was done by Treatment Abroad. It found that about 50,500 UK patients per annum were travelling abroad in the early 2000s: 22,000 for dentistry (43 per cent), 14,500 for cosmetic surgery (29 per cent), 9000 for other surgery (18 per cent), 5000 (10 per cent) for infertility treatment (www.treatment abroad.com). Another study, done for the International Passenger Survey that (subject to security regulations) samples UK nationals leaving UK ports and airports, suggested that the figure was more like 77,000 and growing rapidly. The average spend per UK patient abroad is £3753. Multiplying by 50,500, 77,000, or a soon-to-be reached 200,000, it is a great deal of money.

Just as difficult as the data is, however, the concept. Mode 2 is the act of leaving home expressly in search of good quality diagnosis and affordable medical treatment in a country that is not one's own. The purest type of medical travel is the overseas trip that reflects a conscious and calculative choice. What is involved is non-urgent elective care such as a liver transplant or a root canal job that cannot be postponed forever. A study done for the McKinsey management consultancy suggests that only about 60,000 to 85,000 inpatient medical travellers a year fall into this narrow category: 'Fewer than half of the international inpatients at the providers we visited were true medical travellers' (Ehrbeck et al., 2008). In the real world life is more complicated.

Thus, as noted, some health tourists are also recreational tourists. Although the primary objective is medical, such travellers take advantage of the opportunity to slip in a sightseeing tour or a hill-station breather. The same would be true in reverse where the primary objective is the surf but the traveller nonetheless finds time to buy glasses, try Botox or indulge in cosmetic dentistry to straighten his teeth. In another scenario the primary objective would be business but the secondary objective would be liposuction, a hotel spa or a one-day full-body check-up. The secondary objective makes the definition blurred and ambiguous. Yet the fact is that not all patients, single-minded and focused, secure their intervention and then take the next plane home.

Even more difficult to categorise are the borderline areas. Sometimes a traveller, neither a holiday-maker nor a patient, will go abroad for a meditation class, a temple retreat or a weight-loss clinic. Beauty, exercise, adventure, wellness and relaxation all blend seamlessly into the broad health experience. The definition of health tourism is either/or. Mixed motivation makes it difficult to say where the line should be drawn.

A further complexity is the ubiquity of the unintended. Health tourism is defined as a deliberate and rational act. Yet cross-border medical attention can be required even when the traveller least expects the need. Falling ill while on a foreign holiday is accidental health tourism but not planned health tourism. Emergency surgery for a burst appendix is medical intervention but not cost-effective shopping. Medical treatment for sunburn and malaria, diarrhoea and jet-lag, food poisoning and deep-vein thrombosis is something that has to be consumed without delay. No one goes abroad to seek treatment if he has just been bitten by a snake, is already bleeding from a cut, is in no fit state to travel or is trapped in a pandemic contagion. Divers are attacked by a shark. Explorers fall while climbing a glacier. Some have holiday insurance and some do not. However they pay, there is an urgent need and it has to be met.

Cross-border treatment can also be the concomitant of residence abroad. Students, diplomats, foreign workers and expatriate executives consult doctors in foreign countries because they are already there. It is estimated that up to 20 per cent of Britons will go abroad to live between 2005 and 2025. In 2005 2.41 million British people owned a second or even a primary property abroad. By 2030 the number is likely to reach 12.87 million (Yeoman, 2008: 116). A growing number of foreigners are retiring in the sun. Many of them are long-stay residents registered under programmes such as the Malaysia My Second Home scheme. They are statistically more likely to require medical support wherever they are based.

Some expatriates will have an evacuation clause. Many will have put down roots in their adopted homeland. A small number will have retired in the country of their birth. Language and culture as well as geographical proximity will make care overseas that much more attractive to them. Because expatriates are resident abroad they do not fit the definition of medical *tourists*. Yet they are nonetheless international patients in the literal sense that they hold foreign passports. Americans who live in Mexico may be treated by the statisticians precisely as if they were Americans who went to Mexico for a hip.

Sometimes the same patient entering on three occasions will be counted as one patient disembarking three times and sometimes as three patients, each one landing once. Sometimes the patient will be double-counted if, having arrived in the country, he or she goes to more than one department in the hospital or perhaps to more than one treatment centre. Different countries define medical tourism in different ways. It makes comparisons difficult or impossible. The measure of transnational medicine is therefore inherently problematic.

Mode 2 is the cross-border movement that takes place when American locals are importing hernia repairs from Malaysia, prescription drugs from Canada or cholesterol screens from Germany. American locals have long been importing vodka from Russia, oats from Scotland and silk from China. Mode 2 extends the purchase of goods to the purchase of services. Not all services can cross the exchanges. Long-stay attention in a mental hospital is not something that would usually be sourced abroad. Other services are more amenable to Mode 2.

2.3   MODE 3: CAPITAL

In the case of Mode 3 it is not the patients but the treatment centres that go abroad. Service providers establish a territorial presence in a foreign jurisdiction. They do so in order to trade from that base with the resident middle classes and with international patients from their own or other countries. Mode 3 in that way becomes a complement to Mode 2.

Foreign direct investment may enter through the establishment of a fully-owned new start-up on a green-field site. An American patient in such a case would be importing a service from an American company which happens to have premises abroad. Alternatively, the investment could come in through the acquisition of an existing hospital or a merger with a familiar chain. Foreign capital could conclude a joint venture with a local insurer that wants to expand into provision: both parties would be more willing to invest if they could share risk in this way. Foreign capital could franchise its business model: Princess Beauty and Spa in Thailand has rented out its name to a firm in Laos and has co-invested with the Westin Hotel in a centre in Bangladesh. Construction, acquisition or franchise, it is important not to confuse a change in capacity with a change in ownership. *Ab initio* is new beds. Purchase is a simple transfer of title.

Foreign capital could affiliate its brand name with a locally-operated organisation: the CIMA Hospital in Costa Rica, JCI accredited, has a continuing arrangement with the Baylor University Medical Center (reinforced by a parallel association with the Department of Veterans Affairs in the USA which has an office in the building) in order to ensure that quality is kept up. Foreign capital could set up a new medical school of its own: an example would be the Harvard Medical School Dubai Center which is the overseas subsidiary of a famous United States parent. Foreign capital could, more imaginatively, concentrate on the supply of non-medical services. This would be the case where a multinational network tendered for outsourced ancillaries such as cleaning, catering, laundry, the ambulance service and the blood bank.

Cross-border enterprise could take over management even if does not hold the equity: Al Corniche Hospital in Abu Dhabi is owned by the Government but operated by United Medical. It could operate in a niche market like ophthalmology or cancer: the Magrabi Hospitals chain, based in Saudi Arabia, has seven eye hospitals in Egypt and another in Yemen. It could offer the full range of specialities: a cloned Bumrungrad in Dubai or the Bahamas would provide the same services as in Thailand but would provide them, more conveniently, on the spot. It could confine its operations to a special economic zone: examples are the Subic Bay Metropolitan Authority in the Philippines or the Songdo Free Economic Zone near Incheon Airport in Korea. It could trade exclusively in high-end, high-profit tourist destinations: El Grupo Hospiten, Spanish-owned, operates 12 hospitals in resort areas in Spain, Mexico and Puerto Rico. It could, on the other hand, go nationwide: Parkway Holdings in Singapore has a stake in 11 hospitals throughout East and West Malaysia.

Some foreign investment has a social service motive: Christus Health, based in Dallas, is a Catholic organisation which reinvests its profits in the community, both in the United States and Mexico. Some foreign investment is made to relieve the strain on a network's resources at home: this would be the case of an American insurance company or health maintenance organisation which constructs treatment facilities in Brazil in order to keep down the cost. Some foreign investment, moreover, goes abroad because of the profits that can be made in less saturated markets which are just beginning to take off. Both tourism and health have lucrative long-term prospects. Sunrise sectors in sunrise nations give unsentimental businesspeople the chance to get in on the ground floor.

Money is money. The 500-bed Chang Gung Hospital in Xiamen's Xinyang Industrial Zone is owned by the Formosa Plastics Group in Taiwan. Many Taiwanese are working in South China. The local Chinese are growing more affluent. The new hospital, complemented later on by its own medical school and an eldercare centre, is expected to pay a competitive return. A group of Taiwanese investors is also building a world-class Chinese-language hospital at Subic Bay in the Philippines. Taking advantage of the tax concessions in the special development area, it will cater to medical tourists from mainland China.

Indian investment too is going abroad. Not least among the destinations is health care in Mauritius. While Mauritius internally has generated a certain amount of capital from agriculture, textiles and the hospitality industry, joint ventures and international investment bring in both new reserves and new technology. The Apollo Group from India (which will operate the facility) will put in 26 per cent of the capital for the new Apollo Bramwell Hospital. The bulk of the funding will come from the British-American Investment Company. Investors know that medicine pays. High value-added services will pay even more.

B.R. Shetty, with links to India and Abu Dhabi, owns eight hospitals in the Gulf. Hinduja Ventures, based in London, is investing in Indian hospitals. The Ithmaar Development Company (a subsidiary of the Ithmaar Bank) is putting money into reclamation works for the Health Island in Bahrain. Foreign investment will support local seedcorn once the infrastructure has been put in place.

As always, foreign investment must be situated within a framework of rules. The host country must decide to what extent property rights will be protected and if foreign professionals should be given work permits. It must decide if foreign ownership and control can be 100 per cent (as in Singapore) or no more than 49 per cent (as in Thailand). It must decide if a cap on foreign ownership may legitimately be circumvented through the use of nominees. It must decide if the State should authorise for-profit medicine; or if new entry can be allowed when domestic suppliers already have spare capacity; or if financial guarantees are to be required in order to ensure good order; or if foreign direct investment can be topped up with bank borrowing and new equity; or if reinvestment is to be mandatory. It must decide if net profits can be repatriated without restriction. Investment raises the domestic product. The transfer, however, eats away at the national product. The host country must decide if the gains outweigh the liabilities.

The host country must decide if there is to be a level playing field: should favouritism be shown to locally-owned hospitals in respect of tax holidays, acquisition of land, zoning restrictions, reimbursements from the national insurance fund? It must decide if there are to be market-distorting guidelines. Should local inputs be purchased first and the export drive be given priority? Should State-owned hospitals be protected, subsidised or privatised? Should for-profit investors be allowed to take over not-for-profit foundations? Should disadvantaged social groups be guaranteed affirmative action? Should the spillover training of local staff be made the precondition for a licence? Should it be compulsory to set up an outreach clinic in the forest or to provide free hospital care for the needy? Foreign investment is an exercise in political economy. The State has to promulgate acceptable rules of the game.

Local hospitals will sometimes object that foreign hospitals use better equipment and go in for predatory pricing. They may complain that the foreigners, undercutting them, are driving them out. They may be tempted to invoke the infant industries argument in defence of protection. An alternative view is that local supply cannot keep pace with local demand.

If this is so, then local residents as well as international patients will stand
to gain from new entry.

2.4   MODE 4: LABOUR

In the case of Mode 4, it is natural persons who cross the frontiers. An
organisation is an artificial person. It is a juridical person, distinct in law
from the discrete human beings who make it up. A natural person, on the
other hand, is flesh and blood. He or she is endowed with a pulse and with
a mind. The previous section dealt with the hospitals and investments that
move from place to place. The present section deals with the medical professionals. They too can pack their bags to live abroad.

Many have done so. About 28 per cent of the doctors in the UK, 26.5
per cent in Australia, 25 per cent in the US, 23 per cent in Canada are
international medical graduates. India, the Philippines and Pakistan are
the leading suppliers of medical manpower. About 60 per cent of physician incomers in the US are from lower-income countries. In the UK it
is 75 per cent. British doctors are popular in Canada and Australia: there
the percentage of immigrant physicians from poorer countries is only 43.4
per cent and 40 per cent respectively. Physicians from Canada are the
fifth largest group of international medical graduates in the United States
(Mullan, 2005).

The United States loses very few medical graduates. Other countries
experience a considerable loss. Nine of the 20 countries with the highest
emigration factors are in sub-Saharan Africa or the Caribbean. A sample
of Nigerian medical graduates from the 1995–1997 cohort revealed that
40 per cent of them were living abroad (Ihekweazu et al., 2005: 1847).
Philippine nurses and midwives, English-speaking, adaptable and friendly,
are found throughout the world. There are at least 87,000 Philippine
nurses and midwives working abroad (Arunanondchai and Fink, 2007:
14). At the other end of the spectrum, only 11 per cent of migrating
doctors go from developed to developing nations. For nurses the imbalance is even greater (Eastwood et al., 2005: 1893).

The flow can be permanent or temporary. The former is a topic in citizenship, migration and settlement. It is less convincing to say it is a topic
in international trade. A naturalised American who was born in Iran
cannot realistically be described as an Iranian who is supplying labour to
America. That is why it is more useful for a discussion of Mode 4 to concentrate on the temporary relocation of manpower that will later go on to
a third country or go back to its place of origin. Numbers can be plucked
out of the air to say how long a temporary stay can last. Perhaps from

one to five tax years would be a useful rule of thumb. In practice, what is intended to be a temporary stay often ends up as a permanent relocation. Sometimes it is intermediate migration that uses the first attachment as a step up on the way to a target destination.

The movement is multilateral. India and the Philippines export to Australia and the United Kingdom. Australia and the United Kingdom export to Canada and the United States. Most migration is from the less-developed to the richer countries. There is migration nonetheless from one poorer country to another, from one richer country to another, and even from a richer country to a poorer country which is opening a world-class centre. Many countries both export and import.

Doctors, nurses, pharmacists, technicians and other medical grades go abroad for a variety of reasons. They may be interested in professional development, state-of-the-art equipment, a new skill. They may be curious to sample a different culture or see the world. They may be after better remuneration, better working conditions, better living conditions. Often there is unemployment or under-employment at home: in the absence of a retention strategy they would have had to take a job outside medicine. Often they have parents, siblings and children who are dependent on their remittances.

Some foreigners are on contract to an organisation in the host country. The National Health Service in Britain recruits nurses and doctors world-wide. Some are abroad because their company has a policy of staff rotation. Expatriates through intra-corporate transfers are circulated internally, often in tandem with the capital that makes up Mode 3. The right to bring in aliens, skilled or unskilled, is usually made subject to an 'economic needs test'. The intention is to ensure that no qualified local is available who could do the job. Quotas on overseas manpower, together with restrictions on the repatriation of profits, will often be a bargaining point when foreign direct investment is negotiating to establish a presence.

Some of the short-term assignments take place within the framework of inter-country agreements. In some cases (consider the European Union and the North American Free Trade Agreement) there will be provisions for mutual recognition of qualifications and free movement of labour. In other cases there will be bilateral agreements to bring in a certain number of professionals for a specified number of years to correct a manpower shortage. Contacts give professionals the opportunity to discuss practice variation and local conventions, ethical norms and modes of speech. Even in the absence of uniform international credentials, such an exchange of views is conducive to convergence on a consensual standard of best-practice medicine. As Warner writes: 'Free trade agreements have created a chain of potential reciprocity. . . . A time is coming in which national identity among the professions will be passé. In its place will be the truly world-class physician, engineer, nurse or architect' (Warner, 1998: 74). Quality assurance will become a cross-border public good. It will cease to be nation-based and narrow.

Short-term assignments are often encouraged through special (non-immigrant) visas. Because these limit the length of stay, they are often acceptable to anxious locals who do not want the industry to be destabilised. This does not mean that the support will be ungrudging. Incomers may be accused of snatching jobs that would have gone to residents or of working for wages that undercut the going rate. Unless there is a law guaranteeing equal pay for equal work, foreigners might find themselves hired as cheap labour even within a single grade.

The word 'exploitation' is sometimes used to describe these arrangements. The mathematics that underlies the intuition is complex. If a foreign worker is earning twice what he would have been paid at home but only half what a local worker is being paid for the job, who is better off and who is worse off in his own estimation? In what circumstances should a local union spring to the defence of a foreigner who is relatively deprived compared to a national but in absolute terms is doing well? In what circumstances should the foreigner put up and shut up because the next-best alternative would be herding goats on the family farm?

Employment in a single grade may be remunerated at a lower rate. Similarly, a down-skilled appointment might be offered to an outsider because a lower grade is what the foreign-educated deserve. A doctor will be hired as a nurse. A nurse will be hired as an auxiliary. Incomers might not be given on-the-job training. They might be placed on fixed-term contracts that carry no security or tenure. They might not be allowed to resettle with their children. They might be subject to onerous double taxation. They might be denied public top-ups or tax concessions. They might be cheated by their agencies. They might become used to high-tech capital complements that might not be available in their country of origin. They might develop expertise in gerontology and non-communicable cancers when their home developing countries have a greater problem with malaria and kwashiorkor. Short-term assignments have their downs as well as their ups.

Entry is an obstacle course. The list of barriers extends to language, culture, quotas, stereotyping, racism, professional licences, immigration restrictions. Foreign qualifications are not always recognised. Membership nationality in an economic bloc like the European Union can be made the *sine qua non.* Information about opportunities abroad is not easy to obtain. The psychic and the paid-out cost of moving house is a deterrent to becoming mobile. Trade unions and professional bodies make clear that they do not want the market to be flooded.

Entry is not automatic. There are some who regard a moderately higher fee as the price they are willing to pay for a moderately restricted market. Residents have the advantage of local knowledge and cultural sensitivity. Attitudes differ towards ethically-charged issues like fertilisation, organ transplants, advertising. The bedside manner is unlikely to be the same. It is sometimes said that medical knowledge (in contrast to training in law) covers the same syllabus in all countries. It may not be so if the social-psychological context is taken into account. That is why it is possible to argue in favour of a critical mass of nationals. Conservatives say that citizens should be protected merely because they are citizens. Pragmatists say that locals should retain a core presence precisely because it is they who can listen with the third ear.

2.5   TRADE IN GOODS AND TRADE IN SERVICES

Ricardo's example of wine and textiles is a reminder that the theory of international trade has traditionally been about agriculture and industry. Services, it has been assumed, normally have to be consumed on the spot. Restaurant meals and West End musicals are that way because of what they are:

> The only significant exceptions have been services directly related to the exchange of goods (transport, insurance, etc.) and, more recently, to tourism. The generally low level of trade in services has been attributed to institutional, administrative and/or technical constraints, such as the existence of public monopolies (education, telephone services), strict access regulations and controls (finance, various professional services) and the need for direct physical contact between suppliers and consumers (as in health and other social services) (Adlung and Carzaniga, 2001: 352).

Services, it has generally been assumed, are evanescent ephemerals that cannot be stored and that do not cross the borders well. Of total world trade in 2005, 59.3 per cent was in manufactures and only 19.59 per cent was in services. The share of industry dwarfs that of agriculture (6.9 per cent) or mining (14.1 per cent). Even in the developing countries the share of manufactured exports has exceeded that of primary produce at least since 1980. The tertiary sector has lagged behind. The value of commodity exports is three times as great as the value of traded services worldwide (Krugman and Obstfeld, 2009: 21).

There are exceptions. International tourism accounts for 6 per cent of

total exports (and for 30 per cent of total world service exports) (www.
unwto.org/facts). University education in countries such as Britain and the
United States is a valuable income earner. International finance, insurance
and maritime shipping are also sources of revenue, albeit often regarded
more as complements that facilitate the transportation of goods than as
valued endstates in their own right. Then there is health care. Scholars
like Adlung and Carzaniga seem to think that it proves the rule. Day-care
centres are difficult to pack in boxes. The hands-on-bodies treatments
of the chiropractors and the physiotherapists are simply not possible if
supply and demand are not in the same room. Public provision, strict
licensing, quality minima, social as well as medical objectives, have all
reinforced the idea that trade in health cannot normally cross the water
or the sky.

Yet the GATS, introduced to liberalise trade in services, is more receptive to the new world system. Its mission, Smith writes, is to speed up the
transition to the inevitable. Its objective is

> to ensure transparency, consistency and predictability in international eco-
> nomic policies through creating a credible, reliable and binding system of inter-
> national trade rules, ensuring an equitable treatment of exporters, stimulating
> economic activity and promoting economic development. . . . Its philosophical
> basis is that liberalization will encourage a global increase in efficiency, through
> the traditional economic arguments relating to comparative advantage, ensur-
> ing consumers continued product availability and reducing the economic power
> of individual economic operators (Smith, 2006: 166).

Mode 1 is distance service, virtual and electronic. Mode 2 is personal
service where the consumer crosses the line. Mode 3 is the service of plant
where stateless capital makes a move. Mode 4 is the service of labour
because people and not just things can go abroad. The GATS is on the
side of trade. In respect of all four modes, the GATS wants to see one
hand wash the other across the international divide. Relatively and absolutely, it is a commercially-informed programme that wants to see world
trade in services expand. It is less explicitly committed to universal access,
good outcome indicators or a citizen's right to health. Business is business.
Health is health.

Adam Smith once wrote that a sensible doctrine should not be pushed
too far: 'To expect, indeed, that the freedom of trade should ever be
entirely restored in Great Britain, is as absurd as to expect that an
Oceana or Utopia should ever be established in it' (Smith, 1961 [1776]:
493). The GATS, like Adam Smith, has no objection to making haste
slowly. Pragmatic rather than either/or, it raises no objection to qualified
freedom.

The GATS agreement accepts that foreign suppliers may legitimately be excluded from a subsidy. Land ownership may be made subject to a nationality clause. Foreign equity may be braked or capped. Quality standards may be upheld through bans, proscriptions, licences and certificates. The GATS does not deny member jurisdictions the right to exercise their discretion or to regulate as they see fit. What it does require is the universalisation of all hurdles and concessions. Discrimination that benefits a favoured nation is not allowed. A market opened to one trading partner must be opened to all. This protects the interests of smaller countries. Not all countries have equal bargaining power.

Even citizen suppliers are not to enjoy binding preference: 'Each Member shall accord to services and service providers of any other Member. . . . treatment no less favourable than that it accords to its own like services and service suppliers' (World Trade Organization, 1995: 298). Government procurement should not be limited to local tenders. Gold standard credentialism should not become a non-tariff barrier. Transparency, fair play and common sense should protect the international order.

Here again, however, the GATS agreement is pragmatic enough to leave room for short-run discrimination where the exception is essential for stability and growth. Economic development is an especial concern. Low-income countries are allowed to postpone the open market in order to encourage infant-industry economies of scale. They can restrict foreign capital and labour to protect their own bedstock and professionals. While free trade in the long run will lead to a multilaterally beneficial division of labour, there is also a possibility that in the short run the domestic producers will all be dead.

Cross-national operation can prevent local enterprise from ever gaining a foothold. Loopholes allow poorer countries to opt out of sector-specific clauses that could significantly retard their progress. That said, health care may well be seen as less of a threat. A greater number of developing than First World countries have made GATS commitments in the field of health (Smith, 2006: 168–9).

State monopoly is a further exception. GATS applies only to services which are competitive and commercial. Services provided by the Government on a *pro bono publico* basis are excluded. Examples would be the police, the fire services and the central bank. Free health care on the model of the British National Health Service would also come under this umbrella. Privatisation, as in the case of telecommunications, brings the exemption to an end.

There are, needless to say, grey areas. One of these is the joint venture. If a Government-owned supplier is collaborating in commercial activity with a private profit-seeker, it is all but a conspiracy in restraint of trade to restrict international entry merely because the State holds a share. Another would be an internal market within a National Health monolith. Where the regions compete for vouchers and local bonuses are proportioned to performance, it could be argued that it is inequitable to keep out Modes 1, 2, 3 and 4 merely because the sole capitalist at home is the State.

In the short run there will be quotas and tariffs, restrictions and exemptions. GATS raises no objection to 'appropriate flexibility' where member-States want to use market regulations for social policy, where Governments supply non-tradables without the intention of making a gain, where the Third World needs leeway to prepare for its take-off: 'It is not globalization per se that will be good or bad for the developing world, but how we manage this globalization' (Mutchnick et al., 2005: 43). It is nonetheless the mission of GATS to ensure that in the long run the barriers will ultimately come down. GATS, giving the example of subsidies, summarises its vision in the following words: 'Members recognize that, in certain circumstances, subsidies may have distortive effects on trade in services. Members shall enter into negotiations with a view. . . . to avoid such trade-distortive effects' (World Trade Organization, 1995: 296). Oceana or Utopia will not be established overnight. Yet it is the message of GATS that sooner or later even trade in services will be definitively unblocked.

3. Price

Patients go out of country for a variety of reasons. An obvious reason is the difference in price. A few clinics abroad are more expensive than those in the metropolitan areas of Western Europe, Japan or the United States. Most charge significantly less. Expensive care in high-cost countries creates a market opportunity in countries that can keep their price competitive.

This chapter is concerned with the lure of a lower price. It is divided into six sections. Section 1, 'Comparative cost', says why the prices of international tradables are not globally on a par. Section 2, 'Willingness to travel', asks to what extent the market is imperfect because the consumer is afraid of the unknown. Section 3, 'Insurance', assesses the impact of prepayment on the consumer's preference for a foreign clinic. Section 4, 'Out-of-pocket', speculates that shoppers might be more cost-sensitive if they had to shoulder the whole burden for themselves. Section 5, 'Care and cure', illustrates the discussion of price-differentials with the specific case of long-stay retirement homes. Section 6, 'Price and performance', explains that price influences the quantity demanded, but that other things can do so as well.

3.1 COMPARATIVE COST

The facts speak for themselves. Knee replacement costs US$48,000 in the US but US$15,900 in Canada and US$8500 in India. Heart valve replacement costs US$200,000 in the US but US$9000 in Malaysia. A full facelift costs US$20,000 in the US but US$1250 in South Africa. A hysterectomy costs US$20,000 in the US but US$3000 in Malaysia. Rhinoplasty costs US$4500 in the United States but US$850 in India. A dental filling costs US$400 in the US, US$20 in India. Heart surgery costs US$30,000 in the US, US$6000 in India. Gender reassignment costs US$40,000 in the United States, US$4000 in Thailand. Breast augmentation costs US$10,000 in the United States, as little as US$1500 in Cuba. A three-hour hair transplant costs up to US$12,000 in the United States. It costs up to US$4000 in Brazil. US$4000 is affordable even if US$12,000 is not. A bald man would have to wear a toupee if he did not have the option of Brazil.

The price billed to foreigners might be higher than the local price. There is no clause in the GATS banning price discrimination in a segmented market where arbitrage is impossible, resale out of the question. The real comparison, however, is with the next-best alternative. Untreated complaints can reduce productivity: the net price is less when set alongside the earnings lost due to ill health. Even with the mark-up, moreover, the price will be significantly less than at home. Patients will not travel if the saving is small. There are many interventions where not a small but a large saving can be made.

The price is quoted in the local currency. What really interests the medical traveller is how much of his own money he will have to give up. International prices depend upon the rates of exchange. Between 2005 and 2008 the US dollar fell by 24 per cent against the euro. American patients stay at home when the US dollar falls. Foreign patients take advantage of the weak dollar to come to the United States. The same may be said of airfares: oil prices (quoted in US dollars) go up or down. If America is as cheap as Thailand, if what once was a luxury is now a bargain, there will be an incentive for the international patient to reconsider his destination.

The price is not the same as the spend. The price for total hip replacement in Thailand is one third the price in the United States. Yet the American patient is already in America and Thailand is half a world away. The true outlay would have to factor in return flights and accommodation both for the patient and for accompanying relatives. The add-ons reduce the differential but they need not eliminate it. Cosmetic surgery in Cyprus costs two-thirds what it would cost in the UK: the net figure includes fares, hotels and a two-week period of recuperation on the island. Access has become cheaper due to budget airlines. In Europe, EasyJet and Ryanair fly from Britain and Ireland to Poland and Hungary. In the East, carriers like Tiger, Jetstar and AirAsia offer low fares from Australia and New Zealand to Penang or Phuket where the price of cosmetic surgery is one third the price at home. Even long-haul flights need not be prohibitive. Physical distance is not the barrier that it was.

Travelling in the host country's low season keeps the outlay down. Some hospitals have special arrangements with local hotels. Others provide accommodation of their own. The Matilda Hospital in Hong Kong has serviced apartments within its grounds for caregiver companions and convalescent post-operatives. The M.D. Anderson Cancer Center in Houston operates a hotel on an adjacent site. It is linked to the hospital by a walkway. Raffles Hospital in Singapore does even better. It offers studio apartments at a competitive S$150 per night on the eighth floor of the building. Relatives walk up one floor to visit their loved ones on the ninth.

The total package can be affordable. Yet that is not to deny that the price for medical attention itself can be a significant attraction. Cosmetic surgery in Prague costs half what it would in the United States. The intervention is basically the same. The bill is not. *The Economist* reports monthly to the effect that a Big Mac costs US$3.54 in the United States, US$1.73 in Russia, US$5.79 in Norway. A Big Mac costs US$2.61 in Singapore but only US$1.52 in Malaysia next door. There is much dispersion in a Mac. Health tourism is clearly a horse from the same venerable stable.

Americans pay US$40,000 for a hip replacement. Their counterparts in Canada pay only US$18,000. A cardiac bypass is priced at US$44,000 in Dubai. A very similar bypass can be had in Thailand for only US$11,000. One reason is that labour costs less. Herrick, sampling the receiving nations, found that doctors earn on average 40 per cent less, nurses 80 to 95 per cent less, than they do in the United States (Herrick, 2007: 10). Non-professional labour is cheaper still. Norway and Switzerland, high-wage economies, cannot make money out of the North–South divide. Mexico and Thailand are better placed to coin lower pay into prices and jobs.

Health care is a labour-intensive industry. Yet different grades dwell in different sub-markets. At the top there are the world class professionals. Able credibly to threaten migration to the Upper East Side, they can bargain for something approaching the international going wage. At the bottom there are the unskilled manuals. Radically deficient in human capital, normally in markets where supply exceeds demand, the porters, the cleaners and the gardeners do not have the education or the productivity that would bid them up beyond the minimum wage. In the middle there are the semi-skilled. Third World countries often invest a large share of their development budget in basic literacy and simple skills. The result is that they often have a good-sized pool of low-level technicians and non-specialist paramedics on which to draw. That intermediate stock, although better educated than the unqualified, is not in a position to threaten emigration if their pay is not what they would like.

Medicine means people. In the United States labour accounts for 55 per cent of total cost (*Economist*, 2008). In Singapore it is 44 per cent (Ministry of Trade and Industry, 2003: Annex 1, 8). At Bumrungrad it is 18 per cent. Lower prices are possible because hospital staff cost less. There can also be a quantity effect. Where pay is moderate a hospital can afford more nurses per bed and more cleaners per ward. The result is a more leisured, more personal service.

Labour costs less. It is one reason why medical care is less expensive in some countries than in others. A second reason will be the regulatory environment. Hospitals in Europe and America must often conform to strict guidelines on hours per shift, lines of demarcation, mixed wards, leave allowances. Often there will be entry barriers that restrict the number of beds and the supply of professionals. The net result is a brake on the opportunity to experiment, to innovate and to reassign.

Hospitals in new markets often have more flexibility. They are more likely to be free of laws which prohibit pharmacists from writing prescriptions and prevent nurses from completing the stitches. They are less likely to be subject to mandatory cross-subsidisation which forces them to pass on the overhead. A private hospital that cannot cream-skim has to include a charity mark-up to cover the bad debts of the indigent. It has to price in the deadweight of loss-making Accident and Emergency which the regulators will not allow it to close. Socially desirable as such services are, the implications for doing health business are clear enough. Compulsory transfers make it more difficult for domestic centres to compete price-effectively with their less restricted international counterparts.

A third reason for the lower price will often be the lower cost of malpractice insurance. Litigation (much of it frivolous or opportunistic) introduces a serious wedge into the cost of care. Doctors in the United States can pay as much as US$100,000 annually for their cover. Doctors in Thailand only pay US$5000. There is no need: 'Thailand does not compensate victims of negligence for noneconomic damages, and malpractice awards are far lower than in the United States' (Herrick, 2007: 12). Malpractice insurance costs very little in Mexico. The Mexican legal system makes a successful lawsuit almost impossible. You get what you pay for. It keeps down the price.

Finally, there are the economies of administration. In Canada the hospitals deal with a single insurer. In the United Kingdom medical care is free at the point of consumption. Centralisation in those countries contrasts sharply with the situation in the United States. Administration costs more where hospitals must bill a variety of carriers who follow a variety of practices. Bumrungrad in that sense is the most price-effective of all: 75 per cent of its patients settle their account on the spot.

Occupied beds and rapid turnover squeeze waste out of the system. Canada and the United Kingdom have an economic advantage precisely because they have made it an objective to keep excess capacity to the minimum. Yet there is something else. Waits replace prices as the deterrent that rations the service. Not everyone is prepared to spend the time. Even where the service is free, the patient might still choose India. The time-price at home might make even free care too dear.

Wages, regulations, insurance and administration are four key reasons why the price might be lower abroad. Capital, however, swims against the tide. Customers expect equipment like lasers and scanners to be state-of-the-art. Countries with a severe shortage of domestic savings and foreign exchange might not find it easy to keep up with modern technology. Hospitals in poorer countries might in the circumstances be at a competitive disadvantage even if their price is low.

One solution might be domestic manufacture to take advantage of cheaper labour. Another solution might be maximum throughput to spread the overheads and outrun probable obsolescence. A third solution might be in-service training to raise the productivity of the local staff who interface with the expensive new plant.

There are also Modes 3 and 4. Mode 3 looks to the transnational incomer to make up the capital shortfall. Mode 4 takes the view that skilled immigrants with a track-record abroad might be well placed to make the most of the machines. Thus can Modes 3 and 4 join forces to ensure that the patient who travels through Mode 2 will in the end receive good medical attention at an affordable price.

3.2   WILLINGNESS TO TRAVEL

The old-style medical tourism was expensive. Richer patients from poorer countries made their way to Europe and America. They were charged what the traffic would bear. First World treatment does not come cheap.

The new-style medical tourism is South–North as before. Thais go to Australia for their varicose veins. Indians go to America for an unexpected lump. Yet it is something else too. It is South–South where a Bangladeshi goes to Thailand for his colon or his Lasik. It is North–South where an American goes to India for his facelift or his stent. The flow, in other words, is not just Third World to First World. It is Third World to Third World and First World to Third World too.

The slogan is 'First World treatment at Third World prices'. The necessary condition is that the care is there. The sufficient condition is, however, that the patients should be willing to take the chance. Americans can be treated by American-trained foreigners at less than half the price they would pay at home. That they can do so is not in dispute. The real question is whether they will act as market-economic rationality would seem to suggest.

One obstacle is simple ignorance. Despite higher standards of education and the widespread use of the Internet, would-be consumers might still not know what they can get if they get on a plane. The *Nicolet Bank Business Pulse*, in a small-sample study of 600 top managers in North-Eastern Wisconsin, found that 52 per cent of the respondents had never heard of medical tourism. A further 23 per cent said that they knew little more about it than the name. People who know little or nothing about the services and the prices are unlikely to conduct intelligent arbitrage or to maximise their own well-being.

When, however, the options were spelled out to them, the 600 top managers altered their stance. About a third said they would be interested in medical treatment abroad if the cost were appreciably less. About 19 per cent said they would be interested if the country were user-friendly. Canada scored best. Russia was worst. The positive response was even greater where the medical component such as an annual check-up could be combined with a holiday abroad with their spouse or partner (Bina, 2007: 49).

The proportion in favour – over 50 per cent – is a surprise in the sense that top managers are likely to have more medical insurance and fewer financial concerns. Even the well-padded know about the elasticity of demand. The lesson to be drawn from the study is in general highly positive. Most executives were not aware of cheaper treatment abroad. The majority were nonetheless receptive to the idea once it had been explained to them. As with so much else in the area of health tourism, the unexploited potential is tremendous.

Even when they are informed about the possibilities, still many people are reluctant to desert their comfort zone. Deloitte, polling 3000 Americans aged 18 to 75 in 2008, was able to pinpoint the risk-averters. Age is one characteristic: whereas 51.1 per cent of younger Americans were prepared to consider an elective procedure abroad, only 29.1 per cent of the over-62s said they were willing to do so. Gender was another factor: about 44.5 per cent of the males polled would contemplate medical treatment abroad but only 33.3 per cent of the women would do so (Deloitte Center for Health Solutions, 2008: 5). As for race, about 56.8 per cent of Asians and 51.1 per cent of Hispanics said they were willing to go abroad. Possibly they were less conservative than the Caucasian-Americans (at 37.8 per cent) and the African-Americans (at 36.9 per cent) because many of them had family ties in countries with good medical facilities, such as India or Mexico. The very poor on Medicaid and the very old on Medicare showed hardly any interest in medical attention abroad. The reason is simple. Medicaid and Medicare do not reimburse for treatment in foreign countries.

Respondents to the Deloitte survey specified that the quality of care would have to be comparable. About 43 per cent also said the price difference would have to be 50 per cent or more. At least they were honest about the high threshold that would trigger a response. Scaling upward from the sample, Deloitte nonetheless calculated that more than one American in three was willing to consider medical treatment overseas. The target market was therefore in excess of 40 million. Irrespective of their inertia and their fear, a very large number of Americans, it would appear, were willing to seek care in the unknown darkness of the General Abroad.

Deloitte believed the percentage of Americans willing to travel to be 33 per cent. A Gallup poll in 2009 found it to be, at 29 per cent, almost the same. The average conceals the variations. It was only 10 per cent for cosmetic surgery, 14 per cent for heart bypass surgery and 24 per cent for cancer diagnosis and treatment. When the additional assumption was made that the quality was just as good but the price was less, the interest went up: 29 became 40, 10 became 20, 14 became 27 and 24 became 37. Americans without health insurance were more likely than those with health insurance to say they were willing: 44 per cent, as compared with 26 per cent. When the additional assumption of American-standard quality, lower price was made, the 44 per cent became 51 (Khoury, 2009).

Words, however, do not add up to deeds. Deloitte found that 88 per cent of the respondents to its survey said that they would consider going out of community if the prognosis was expected to be better and the cost no more (Deloitte Center for Health Solutions, 2008: 5). Only 8 to 12 per cent, however, had done so. Only 1 to 3 per cent had gone overseas. Less than a quarter of Americans in 2008 actually held a passport. Very few indeed had actually sought diagnosis or care outside the United States. Yet they knew that the option was there.

Other studies confirm the Deloitte result. Thus Thompson Reuters in their 2008 PULSE Survey found that 71 per cent of their 23,000 American respondents were aware of the possibility. As for their willingness to travel, it went up with income level. Nearly 30 per cent of Americans who self-reported an interest in securing medical care overseas had an income of US$150,000 or more. For respondents with incomes from US$75,000 to US$90,000 the figure was 23.7 per cent (*International Medical Travel Journal*, 2008c). Presumably, the future will be different. Incomes are rising across the board.

The European experience is in line with the American evidence. The National Dental Survey in the UK found in 2008 that 16 per cent of Britons (more than 16 per cent among younger people) said they were willing to travel abroad for dental treatment. The savings that could be made on dental implants were as much as 60 per cent; on a full set of acrylic dentures 44 per cent. Dental treatment in Hungary (including hotel accommodation) is less than half the price in Germany. These figures are similar to the threshold of 50 per cent that was reported by Deloitte.

In the European Union, a Eurobarometer random sample of 27,200 respondents conducted by Gallup in 2007 discovered that 54 per cent of

EU citizens in the 27 member states said that they were willing to seek medical treatment in another EU country. The figure went up to 57 per cent for the self-employed. It is, however, a question of words and deeds again. Although 54 per cent of respondents told Gallup that they were willing to go abroad for care, only 4 per cent on average had actually done so in the previous 12 months. The exception was tiny Luxemburg. There the proportion jumped to 20 per cent.

In common with the Deloitte study, the willingness to travel rises with education and falls with age. Two-thirds of the 15–24s but only 43 per cent of the over-55s in the Gallup survey were prepared to travel. Geographical distances played a part. In Cyprus 89 per cent were prepared to go abroad. In Finland the figure fell to 27 per cent. Willingness to go abroad went up for patients who had received treatment overseas on a previous occasion.

As for price sensitivity, the Portuguese (68 per cent) and the British (66 per cent) were the most likely to say that they would travel abroad for cheaper treatment. The Hungarians (22 per cent) and the Latvians (21 per cent) were the least likely to say this. Treatment was already relatively cheap in their country. The country where most Britons (60 per cent) would like to receive treatment was Germany. Romania came last: 3 per cent (Gallup Organization, 2007: 9, 16).

Money is not the whole story. What is important is that they got what they wanted. About 74 per cent in the Treatment Abroad study were 'very satisfied'. A further 16 per cent were 'quite satisfied'. About 97 per cent of the 650 medical tourists polled said they would definitely or probably go abroad for treatment again (Treatment Abroad, 2008). In a study conducted by the Medical Tourism Association the equivalent percentage was 88 per cent. About 93 per cent of the respondents in the MTA survey told the investigators that they would encourage a friend, relative or acquaintance to travel internationally for care. The same study found that 63 per cent believed the treatment abroad was better than the care they would have received in the United States, while 37 per cent said that the medical experience was about the same. Not one said it was worse (Medical Tourism Association, 2009: 35, 36).

A British survey in 2008 established that 91 per cent of the respondents were satisfied with their dental treatment (top destinations: Hungary, Poland, Turkey), 87 per cent with cosmetic surgery (top destinations: Spain, Belgium, Cyprus), 85 per cent with fertility treatment (top destinations: Spain, Cyprus, Turkey) (Eturbonews, 2008). McKinsey found the same positive reaction: 'The medical travellers we interviewed were uniformly quite satisfied with their experience. They wouldn't hesitate to go abroad for care should they need it again and would strongly recommend that friends and family members do so as well' (Ehrbeck et al., 2008).

They would do so, they reported, even if care were accessible and quickly available at home.

3.3 INSURANCE

The precondition is payment. A foreign hospital will probably be willing to provide emergency stabilisation without first seeing an insurance policy or a credit card. It is unlikely that the foreign hospital will be prepared to provide much else. That is what the market mechanism means.

Health tourism costs money. Different territories offer different things. International insurance is most successful where it empowers the patient either to buy a cheaper product or to compensate for a domestic void. This section explains how risk-pooling and prepaid policies make it possible for the patient to purchase medical and dental treatment in the global and not just the local market. The next section discusses payment out-of-pocket when there is no faceless third party to foot the bill.

3.3.1 Combinations and Permutations

Insuring agencies will not always reimburse for cross-border treatment. Their refusal is a wedge that is every bit as protectionist as a tariff. If the consumer must pay 100 per cent of the price abroad but only 20 per cent of the price at home, the lack of portability is an economic reason to turn down a bargain that would have been a cost-saving gain from trade.

Some consumers will be satisfied with policies that protect them in a single country alone. Others will shop around for policies that give them an international option. It is the great advantage of a competitive market that different carriers will offer different plans. Product differentiation allows niche suppliers to satisfy different needs.

In some cases the international option will extend to the whole range of medical services. No distinction will be made between core and periphery. In other cases the insurer will restrict the package to services that are not on offer in the patient's own country. Here the test is simple availability and not perceived quality of care. The proviso would be that the procedure is not banned because it is deemed dangerous or immoral at home. Few insurance companies will refund the cost of an organ transplanted abroad from an executed criminal.

Some insurers reimburse retrospectively and do not query the bill. Other insurers reimburse prospectively on the basis of agreed-upon diagnostic related groups. Transparency, written quotes and all-in packages make it easier to budget. They also block off the temptation to multiply the discretionary add-ons. Some insurers refund a standard sum per service irrespective of the treatment centre. Other insurers refund less for Mode 2 treatment in a lower-cost country. Such cheese-paring is counter-productive. It is a disincentive to seek medical care where the financial burden is the least. Or the most: hospital stays in Japan can be three times as long as in the United States. Attitudes to technology and drugs differ. Given the cross-national variation, it is not clear what the insurers should agree to refund.

Some insurers cap the cross-border refund at the cost of the public package at home. Other insurers, non-discriminatory, impose the same deductibles, ceilings and restrictions irrespective of whether the consultation takes place domestically or worldwide. Some insurers are more generous: the package may include Lasik surgery, experimental drugs or costly complications. Others insurers will refund less but charge less. They may cover routine dental care abroad but may exclude implants: an implant is not a natural tooth and must therefore be counted as cosmetic. They may ask the patient to prove that he is seeing a dentist at least once a year. Their argument is that, resistant to moral hazard, they will not look after a patient who has consistently neglected his teeth.

Some insurers will not see the need for treatment abroad. Others will go out of their way to encourage it. Some offer lower premiums to patients willing to travel to a lower-cost centre. Some pay for flights, hotels and accompanying caregivers. Some waive the cost-shares. Some guarantee a more comprehensive package. Some give a cash incentive. Some promise legal aid in case the knife slips.

Some insurers will pay for a further foreign appointment in case of complications within 12 months. Some will cover necessary follow-up or corrective treatment in the patient's country of residence. Some will have bilateral agreements of their own (including clauses on quantity discounts) with specific foreign hospitals. Some will have purchased a foreign treatment centre in the expectation that elective surgery conducted in a subsidiary abroad will cost them less.

Some business corporations with a self-administered group plan take an active interest in treatment abroad. It is mainly American companies that are exploring the overseas route. No major UK insurer currently allows companies to send employees overseas. The US shows a greater sensitivity to the price advantage in the face of rapidly rising cost. Treatment abroad allows employers to choose more comprehensive plans and to pay more affordable premiums.

Approximately a third of the larger employers in the United States believe that the option is viable. At least two American states, Colorado and West Virginia, allow their civil servants to have surgery abroad. While the precise figure is not known, one sample survey found that 11 per cent of company plans in the United States cover medical care in foreign countries (*International Medical Travel Journal*, 2008e). Serigraph in Wisconsin uses Healthbase, a Boston-based agency, to send customers to Apollo in India: the self-funded plan covers not only the medical and post-operative care but airfare, accommodation and concierge services on the spot. In the American North-West some company-based plans are using a specialised agency, Medtral, to send their employees to New Zealand for care. Financial intermediaries such as Swiss Re are prepared to reinsure them against cost-overruns. Conditions are imposed. The foreign hospital must, for example, be properly accredited and the foreign option must be managed by an approved agent such as WorldMed Assist.

Financial intermediaries are themselves a topic in borderless exchange. Just as trade in medical services has been liberalised on the precedent of trade in things, so trade in insurance has been opened up to international competition. New players threaten cosy cartels. They keep the premiums reasonable. New players, furthermore, offer new products. Foreign insurers might offer first-dollar cover where domestic insurers insist on high co-pays. Locals have more choices. So long as the carriers are adequately regulated and cross-border disputes expeditiously settled, there is no reason to think that domestic insurers will be more reliable or more cost-effective than insuring agencies with their headquarters abroad.

Variety is the spice of life. It is attractive that insurance arrangements should expand the choice-sets rather than stifle the opportunity to buy and sell. One thing, however, is a constant. All insurance companies will specify that the quality of care should be good. Normally they will insist that the hospital should be an internationally-accredited one. An example would be Bumrungrad: Blue Cross Blue Shield of South Carolina, Anthem Blue Cross and Blue Cross of Wisconsin have put it on their list of approved providers in no small measure because it has JCI status. JCI is not, of course, the only accrediting body. Nor should it be forgotten that many diagnostic and therapeutic centres forgo accreditation in order to plough the money back into care. Referrals are in that way constrained by the insistence on a hurdle higher than that which the consumer, if fully informed, might conceivably have preferred. Even in the case of quality control, variety is the spice of insurance. The consumer should have a choice.

3.3.2 Health Insurance: Holidays Abroad

Many people buy health insurance for a short trip abroad. It is not the same as the indemnity they would buy if they were in the market for

medical travel, targeted and focused. Holiday insurance covers the poli-
cyholders for emergency medical care and unforeseen medical evacuation.
It does not cover them for planned medical interventions, whether dental,
aesthetic or surgical. Holiday insurance is easy to obtain: the motive is
the holiday, the medical claims stochastic. Insurance for a known medical
problem is more difficult to arrange. Where there is a pre-existent condition or where the patient has already decided upon elective surgery, the
insurer will refuse the policy because the probability of a claim will be too
high.

Yet even medical tourists who are paying out-of-pocket will need
travel insurance. Their baggage might be lost. Their hotel might be over-
booked. A missed flight can mean a cancelled appointment. A cancelled
flight can mean the abandonment of a prepaid procedure. A trip abroad
for hernia repair can necessitate additional days in hospital if the patient
slips accidentally and breaks a leg. Even if insurance cannot be obtained
to cover the prearranged medical component, insurance may nonetheless
be bought and sold to cover the unanticipated contingencies and the non-
refundable prepayments that circumscribe the trip.

Inevitably, there will be disputes. Travel insurance might cover the
repatriation of the body: does this extend to a patient who dies during elective surgery? Travel insurance might promise an emergency airlift: will it
pay if a discretionary intervention fails? Travel insurance might guarantee
extra nights in case of *force majeure*: do complications in breast augmentation count as *force majeure*? Eventualities such as these will be subject
to the law of large numbers. Predictability is not the issue. The issue is
the extent to which holiday insurance can reasonably be used as medical
tourism insurance even if the death, the airlift and the extended stay are
explicitly included in the contract.

There will always be people who conceal chronic complaints in order
to claim back planned interventions from their holiday cover. Fraud is
sometimes detected and sometimes not. What is important is that honest
people should have access to proper protection even if the planned medical
component is in no way covered by their policy. As always, the insurer has
to separate the sheep from the goats.

The insurer can do this by confining health travel insurance to
group plans. It can cap permitted claims and impose a high excess. It can
exclude medical treatment in the United States. It can refuse all applica-
tions from the 65-plus. In ways such as these the insurer can protect itself
against statistical loss-makers while also protecting the policyholder
against unforeseen contingencies not related to the medical episode
per se.

3.3.3 Health Insurance: Resident Aliens

Life in a global village is increasingly cosmopolitan. Insurance will increasingly be required for the mobile and the uprooted who have links to more than a single jurisdiction.

One such group would be the retired. American pensioners are in Mexico. British pensioners are in Spain. They are there because of the lower cost of living, the more affordable rentals and the warmer climate. In some cases they will remain covered by their home Government, by an existing private policy or by their former group plan. The California Public Employees' Retirement System (CalPERS) covers retired California State employees anywhere in the world. In other cases their public-sector protection stops at the border. The retired must take out private insurance to cover their new life abroad. Those who cannot will face underwriting, exclusion clauses and higher premiums. In some cases they will be refused.

Another group with multiple links is non-resident manpower. The labour market is a cosmopolitan net. Unskilled, executive or professional, all grades now move about for work. In some cases their health insurance will be arranged by their company. In other cases they will be eligible to join the local State insurance system. Some land on their feet. Some do not. Uninsured foreign workers who come to the United States from Mexico, El Salvador and the Philippines are very exposed. There are 4 million of them in California alone.

Cross-border medical insurance may be an attractive solution for the transnational. Diaspora, issued by the medical travel agency PlanetHospital, is a low-cost plan marketed to uninsured Hispanics. Members are entitled to a basic package of up to three hours of telephone conversation per month with a fully-qualified doctor, plus up to three doctor visits per month in the United States, plus a limited amount of emergency care. After that the members are instructed to seek medical attention with low or no deductibles in their country of origin. The attraction of the policy is that the premiums are more affordable than would be the case if the patient had to undergo treatment in the high-cost United States. Many Hispanics actually prefer care in Mexico. The doctors are Spanish-speaking. The food and culture are familiar to them.

The insurers cross in both directions. Sistemas Medicos Nacionales S.A. is a Mexican health maintenance organisation licensed to operate in Southern California. It has 19,000 members in San Diego. They cross to Tijuana for urgent attention within the SMN network. BlueCross BlueShield of California offers a similar package, Access Baja. Typically employer-based, this binational policy provides for limited attention on the American side followed by more extensive (elective) treatment at BlueCross BlueShield centres in Tijuana, Mexicali and elsewhere in northern Mexico. Premiums would be at least one third higher if the medical attention were to be delivered exclusively on the California side.

Not all Hispanics, needless to say, live near the Mexican border. Not all will have families close enough to Baja to visit them. Illegal immigrants will not risk deporting themselves to Mexico in case they never come back. Itinerant labourers and domestic servants might not in any case be able to pay. For them the outpatients room and the free clinic might be all they can afford.

Despite its shortcomings, cross-border insurance can be a popular choice. Bustamante, in his survey of Mexican immigrants living in the United States, found that 62 per cent were in favour of this protection. They were willing to pay up to US$125 per month for insurance reimbursing services in Mexico in public hospitals. A minority were willing to pay up to US$250 per month for services delivered in private hospitals (Bustamante et al., 2008: 169). The Latino population in the United States is expected to double from 14 per cent of the population in 2005 to 29 per cent in 2050. New Latinos are one third as likely to have health insurance as the native-born population. About 62 per cent of Mexican immigrants in America for more than 10 years, 43 per cent of those in America for less than ten years, had health insurance. The rest did not.

The highest concentration of uninsured persons in the US is along the US–Mexico border. The border states account for 30 per cent of the total US uninsured population. Also, 'within border states, uninsurance is higher in the border regions than in other regions away from the border' (Brown, 2008: 2037). Brown argues that the lower level of insurance is a direct consequence of the ability of Mexican immigrants to return to lower-cost Mexico in the event of catastrophic illness. The native-born population faces a greater psychological barrier to going abroad. They are the ones who are the more likely to hold out for a health plan.

3.3.4   Health Insurance: The Multinational Union

Multinational blocs put teeth into the freedom of trade. The North American Free Trade Area and the ASEAN Free Trade Area are two of the groupings that are making themselves customs unions in order to bring into being a single market in goods, services and capital. Even more ambitious is the European Union: it has common economic policies, a European Parliament and a European Central Bank. The European Union is committed to borderless trade. Article 49 of the EC Treaty prohibits restrictions on the freedom to provide services across frontiers.

Medical care will be one of the good things that will have to break loose from its nation-State moorings. Not only is this in keeping with the European ideal, it is also of great benefit to patients in border areas, or who have gone abroad for work, or who need specialist care not available in their country of residence.

There is considerable variation in prices even within the EU. Hip replacement costs £948 in Hungary but £6422 in the Netherlands. Privately-insured patients together with some out-of-pocket clients are already crossing the borders to take advantage of the differential. The next hurdle will be EU residents insured under their home country's public plan.

Emergencies are always reimbursed. Unforeseen eventualities are covered by the European Health Insurance Card (EHIC). As for non-emergency treatments, however, the rule is that cross-border patients are only able to claim for procedures that are offered in their country of origin. They have no entitlement to cancer drugs or other medication that is not available at home. Rare diseases and treatments are a problem. Often patients go to a foreign country for a different product. The EU directive does not make provision for reimbursement in such cases. Nor does the EU system cover organ transplants and long-term care.

Each member-State defines the services to which its citizens have a right. Patients are reimbursed up to the cost of their treatment in their home country. Accommodation and travel are discretionary, as are the higher costs incurred by patients with disabilities. One consequence is that over-seas centres have a financial incentive to treat international patients with a view to the reimbursable rather than the local norm. Incomers cannot jump the queue where locals are waiting for care. A medical professional is expected to certify that the intervention is necessary. Patients are required to demonstrate that the delay at home has been excessive.

The European Court of Justice in 1998 (the Decker Case) ruled that Decker, living in Luxemburg, had a right to claim reimbursement in Luxemburg for prescription spectacles he had bought in Belgium. In 2006 (the Watts Case) it ruled in favour of a British citizen who had gone to France for a hip replacement after a year's wait in the National Health Service. A year's wait, it decreed, is medically unacceptable ('undue delay') even if it is within the home Government's country-specific targets. British patients who can access a private but not a National Health dentist are entitled to claim for dental work done in any of the EU-27 member-States. The criteria applied are not, however, necessarily clear or transparent.

The opportunities are there but they are limited. Cross-border health in 2007 is believed to have accounted for only 1 per cent of total public spending on care in the EU-27. Reliable data is not available. In the UK, only

552 official ('E112') permits were issued to UK residents for treatment in Europe (House of Lords, 2009: 13). Patients pay for their own interpreters.

Intending inpatients must seek prior authorisation from their health authorities where an overnight hospital stay is involved. Such permission constrains the patient's freedom to choose. A Committee of the House of Lords affirmed that the gatekeeper function was nonetheless in the social interest:

> We think that a system of prior authorisation is necessary. This will protect the financial resources of Member States' healthcare systems. It will also allow clinicians to explain clearly to patients the treatment options available to them, including their respective advantages and disadvantages. This is particularly important to enable patients to make an informed decision (House of Lords, 2009: 26).

Patients might make a decision based on a small number of considerations. Without guidance it might be a decision that they would live to regret. It is unclear who in each member-State will be in a position to advise on other members' health care systems. It is unclear whether the notes would be kept in the patient's own language so that doctors after repatriation will be able to read them for continuity of care. It is unclear whether a British patient in Poland will be asked to sign a consent form in Polish. Mistakes are bound to occur where a prescription drug with the generic name of captopril is called acepril in the UK, enalapril in Switzerland and lisinopril in Denmark. It is unclear where the liability for negligence will lie when a home patient is given the go-ahead to go abroad for care.

A member-State can complain that patient outflow is badly disrupting its hospital services. Liberalisation might lead to pan-European harmonisation or at the very least to local upgrading. Hospital trusts at home might be shamed into improving quality standards or reducing waiting lists. If they do so, the outflow could be self-correcting. On the other hand, health care systems remain national. Until such a time as there is a Europe-wide Ministry of Health, it might be premature to undermine the unique national base. Even 'prior authorisation' and 'undue delay' might have to be defined separately in each discrete jurisdiction.

Liberalisation will entitle the EU resident to reimbursable treatment in any member-State. The idea is not without its critics. Some feel that it limits member-States' discretion and autonomy. Some say that it in that way violates the principle of 'subsidiarity' or tolerance of member-State diversity. Some object that obligatory reimbursement within the EU makes it less likely that there will be NHS reimbursement for even cheaper care in Asia. Some say that an internal market puts competition before disinterested care. Some say that it does not go far enough. Until there is a single insurance system, it is argued, there will never be a single market in hips and teeth.

3.3.5   Health Insurance: Purchase and Provision

In some countries the two functions of payment and treatment are separate: Blue Cross insures but Cedars-Sinai delivers. In other countries the two functions are linked: the British National Health Service both finances and operates the medical facilities. An insurer can conceivably pay for its subscribers to be treated in a foreign hospital. It is much more difficult for the NHS to do this. Combining purchase with provision, the NHS is in the business of supplying medical care free of charge at the point of consumption. It is in the business of treating the sick through its own integrated network of hospitals and outpatient centres. It is not in the business of paying for care outside. To do this would make it a national health insurance agency and not a National Health Service at all.

Yet there is a new cooperation between the public and private sectors in the UK that is blurring the borders. NHS patients on long waiting lists are already having elective surgery in underutilised private hospitals. Willing to retain economic responsibility for payment but prepared to delegate the medical technicalities of provision, it is possible that the NHS is repositioning itself in such a way as to make treatment in India only a logical extension of treatment in Wimpole Street or the Wellington Road.

If the NHS were to pay for British residents to have their cataract removed in Chennai, the gain would be a dual one. The Service would save on the paid-out cost. The patient would not have to bear the psychic and physical burden of a wait. Apart from the anxiety and the pain, the condition could become worse if left untreated.

In 2006 some 50,000 British patients received treatment abroad. Of those, only 357 received financial support from the NHS. It was only the tip of the iceberg. In the United Arab Emirates the patients can claim from their Government for treatment abroad as well as treatment at home. In the United Kingdom the patients are given free care at home but they have to wait. There are currently 1.2 million patients on the NHS waiting lists. Treatment abroad would be a way of reducing the blockage.

If Britain were to adapt the Emirati practice, the NHS would build up a network of trusted providers at home and abroad. Although not proper subsidiaries of the British parent, the foreign hospitals would in effect have some of the properties of an external NHS. They would resemble the Costa Brava hotels with which the tour operators make their arrangements. One coachload leaves. Another coachload arrives. If the holiday-makers are satisfied with their experience, it seems rather unkind to say that they ought to have gone to Blackpool instead.

Creeping internationalisation can be no more than market socialism played out on the world stage. Yet it can also be a topic in the creeping privatisation that is already a feature of the British health care scene. About 13 per cent of British residents (7.3 million persons) already have private insurance. Three-quarters of that insurance is company-sponsored. As for the strictly NHS cases, significant numbers are paying out-of-pocket. What is happening is more than the internal market, inter-trust competition and the devolution of hospital budgets. What is happening is a tentative groping towards supply and demand because money makes the world go round.

Expectations are rising. State budgets are constrained. Patients want choices. NHS dentists are hard to find. Taxpayers are frustrated because they fund the system but cannot claim for the immediate, the aesthetic and the discretionary. Not everyone would still share with the founding fathers the conviction that State supply will one day match citizenship demand because social planning must ultimately triumph over moving disequilibrium. What many would say is that creeping privatisation is the inevitable consequence of high income elasticity. Creeping internationalisation may be just another way in which the unsatisfied are resorting to exit because voice and loyalty do not slake their thirst.

It may be the thin end of the wedge. If so, it may be more than a safety valve for a determined minority that in the end leaves the surrounding structure intact. Serious difficulties would arise if small-scale shuttles were to escalate into the norm, the demand and the expectation. The NHS is purchase *and* provision. It cannot be the same NHS if the majority of its clients are asking to be transferred out.

One difficulty is the inconvenience. Languages, cultures, even medical routines might not be the same abroad. Legal redress and compensation can be a minefield. Flight times to Asia are not two or three hours but more like ten. Continuity of care is a problem. Social workers, district nurses, community services and family doctors are not in a position to build up a relationship until their client has returned to the seamless web.

Another difficulty is cash flow. Where the patient pays on the spot and claims reimbursement later, there may be a conflict with the core NHS ideal of equal access for equal need. Not all patients have the cushion of savings and family that would allow them to pay upfront for the foreign hospital or to cover the overheads of travel and accommodation. There may be a considerable delay before the claim is processed and repayment received. Some post-operatives will be in urgent need of the cash.

A related difficulty is the price barrier. There is no guarantee that reimbursement will cover the whole of the outlay. If the treatment costs more abroad than the guide-price allowed, the patient will have to absorb the difference out-of-pocket or do without. Some will pay for private insurance in order to top up their NHS entitlement. Some will remain stranded on the waiting list at home because the queue at least is free. The result will be a two-tier service that tracks unequal incomes and the poor person's inability to pay. Such an inequity is incompatible with the levelling ethos of the citizen's right. It is also incompatible with the philo-sophical commitment to a common experience in a common ward with a common wait that made the NHS an architect of nationhood in the eyes of its founding fathers: 'There must be no allocation of resources which could create a sense of separateness between people' (Titmuss, 1970: 225). If the boss goes A-class in India and the worker goes B-class in Singapore, the quality might be the same but still the fellow Britons might be missing out on a priceless gift.

A fourth difficulty would be the economic threat to the NHS itself. If the patients are in India, there will be pressure to shut down some capacity at home. Cheap beds over there can mean expensive beds over here where loss of volume raises the average cost because the fixed overhead is not being spread economically. The NHS will find it difficult to plan ahead: it cannot predict what demands will be made upon it at any given time. The Government will be embarrassed: no Prime Minister wants to say that costs are out of control or that waiting times have become intolerable.

Even so, the pressures are there. Subcontracting to India or outsourc-ing to Thailand would reduce the burden on the British taxpayer: while quantities might expand to take up the slack, at least the external arm would keep down the price per unit of care. The same would be true in the United States where about half of total spending on health is Government spending. If Medicaid and Medicare were released for treatment abroad, it would make medical care more affordable. It would also have a dem-onstration effect. It would put the example of the State behind medical tourism and private payment abroad. Company plans and insurance companies might emulate the role model and follow suit.

The NHS could send registered residents abroad. Yet patients are also coming in, and not all of them pay. NHS care is free at the point of consumption. It is an open invitation. Outsiders from countries without reciprocal arrangements might enter the United Kingdom with the clearly-defined purpose of riding free.

There are people who use their savings to buy a plane ticket, enter on a tourist visa and then unexpectedly give birth or need a quadruple bypass. Accident and emergency clinics are unlikely to turn away such patients despite their lack of medical insurance or a credit card. Non-emergency cases can be asked for a deposit. Since they are free to leave the country without settling in full, the bad debt will have to be absorbed by the health authority. The burden is heaviest in the most heavily-touristed regions. In Taiwan where there is a national insurance rather than a national health system, non-residents are charged twice what the locals pay. It does not solve the problem. Genuine opportunists will be gone before the money changes hands.

3.4   OUT-OF-POCKET

America has private insurance and Britain has the National Health. In spite of that, there are patients in both countries who fall through the cracks. The invisible import fills a social void.

About 48 million Americans (16 per cent of the total) do not have medical insurance. About 120 million (39 per cent) do not have dental cover. The figure includes 9 million children. While many are too poor, others do not qualify because of a pre-existent condition. Some are low-level owner-entrepreneurs, discouraged by the cost of a personal plan (Adams et al., 2007: 1). Company-based plans do not protect the self-employed, the unemployed and the employee of the small firm. Out-of-pocket is their first and last resort.

Being insured is only the tip of the iceberg. Approximately 15.6 million Americans (18 per cent of the insured population) are medically under-insured. Although they have insurance, they will have reached their ceiling entitlement or are subject to an exclusion clause. A study in 2008 found that 43 per cent of chronically ill patients in America were missing out on needed care because they did not have the money.

Dentistry, physiotherapy and cosmetic surgery are extras. Plan administrators turn down a borderline intervention. The underinsured are under-protected. They spend more than they can afford or dispense altogether with treatment. An international study conducted by the Commonwealth Fund in 2008 demonstrates clearly what this can mean:

> More than half (54 per cent) of U.S. chronically ill patients did not get recommended care, fill prescriptions, or see a doctor when sick because of costs, compared to 7 to 36 per cent in other countries. . . . 41 per cent of U.S. patients spent more than $1000 in the past year on out-of-pocket medical costs, compared with 4 per cent in the U.K. and 8 per cent in the Netherlands (*Health Affairs*, 2008).

The average health insurance policy for an American family costs about US$12,680. Even if the company has a group insurance plan for its staff, often family members will not be included. Additional cover will have to be secured. A large segment of the population will not be able to afford the top-up. Health in America can cost a great deal of money: 'The year 2006 is a watershed year for U.S. employers and employees. Their combined average health care spending for a family of four exceeds the annual earnings of a minimum-wage worker' (Milstein and Smith, 2007: 137).

Employers are increasingly dropping health insurance altogether. About 63 per cent of firms in the year 2008 still sponsored group plans for working age adults. By 2015 it is estimated that only 50 per cent will be doing so (Adams et al., 2007: 5). Some businesses are being driven overseas, as Marvin Cetron, a specialist consultant, has reported: 'Virtually every entrepreneur I spoke with cited soaring and uncontrollable health costs in America as a reason to move factories abroad to countries where benefits were more limited, or nonexistent or where there was national health insurance' (Cetron, cited in York, 2008: 100). For those that remain there is a move towards high-deductible, high co-pay policies. Cost shares have quadrupled since 2000.

Even if an American has insurance, an excess of US$10,000 followed by a 20 per cent contribution can effectively price him or her out of the market. Himmelstein and his collaborators describe how one worker with a broken leg and torn ligaments faced financial ruin when he had to find $13,000 for deductibles, cost shares and uncovered services (Himmelstein et al., 2005). The worker in question was insured through his work. It was the co-payments that were beyond his means.

Commitments to the retired are being weakened. In 1986 66 per cent of American organisations with 200 or more employees were providing health benefits for their retired been-and-gone. By 2008 the figure had fallen to 31 per cent (Edelheit, 2008: 22). Eventually the lifelong protection may have to be phased out. Credit squeeze and recession will force firms to trim their costs. The sheer numbers will drive a coach and horses through the fringe benefit. Between 1997 and 2025 the headcount of Americans aged 60 and above will increase by nearly 90 per cent. The headcount of the over-65s will double. Older people make more use of expensive medical attention (Reisman, 2009: 22–33). Unit costs are themselves going up. Medical inflation was 8 per cent per annum in the United States in 2008. Rising premiums and rising prices will make it uneconomic for the former employer to continue care for the old.

The consequence will be that a large number of elderly pensioners will be left with State Medicare but no other medical insurance. They are unlikely to have a significant precautionary reserve. A couple retiring in 2016 at age 65 would need at least US$560,000 to supplement their Medicare entitlement if they matched the average American's life expectancy at birth of 82 for men, 85 for women. In fact, over 40 per cent of Americans have savings of US$50,000 or less (Adams et al., 2007: 7). Marginal patients such as these will have an economic incentive to try something new.

It is believed that as many as 18,000 Americans die every year because they cannot afford an insurance policy. As many as 2 million debtors (the figure includes their dependants) are driven into personal bankruptcy because of the cost of medical attention (Wolff, 2007). Medical bills are responsible for half of all personal bankruptcies in the United States. Surprisingly, according to a sample survey conducted by the Harvard Law and Harvard Medical Schools, more than 75 per cent of those officially bankrupted by sickness had health insurance when the medical catastrophe first struck. The cover lapsed once Americans on the way to a bankruptcy filing were having to pay on average US$11,854 out-of-pocket. People with cancer had average medical debts of US$35,878. Affordable premiums will be especially problematic for Americans uninsured because of a medical condition. A heart attack may have been the reason why they lost their job and with it their occupational cover (Himmelstein et al., 2005).

Americans on low incomes are the hardest hit. That said, the average bankrupt in the Harvard study was a 41-year-old woman with children, an owner-occupied home and some tertiary education. Being middle class was not enough. It may be part of the problem. The well-to-do can afford medical insurance. The destitute qualify for Medicaid. It is the income group in the middle that is the most at risk. The telephone had often been disconnected. The mortgage was in arrears. Income had dried up where the sick person had to take time off work. Surgery in Mexico or drugs in Canada are a safety valve and even a life-saver for Americans who face financial ruin because they cannot square the circle.

A quadruple bypass costs the uninsured US$122,000 at a medium priced hospital in South Carolina. It would cost them US$15,000 at an accredited, certified hospital in Bangkok or Kuala Lumpur. About 95 per cent of medical tourists in Costa Rica are Americans. Most are uninsured or underinsured. The great majority are not so much attracted by the low cost abroad as repelled by the unsupportable burden at home. If price-effective treatment cannot be found domestically, it is reassuring to think that it can be obtained somewhere else. The result is an equalisation in access and outcome which corresponds to the National Health ideal and yet is paid for out-of-pocket. It is supplied through capitalist supply and demand.

Out-of-pocket has the attraction that it makes a market. Where Governments and insurers settle the bills, the patient has no real incentive to search out value for money. Reimbursements, not market-clearing prices, tend to follow a negotiated, predetermined scale. In the United States about 87 per cent of health care in aggregate is funded by third parties. Chief among these are private insurance (35 per cent), Medicare for the elderly and the disabled (19 per cent), Medicaid for the poor (15 per cent). American bodyholders spend only 13 cents out-of-pocket for each dollar of care that they receive. Medicaid and Medicare enrollees pay nothing at all at the point of consumption: 'As a result, they do not shop like consumers do when they are spending their own money, and the providers who serve them rarely compete for their business based on price' (Herrick, 2007: 10).

Health care spending in the United States has risen in the last 60 years at twice the rate of the national income. Medical prices have risen at three times the rate of inflation. The acceleration in cost cannot be explained in terms of improvements in indicators: 'Regions of the country with the best outcomes for Medicare patients with chronic conditions typically spend less per patient than areas that have worse outcomes' (Herrick, 2008: 6). The runaway rise has been due in no small measure to the fact that out-of-pocket was 47 per cent 60 years ago and rational bodyholders were sensitive to price. It is still the case in the market for cosmetic surgery where prudent consumers are paying with cash that is their own: 'From 1992 to 2005, a price index of common cosmetic surgeon fees rose only 22 per cent while the average increase for medical services was 77 per cent; overall, prices for all goods increased 39 per cent' (Herrick, 2008: 8).

Prepaid markets tend to be sluggish. In the American domestic market (despite the fact that health care in 2008 accounted for approximately 16.6 per cent of the US GDP) protected consumers tend not to know what a particular intervention will actually cost: 'Consumers can guess the price of a new Honda Accord within $1000, but when asked to estimate the cost of a four-day hospital stay, those same consumers were off by $12,000' (Herrick, 2007: 10). Direct-pay consumers are different. They have no choice but to compare the prices and the services. The money they are spending is exclusively their own.

About 78 per cent of health spending in India and 51 per cent in Mexico is direct-pay spending of this kind. The bulk of international health outlays are subject to the same hard-nosed pay-as-you-go. Price sensitive and cost aware, paying patients are the most likely to demand that a good estimate be disclosed in advance. They will want to ensure that the medical entrepreneurs deliver more for less and do not make them wait.

Reinforcing the tendency of customers to look the medical mystique unceremoniously in the mouth is the counterpart propensity of professional managers to streamline their product. Some of the hospitals that do an international business are run by unsentimental executives from the hotel or car industry. Unlike doctors, they have never been exposed to the service ethic. What they do know is marketing, efficiency and salesmanship. They know that they have to please their customers to survive. They know that they have to make care affordable and good if they are to compete.

It is tempting to say that sick people in South Carolina would not have to go to Bangkok for their bypass if America had a comprehensive system of national health insurance. Mandatory insurance, making basic care a universal entitlement, would mean that outsider Americans would no longer have to search worldwide for the option they can afford. It would be a mixed blessing. While it is of incalculable value that the lives of as many as 18,000 Americans should be saved, the downside would be a reduced incentive to scour the globe for the best deal around. More demand chasing limited supply would mean a rise in the unit price of care. Opening the flood-gates would mean that the crowds flood in.

Citizenship-wide insurance can lead to higher prices and longer waits. One solution would be to combine universal coverage with the guaranteed reimbursement of approved health care abroad. Another solution would be to confine the national service within the national boundaries but to encourage patients to pay out-of-pocket if they want something more. Even in a top-class national system like the British National Health there are always going to be non-standard requirements that do not mesh well with the norm. In such circumstances the minority member, paying twice, will have go out of the network to satisfy an idiosyncratic want.

One patient is willing to pay for a shorter wait: since the NHS rations not by price but by time and cannot therefore auction queue-jumps to the highest bidder, the patient under stress, in pain or in a hurry must find an answer outside. Another patient has a need for a shadow service: interventions not on the NHS list such as experimental drugs or organ purchases might be tradable through free-market international exchange. Then there is the British pensioner retired abroad. He or she will often be paying cash because even British citizens cannot return for their National Health once they have been spending more than six months out of 12 in the European Economic Area, more than three months out of 12 anywhere else. It seems rather unkind to deny British people living in the sun the rights towards which they have contributed all their life. Be that as it may, payment out-of-pocket is their way of buying themselves back into health.

Some will have the money. Some will not. It is a useful reminder that even care that is cheap in relative terms can nonetheless be expensive in terms of the absolute outlay. For that reason medical tourism does presuppose a threshold level of resources. In some cases there will be savings. In other cases there will be family. In extreme cases it will have to be a loan.

Interest puts up the cost of the procedures. Instalments are a psychic burden on a post-operative trying to get well. Many observers find it distasteful or even unethical when the surgeon himself brokers the introduction to a finance company. Collateral might be a second mortgage on an owner-occupied home. Borrowers without marketable assets will find it more difficult to raise capital, while even an owner-occupied home can be too illiquid to appeal to a risk-conscious bank. Governments in economic emergencies have been known to underwrite bad debt. In normal times they leave it to the banks to operate their own profit and loss account. Systemic protection against moral hazard is not much comfort to the patient who, turned away, has no alternative but the loan sharks and the criminals. Even they might not want to lend.

Whether from savings, family or loans, the more affluent among the uninsured might just be able to get together the US$15,000 they need for the bypass in Bangkok that would have cost them US$122,000 at home. The unskilled, the deserted, the severely disabled without a job, the sweat-shopper on US$1 a day will find it more difficult to jump the hurdle. Out-of-pocket is not a promise of service. Replacing the upbeat name of 'medical tourist' with the downbeat description of 'medical refugee' should not be allowed to conceal the fact that there are many throughout the world who cannot afford to pay for the last refuge. The poorest of the poor will not stand a chance.

3.5   CARE AND CURE

Residential care is a field in which an overseas centre will often be able to quote a lower price:

> In most areas of the United States, the cost of nursing home care can easily surpass $60,000 per year. But in Mexico, high quality long-term care costs only about one-fourth as much. For about $1,300 per month, a senior can get a studio apartment that includes laundry service, cleaning, meal preparation and access to around-the-clock nursing care (Herrick, 2007: 3).

The average fee in the United States is four times as much. About 80,000 American seniors now live in Mexico. Since they are not covered by Medicare, they are obliged to live cost-effectively. They are reassured by the knowledge that long-stay care in Mexico is both available and affordable should they not be able to manage on their own.

Residential care is a sunrise area in India as well. There medical chains such as Apollo Hospitals and business corporations like Impact Senior Living are investing in retirement communities. It is a break with the cultural tradition of caregiving in the family but also a recognition that the ties of kinship are looser than they were. The cost of a place in the retirement village will be lower than in the West: a deposit of US$85,000 and a monthly fee of US$250 have been cited (Rai, 2008: 66). The general ambiance will be more Indian. Initially the homes will appeal to affluent locals. There will be over 200 million over-65s in India by 2030. A number of ethnic Indians have emigrated to make their careers abroad. The homes will appeal to returnees such as these. Over the years, there is no reason why other nationalities could not move in as well.

Singapore does not have the resources that would make it an obvious centre for incomers in search of assisted living. Unlike the Philippines or Thailand, it is unable to provide affordable nursing homes for retired Japanese or Americans. What it does have is an ageing population that is anxious about life's final act. A study of the baby-boomer generation has shown that only 37 per cent expect to be living with one of their children; that 14 per cent would not mind staying in a nursing home and that 25 per cent were prepared in due course to move into a retirement village (Chan and Yap, 2009: 69). About 93 per cent said they expected to continue living in Singapore. Malaysia, however, is just across the Causeway. Residential care in Malaysia costs only half what it does in Singapore. A cross-border solution would save a considerable sum of money.

Cross-border care can mean an indeterminate stay. It can also mean an extended visit sandwiched between spells spent in the resident's own country. An example would be a long-stay holiday in sheltered accommodation or in an adapted hotel situated near a foreign hospital. In some cases the insurers in the home country will actually pay, on the assumption that it costs them less if the client spends the cold winter months in Turkey or Thailand than at home in Norway or Finland. Long-stay tourism has the advantage that it is contra-seasonal and contra-cyclical. When it is low season for the holiday-makers or when holiday bookings are cut because of a recession, the rooms can be discounted for block-booked cross-border retirees.

3.6   PRICE AND PERFORMANCE

Prices matter. Other things matter too. It is the task of this concluding section to say whether price matters most or whether price is just one attribute among many in the demand function for health care abroad.

3.6.1   Comparative Advantage

In his *Principles of Political Economy* David Ricardo showed that efficiency gains would be at their maximum where each trading nation specialised in what it did best relative to the alternative economic activities in
which its fully-employed inputs would be comparatively less productive:
'It is this principle which determines that wine shall be made in France
and Portugal, that corn shall be grown in America and Poland, and that
hardware and other goods shall be manufactured in England' (Ricardo,
1951 [1817]: 134).

Countries specialise in the areas in which each is relatively even if not
absolutely superior. The result is that standards of living are higher across
the board. Autarky means lower productivity and higher cost. Countries
that shelter behind non-tariff barriers such as unnecessarily high medical
qualifications should take this lesson to heart.

It is easy to understand what comparative advantage would mean in an
early economic order where exports were stamped by climate, soil and mineral
resources. The United States, with plentiful land, exported food to densely
populated England. England, with substantial capital, exported locomotives
to agrarian Brazil. Saudi Arabia has oil. Bali has beaches. The will of whimsi-
cal nature endows them with a surplus that they can use in trade.

A later economic order is more difficult to read:

> The concentration of computer companies around Silicon Valley. . . . has
> nothing to do with bountiful natural deposits of silicon; it has to do with Xerox's
> fabled Palo Alto Research Center, the proximity of Stanford University, and
> the arrival of two young men named Hewlett and Packard. Silicon Valley could
> have sprouted up elsewhere (Blinder, 2006).

In the later economic order nature is marginalised, even eclipsed by the
human input. Productive advantage is in no small measure man-made. It
can change over time. It can be changed by public policy.

Bhagwati uses the phrase 'kaleidoscopic comparative advantage'
(Bhagwati, 1998: 40) to pick up the transient nature of a nation's unique
potential. Dynamic and not static, the nation's strongest selling-point can
alter over time as capital accumulates, skills are built up and subsistence
farming gives way to new technology. Nowhere is the mutability more
in evidence than in the case of medical care. Mexico has more land and
more labour, cheaper rents and lower wages. On the other hand, it has less
physical capital and less human capital, higher bank rates and fewer specialists. It is not clear how to transform this bundle of pluses and minuses
into comparative cost or even market price. It is what it is until it becomes
something else.

3.6.2   Trade Diversion

Health tourism in the United States is in part a response to the high cost
of care at home. Companies' profits are evaporating into fringe benefits.
Disposable incomes are being absorbed by out-of-pocket payments. Prices
are rising by 8 per cent a year. It is no surprise that consumers are becoming desperate. The number of medical tourists leaving the United States
is growing faster than the number of foreign patients coming in to the
United States for care: 'If the trend continues, it is likely to mean the loss
of billions of dollars annually for U.S. healthcare providers' (Rhea, 2008).
US health care providers in 2008 lost approximately US$16 billion in
revenue forgone to outbound medical tourism: 'That figure is expected to
grow to $68 billion by 2010, up 325 per cent' (ibid.). This represents trade
diversion from home to foreign hospitals of 3 per cent within the space of
only three years.

Yet market economics is the science of turning points. A tendency
to globalisation can mean a tendency to equalisation precisely because
the inputs and the consumers are mobile and free. Within the European
Union dental care is cheapest in Hungary and most expensive in England.
Arbitrage and rational choice suggest that it will not always be so. As the
dentists move out and the patients move in, the prices are likely to come
closer together. India and Thailand cannot assume that their hospitals will
be cost-effective forever. Even in America some health care providers are
already matching the prices quoted abroad. Connell is speaking too soon
when he says that the writing is on the wall: 'Rich countries can rarely
compete, and restore the old order. . . . Medical tourism has reversed direction. . . . Economics effectively calibrates the rise of medical tourism. Price
differentials between most Asian states and more developed countries are
considerable and are presently diverging even further' (Connell, 2006:
1095, 1097).

If Silicon Valley were built on silicon and Bangkok Health were built on
Bangkok, they could plead that they had a durable comparative advantage. This, however, is not the case. The most the care providers can do is
to lower their price for services provided internationally and then recoup
the loss by putting up the price for procedures that do not lend themselves to Modes 1 to 4. Hernias gravitate to the going price. Accident and
Emergency, hospital kidney dialysis and chronic pulmonary disease go for
all the traffic will bear.

Prices will come closer together. Whether they will become the same
is less certain. There will always be the add-on of transportation and the
overhead of accommodation. The first-mover will have brand-name recognition that seals in a rent. Unfamiliar destinations will be discounted

because of the differences in way of life, language, medical liability and personal safety. Markets will not be contestable where providers and professionals face barriers to entry. Patients (especially long-stay patients) do not want to be separated from the support system of friends and family. A long-haul flight can be unpleasant. Some people have never flown before. Some people are simply afraid of the General Abroad. Perhaps this will become less important as more people take holidays in foreign countries.

International politics and geopolitical calamities will mean delays in vetting patients before visas are issued. Insurance companies often will not refund: 'If payors covered medical travel, the potential US market would probably range from 500,000 to 700,000 patients a year. . . . The savings might be on the order of $20 billion' (Ehrbeck et al., 2008). Exchange controls and lack of transparency stand in the way of a single price. So do doubts about the continuity of (chronic) care where the original surgeon will not be in a position to deliver follow-up operations. It is tempting to say that the market for health is not national and not regional but fully international. Hurdles such as these, however, suggest that the law of one price might not be just round the corner.

The hurdles are there and they are a deterrent. The result is that patients do not pursue care abroad in borderline or break-even circumstances: 'The required savings for patients are likely to be more than $10,000 a case, the threshold reported by today's uninsured US medical travellers' (Ehrbeck et al., 2008). Prices converge where the deviation is great. The dispersion is sealed in by inertia where the difference is less than US$10,000.

3.6.3 Demand Curve and Medical Travel

Price matters: 83 per cent of the respondents in a British survey in 2008 said that they had gone abroad expressly to save on the cost of private treatment. Some reported considerable success: 17 per cent had saved upwards of £10,000. Even after allowing for travel and a hotel, some had made a saving of almost 60 per cent on breast augmentation and knee replacement (Treatment Abroad, 2008).

The full story is, however, more complex. In Gallup's Eurobarometer study only 48 per cent of the sample said that the primary reason for medical travel was a lower price. However attractive in itself, a lower price was not the selling-point that attracted them first. More important to them were access abroad to a service not available at home (91 per cent), better quality of service (78 per cent), treatment by a renowned specialist (69 per cent) or a shorter waiting time (64 per cent) (Gallup Organization, 2007: 5, 11).

McKinsey in 2008 did a multi-nation survey of the reasons why medical travellers, strictly defined, sought inpatient treatment abroad. It found that 40 per cent went international because they wanted the most advanced technology. The second largest segment, at 32 per cent, wanted better care than they could find in their own (often less developed) countries. The third largest group, 15 per cent of the total, were deterred by long waits at home. At the bottom of the list were the price-sensitive. Only 9 per cent travelled because of the lower cost of medically necessary procedures. Only 4 per cent went abroad because discretionary procedures cost less. Only 13 per cent, in short, had selected medical tourism because the price was right (Ehrbeck et al., 2008).

US patients made up almost all of the respondents in the price-sensitive group. They were disproportionately consumers of discretionary procedures such as tummy tucks, liposuction and rhinoplasty. As incomes rise, this market sector is likely to show considerable growth. Even so, 13 per cent is a relatively small proportion. McKinsey's result might have been different if they had included outpatient care or broadened their definition to include wellness treatments. What the McKinsey investigators found is nonetheless striking. A street busker is cheaper than Covent Garden. A hamburger is cheaper than the Savoy. Price matters. Other things matter more.

4.   Quality

A second reason why patients go abroad is to enjoy a high standard of service. Some medical centres in the sending nations are among the best in the world. Not all, however, may be said to match the front runner's level of excellence. A top-tier hospital in India or Thailand might have better capital equipment and more specialist manpower than an under-resourced provincial infirmary in rural Tennessee. The rapid expansion in health tourism has been made possible by the improvement in the quality of care in the foreign host countries. Otherwise there would be ethical concerns which doctors and insurers might find difficult to reconcile with their professional commitment.

The standard of service might be better. At the very least it might be just as good. Milstein and Smith, comparing median care at home with median care abroad, speak of 'lower-cost surgery at levels of quality that cannot be readily distinguished from domestic care' (Milstein and Smith, 2006: 141). It is value for money. Curtis Schroeder, former CEO of Bumrungrad, has put it as follows: 'We're selling Cadillacs at Chevy prices' (*Economist*, 2008). Something that is just as good but not nearly as dear should not automatically be dismissed out of hand merely because the view from the window is of palm trees and not the Golden Gate.

This chapter, concerned with the quality of care, is divided into six sections. Section 1, 'Perception and reality', asks what travellers want and what they are likely to find. Section 2, 'Malpractice', explores the worst-case scenario when something goes badly wrong. Section 3, 'Information', shows how customers can learn the specifications of the product they are planning to buy. Section 4, 'Principal and agent', explains that there are advisers who can counsel the patient on the spectrum of choice. Section 5, 'International collaboration', says that cooperation with a famous name is an indication that a local player has entered into a certain class. Section 6, 'Accreditation and certification', demonstrates that both hospitals and professionals can be tested to see if they are good.

4.1   PERCEPTION AND REALITY

Treatment abroad can mean better treatment. It can also mean human error and avoidable complications. No one wants to leave the hospital in worse shape than he or she came in. No one by the same token can predict with certainty what the outcome of a medical intervention will be. Medical care is an unusual industry. Customers still have to pay even if they die on the table. That is why, in considering medical treatment abroad, they have to make an informed guess about the difference in quality that a lower or a higher price will buy.

4.1.1   It Can Happen Here

Treatment abroad may involve risks and dangers. The same, however, may be said about treatment at home. Sample evidence from the United States suggests that the likelihood of a patient receiving clinically appropriate care was only 53 per cent. The proportion was the same whether the patient had private insurance, government-sponsored insurance or no insurance at all. It is tempting to make the US or the UK the benchmark standard of medical excellence. The reality is less reassuring. Even in the US the doctors have performed unnecessary surgery for money. Even in the UK MRSA resists the antibiotics in the National Health.

Medical errors in the USA, according to the Institute of Medicine, are causing between 48,000 and 98,000 patient deaths a year: 'Even when using the lower estimate. . . . deaths due to preventable adverse events exceed the deaths attributable to motor vehicle accidents (43,458), breast cancer (42,297) or AIDS (16,516)' (Institute of Medicine, 2000: 26). A Johns Hopkins Study puts the figure at 225,000, 'making America's health system the third-leading cause of death in the nation' (*International Medical Travel Journal*, 2008e). There are errors of omission: only 24 to 29 per cent of known diabetics regularly receive haemoglobin tests, essential for the early detection of complications. There are errors of commission: MRI is ordered when a simple X-ray would be enough. Medication errors in the USA are costing over US\$3.5 billion annually (Adams et al., 2007: 1, 11). Things, in other words, regularly go wrong: 'One-third of U.S. patients. . . . reported either being given the wrong medication or dosage, experiencing a medical error, receiving incorrect test results, or facing delays in hearing about abnormal test results' (*Health Affairs*, 2008). Slippages were less frequent in the Netherlands (17 per cent), France (18 per cent) or Germany (19 per cent). The patient has approximately an 80 per cent chance in the Netherlands, France or Germany that the doctors will not make a mistake. While it is better than in the United States, it is nonetheless not very reassuring.

The Healthcare Commission in the UK estimates that one hospital patient in ten in developed countries will fall victim to mistakes and slip-ups. An incorrect diagnosis is made. The wrong dose or drug is prescribed.

The surgeon operates on the wrong part of the body. The paperwork is misplaced. A third of the inpatients affected will suffer severe illness or even die. A high proportion of the adverse side-effects could have been avoided if the lessons of unsafe practice in the past had been learned.

In Britain in 2006–07, despite the vigilance of the watchdog Human Fertilisation and Embryology Authority, there were 40 mistakes for every 10,000 cycles of in-vitro fertilisation. In 2003–04 there had been 15 (Leach, 2009). In one case the twins were black but the couple was not. As for primary care, medical errors occur up to 80 times per 100,000 consultations. Up to 20 per cent of these actually damage the patient's health: 'The cost of clinical negligence in England was £579 million in 2006/7' (Healthcare Commission, 2008: 30). Only half – 49 per cent – of NHS trusts comply with all safety standards.

The National Patient Safety Agency in the UK received 959,590 reports of errors and 'near misses' between April 2007 and March 2008. There were 7660 reported cases of severe harm. There were 3471 deaths. The Patients Association, describing soiled bedclothes, cancelled operations, inadequate food, bungled referrals, inaccurate diagnoses and dismissive staff, extrapolated from its sample to the effect that as many as one million NHS patients between 2002 and 2008 may have been given care that was demeaning and poor (Patients Association, 2009: 3). A specialist unit in a top-of-the-range Third World hospital may have a better success rate than that.

4.1.2 Better Quality Care

Even in the First World the treatment centres can leave behind a surgical clip or pass on the free gift of septicaemia. Even in the First World bad blood can be the cause of hepatitis or AIDS. The fact remains that developed people do not normally regard treatment in Dubai or Chennai as a step up to a higher plane. Underdeveloped people are different. They tend to regard medical care in the West as the best-quality treatment they can buy.

Treatment centres in the First World are still in the game. The McKinsey study found that 40 per cent of medical travellers sampled had gone abroad because they had a felt need for gold-standard technology. A further 32 per cent had gone abroad because they wanted a higher standard of care than they believed to be on offer at home. The bulk of the patients who had travelled for performance had travelled to the United States. They had originated in Latin America (38 per cent), the Middle East (35 per cent), Europe (16 per cent) and Canada (7 per cent) (Ehrbeck et al., 2008). Medical travellers to the United States come disproportionately from poorer countries.

Yet the less developed countries are themselves developing a profile in the quality niche. They can increasingly compete on outcomes and amenities. An underdeveloped country must not be confused with an underdeveloped hospital. Camels may be delivering the supplies and the five-foot way may be doubling as a public toilet. What goes on in the treatment room may nonetheless be state-of-the-art through and through. The death rate at the Escorts Heart Institute in Delhi is less than half that for heart operations performed in the United States (York, 2008: 100). In the case of operations performed in New York, it is about a third: 0.8 per cent as compared with 2.35 per cent (Hotel Marketing Newsletter, 2006). At the Asian Hospital and Medical Center in Manila, the mortality rate in heart surgery is 1.4 per cent. For the United States as a whole it is 3.09 per cent (Santos, 2008: 25).

Some treatment centres in the Third World have well-publicised weaknesses in personnel and supplies. The treatment centres that service an international clientele will be not one but many cuts above. At the higher end, there has been levelling up towards international standards of care and safety. Hospitals will screen transfusions for HIV, syphilis and malaria. They will dispense alcohol disinfectant from the foot of every bed. The doctors are likely to have trained or done specialist work in recognised hospitals in America or Europe. They will be working with up-to-date electronic and diagnostic equipment, US- or EU-certified. They will have years of experience in the correction of a squint or the delivery of a bypass. Doctors and other professionals will not only speak good English (the present-day lingua franca) but, frequently, other languages as well. Mandarin and Arabic are particularly valuable if the patients being treated are from Greater China or the Middle East. Bumrungrad in Bangkok can draw upon a number of Chinese-speaking Thais. The Dubai Healthcare City has Arabic-speakers on its staff.

Patients who go abroad for care can be confident that they will be seen by the consultant and not just a houseman. About 85 per cent of American patients told a survey that the service was more personalised than at home (Medical Tourism Association, 2009: 35). There might be a guarantee of 24-hour personal on-call from the attending physician. There might be a higher nurse-to-patient ratio. Single rooms might more frequently be the norm. A cot might be put in the room for an apprehensive relative. The receptionists might be more welcoming. Appointments might last longer. Treatments might be provided without a wait. A range of specialities might be available in-house should a blood-test for anaemia unexpectedly turn up HIV. Safety, cleanliness and food might be selling points. Even abstracting from the much lower price, these are attractive features in themselves. The customer will not just be paying less but receiving more.

The fact that professionals in less-developed countries are frequently of a different race need not count against them. The patient from England (where 34 per cent of the medical workforce is from the ethnic minorities and 70 per cent of all locums qualified overseas) or America (where a quarter of all medical students are foreigners, most of them Third World) will take it in his stride that his doctor in India is an Indian. One out of every five doctors in the world is ethnically an Indian. There are more than 37,000 ethnic Indian doctors in the American Medical Association alone. Only half of the doctors of Indian nationality who receive their training in foreign countries actually return to India later on (Gupta et al., 1998: 219). A patient in America or Britain will already know what it means to be examined by an Iranian, injected by a Philippina and fed by an African. In some First World hospitals the patients would be moderately surprised if their doctor were named Smith and their nurse were a WASP. Going to the Third World is not all that different from being treated by the Third World at home.

Patients from the First World can experience a good quality of service even if cows forage in the streets. The same is true of patients from comparable Third World countries where the standard is not as high. A Bangladeshi who goes to India for an angioplasty is doing so not just because the provider is cheap but because the treatment is reliable. Cross-infection will be less prevalent. Misdiagnosis will be less likely. Transfusions will not be contaminated. Wonder drugs will be in stock. Tests will be possible that cannot be delivered in Bangladesh. Surveys cited in the previous chapter show that patients are generally satisfied with the care they receive.

4.1.3 Risks and Hazards

Quality can be good in Third World treatment centres. Even the grandson of a rubber tapper can be an experienced surgeon. Even in the heart of darkness there can be evidence-based medicine. Yet there are also some risks. Section 4.1.1 showed that bugs and lost records can be real concerns even in countries where the supplies are not delivered by camel. This section spotlights unique shortcomings in the poorer countries which might convince both a First World and a Third World patient to opt for costly Harley Street instead.

There are different diseases in a foreign country: the new arrival will not have built up an immunity before he braves the crowded airport, the taxi and the ward. There are unfamiliar germs in the water and the air: incomers should have hepatitis injections, use high-factor sunblock and take appropriate antimalarials. Outside the airconditioned hospital there will be the heat and dust. Restaurant food can trigger diarrhoea. Different patients will react in different ways to environmental factors such as these.

Although time is limited, too many procedures should not be squeezed into a single visit: it is a strain on the system to have too much cosmetic surgery at once. Although the beach is tempting, the post-operative should avoid over-exposure to the rays: patients wanting a tan should schedule the sunbathing before the surgery. Although there are good reasons to go home, unexpected complications can prolong a stay abroad. Proper convalescence may be a part of the healing process. Jet-lag disrupts sleep patterns. Travel sickness is debilitating. Sitting upright can be painful. Blood clots and pulmonary embolisms can develop on long-haul flights. Diabetics on insulin will need to rethink their schedule.

Once the patient has returned to base, the foreign physician can no longer provide the follow-up. Professionals in the home country may have to take over the function. Taking on another doctor's case, always problematic, is especially difficult when the first-line doctor is far away. The new doctor might not know what techniques, implants, drugs or materials the overseas doctor has used. The new doctor might not want to become involved at all if professional negligence is suspected and genuine harm has been done. If the foreign doctor has botched the breast enlargement, the home doctor who promises to put things right may become liable for crippling damages himself.

Some doctors in developed countries have expressed serious reservations about the untested backwater. A minority, as one patient has stated, have gone so far as to refuse continuing care: 'When I returned and went to see my doctor, he was furious. He said no American doctor would treat someone who had had surgery overseas' (quoted in York, 2008: 101). Doctors have no economic incentive to promote international mobility and competition. Returnees have been sent to the hospital emergency room or to an unfamiliar practitioner with whom the patient will not have an ongoing relationship. It is hard to reconcile this intransigence with the Hippocratic Oath. As the President of the International Medical Travel Association has said: 'International patients are often treated like pariahs. Continuity of care is the number one concern of patients and they often need their hometown doctor's support. . . . International patients should not be penalised and should be treated the same as any other patient for after-care' (*International Medical Travel Journal*, 2008c).

'To treat the sick' enjoys the official endorsement of the American College of Surgeons. The ACS advises patients to consider carefully the 'medical, social, cultural, and legal implications of seeking medical treatment abroad' but it also opposes the erection of a new Berlin Wall: 'The

ACS encourages patients to seek care of the highest quality and supports their rights to select their surgeons and health care institutions without restriction' (American College of Surgeons, 2009). The problem is that not all doctors have been as open-minded about cross-border care.

There is a further set of risks that come into play when the patient goes abroad for care. These relate not to established centres of excellence like Bumrungrad or Apollo but to the cheaper second-string that may be cutting corners to stay in the game. Internet sites might exaggerate success rates because business is business. Representatives might disappear if the fees and deposits are paid in advance. Confidentiality might be breached. Kitchens might be unhygienic. Specialist skills might atrophy where patient throughput is low. Locally-produced equipment might not be finely calibrated. Locally-produced generics might not have been rigorously tested. An imported scanner might turn out to be second-hand. General practitioners or even medical students might be roped in to do surgery. Interpreters might be schoolteachers who make mistakes because medical terminology is not their field.

Foreign qualifications might not be easy to assess and might not be very good. Examiners might have been bribed. Certificates might have been faked. In 2004 the Delhi Medical Association determined that as many as 40,000 unqualified persons with fraudulent credentials were practising medicine in Delhi alone. Every 10 minutes a patient in Delhi was losing his life or undergoing irreparable damage at the hands of a fraud. In 2007 the Health Ministry in Saudi Arabia discovered 4000 forged certificates in a sample of 20,870 (Timmons, 2008: 12). Persons seeking care abroad should research carefully the doctor they will be seeing.

Ranging more widely, there can be violent demonstrations, inconvenient curfews, opportunistic violence, gang warfare and political instability. An urgent procedure might have to be cancelled because of civil disturbance. Recovering patients might be trapped abroad by an airport sit-in. Internet warnings posted by Government bodies such as the British Foreign Office will often be disregarded until it is too late by health tourists who only want to see their doctor and go home.

Pirates, kidnappers and hurricanes are all good reasons to stick with the devil one knows. Even so, there is a school of thought that would treat exaggerations and one-offs as special pleading aimed at discrediting foreign rivals in order to seal in high fees at home. Where it is illegal for national legislation to restrict transnational competition, horror-stories about permanent scarring and anaesthetics that starve the brain might be the non-tariff barriers that sitting tenants raise up in order to block off market penetration. A more balanced view would therefore be that medicine is always and everywhere a minefield of *ifs*. Inferior foreign institutions can seriously damage the patient's health. So can inferior doctors and hospitals at home. All things considered, it is better not to fall ill.

4.1.4 Market Correctives

Treatment abroad can mean that medical documentation is incomplete. A full medical history might have to be taken and the whole battery of tests conducted. Misdiagnosis, delay, wasteful repetition, allergic reactions, incompatible drugs all put an uneconomic burden on the patient's health and wealth.

It would, however, be premature to throw out the treatment baby with the documentation bathwater. Solutions can be found. Already the referring doctors can send their own notes ahead. At the very least the foreign centre will have been told the patient's blood-type. It will have been warned that peanuts can kill. As records become computerised, so treatment centres worldwide will be able to access the entire data-set. Patients themselves could carry a complete set of medical records in a portable memory stick. If the data were encoded in a wristwatch or a mobile phone, it could be downloaded even if the patient were unconscious. Thus does the electronic revolution make its own small contribution to the reduction of human error abroad.

Multinationalism too ensures that home data will go abroad. An illustration would be the Mills & Mills Medical Group. It has hospitals both in Spain and in Britain. Its principal area of expertise is cosmetic dentistry and aesthetic surgery. Since Mills & Mills draws its clients disproportionately from the United Kingdom and Ireland, it strives to offer preliminary consultations and appropriate aftercare in the patients' home territory. Even if the treatment is delivered in Marbella, the providers have a physical presence on the patient's home turf.

Oxygen Zone, similarly, has made an arrangement with a clinic in Manchester for preliminary assessment and necessary follow-up. Oxygen Zone offers aesthetic and dental surgery in Serbia. It provides a twelve-month guarantee. It discounts its charges in the slack season. It pays for additional flights and accommodation in Serbia if its Manchester partner concludes that further work is required.

VitalEurope offers pre-treatment consultations and aftercare follow-up in London. About 95 per cent of its clients come from the UK. The dentistry itself takes place in Budapest. Implants come with a seven-year guarantee. Patients wishing to discuss their treatment are able to contact their provider on the telephone or by email. Trained staff sometimes travel to major markets abroad. They provide a diagnosis, recommend procedures and flag up complications. Patients are often given an assurance that the same professional they are seeing in London will continue to treat them in Budapest. VitalEurope offers its two-centre option because it understands the logic of its market. Each provider must do something to differentiate its product from that of other international clinics which are competing for the same client base. Some doctors go so far as to promise lifetime after-sales service. They keep in touch with their patient by email and fax.

4.2 MALPRACTICE

Things can go wrong. Neighbouring organs are damaged. The healthy leg is amputated. The babies are mixed up at birth. Doctors are human. People are fallible. While some systems do better than others, no medical system will ever have a perfect score. That is why the prospective patient should have a detailed contract. It should specify that the supplier will cover the fees if unsatisfactory workmanship has later to be corrected. It should specify that the provider will pay proper compensation if there is no other way to make good the loss.

If genuine negligence can be demonstrated there is a right to redress. It is easier said than done. The doctor–patient relationship does not come with a money-back guarantee. Outcomes vary: no two patients are identical. The body is full of secrets: a pre-existent weakness, not spotted or declared, might make the operation unsuccessful. Time hides the clues: it is hard to assign blame for latent infections and lagged complications where they lie dormant in their incubation phase. It is never easy to prove that the patient was given all relevant information before he or she signed the consent form: relevance is relative when the client is too distraught to listen. It is never easy to sue a practitioner for something he never promised to do. The dentist contracts to fill a tooth. Can he be taken to court for failing to notice that the patient has cancer of the mouth?

Information asymmetry, the fee-for-service incentive, supplier-induced demand (Reisman, 2007: 56–64) are an invitation to abuse in the patient's home country and not just abroad. Services are heterogeneous. The providers have a head start. It is hard enough to monitor abuse in one's own country. It is even more difficult to sue successfully in a far-away place where the language, the laws, the court system are not the same.

Foreign cultures may have a different interpretation of anxiety, pain or inconvenience. The patient weighing home and abroad will want to know how satisfactorily medical claims were settled in the past. Even, moreover, if the court decides for the plaintiff, the compensation might still not be up to the tariff in the patient's own country. In the United States, in particular, settlements can be substantial. Foreign courts, however generous, will seldom make comparable awards. Nor will foreign doctors have the malpractice insurance that would allow them to meet American-style claims. It is swings and roundabouts. Less insurance means a lower price.

It is tempting to say that patients from the First World should avoid medical treatment in the Third World unless they are prepared to take a chance. All but 5 per cent of the respondents to a survey said that they were 'concerned' (76 per cent) or 'somewhat concerned' (19 per cent) about the pitfalls of a lawsuit in a foreign country (Medical Tourism Association, 2009). In fact, however, the legal position is much stronger worldwide than one might suppose.

The foreign defendant for one thing might have a physical presence in the plaintiff's home country. Doing assessment and follow-up in an overseas capital, opening local offices to market the name or simply dialoguing with patients on an interactive website, the foreign supplier will come within the home country's jurisdiction. It may be possible for a medical multinational to be taken to court in Dallas for a procedure that was delivered in Monterrey. Even if there is no local presence, cross-border litigation is greatly simplified where the countries have formally agreed to cooperate in civil law.

A local law, moreover, will often uphold the client's rights. Thailand's Procedural Act for Consumer Protection Cases, introduced in 2008, is such a law. Article 13 offers a statutory guarantee that the burden of medical negligence will not lie where it falls: 'The medical service provider, who committed the error that had an effect on a patient's life and health, must take responsibility for the victim for a maximum period of 10 years even if the adverse health condition caused by the medical error shows up later'. Article 40 says that the victim must never again suffer in silence: 'The judge can increase the compensation for a patient who wins a lawsuit if they find more damage. The judge can revise the verdict within 10 years.' In addition to that, Sarnsamak writes, the new Act effectively reverses the onus of proof:

> In the past, when plaintiffs filed a suit with the civil court, they had to prove the medical malpractice was caused by a doctor or medical service provider. This was a complicated process because most doctors and medical service providers did not give any evidence that could prove professional error. The patient had to wait a long time to receive compensation. But under the new law, doctors and medical service providers will have to prove that the error was not caused by them. If they cannot do so, the court will order them to pay compensation to the victim as soon as possible (Sarnsamak, 2008).

Costly defensive medicine, more frequent lawsuits and higher malpractice premiums are bound to be the ugly face of the new patient's charter. The advantage is the protection afforded by the legislation even to the foreign patient whose Thai doctor has made a mistake.

Furthermore, patients themselves (or, for group plans, their employers) may have taken out a rider against malpractice committed abroad. Here as elsewhere, one market sells a product that will correct another market's failure. Some packages cover the cost of a lawsuit in a foreign country. Others reimburse treatment for aftercare, repair surgery and complications. Others pay for lost wages, breach of confidentiality, severe disfigurement and accidental death. Even if a claim cannot be made against a professional abroad, insurance makes it possible to obtain the appropriate sum at home.

Foreign professionals too might choose to buy international policies. It is a selling point in their publicity that they can afford to pay American-standard indemnities. It is less of a selling point that their insurance will also cover the excrescences of moral hazard and the cost of malpractice litigation. The downside is the expense. The upside is that the patient feels more confident because the protection is there.

Additional protection is provided by the medical facilitator who makes the booking. The position is not clear: since the intermediary is only a broker, it might deny professional liability as the malpractice was not committed by its staff. On the other hand, there is a recommendation and a contract: the client might sue on the grounds that he was misdirected or badly advised. Travel agents take out insurance against contingencies such as cancellation due to freak weather. It is possible that they should also have insurance against claims of medical negligence in a foreign country or unintentional misrepresentation at home. Documents can be lost. Legionnaires' disease can spread through the air conditioners. The policy pays an agreed sum if the unexpected happens. Costly litigation could make a small travel agency bankrupt. Immediate reparations might dissuade clients from taking the matter to court.

The underwriter, needless to say, will only cover an agency that can prove it selects licensed practitioners with a sound professional record. In this way the insurer is protecting the patient *ex ante* as well as *ex post*. The underwriter might further secure its own interests by prespecifying the jurisdiction. What is the norm in one country might not be acceptable in another. An American patient suing an Indian clinic will prefer the American-style compensation that would be awarded by an American court. The Indian clinic and its insurers will prefer India where the damages are less. Either way, the domicile of the contract must be agreed upon in advance.

In some cases the intermediary voluntarily accepts some liability as a part of its service. An example would be LasikAbroad.co.uk. This specialist agency, operated by the Swedish parent Salveo Travel, not only books competitively-priced laser eye surgery in Istanbul but also offers a full refund if the surgery does not go ahead and a five-year guarantee of a second treatment if the patient's eyesight deteriorates. The agency protects itself by dealing with Dr Bas. Dr Bas is a member of professional bodies in both Europe and America and is a highly experienced practitioner. He has personally performed the procedure more than 50,000 times.

When all else fails, the employee covered by a group plan can sue the employer. Employers, reinsured or self-funded, are understandably nervous about vicarious liability. Terrorism, flash floods, road accidents, medical malpractice – the employer may not be prepared to take the chance. Nor might a referring physician in the country of origin. Unfamiliar with the clinic abroad and in two minds about risky therapies not approved by bodies like the Food and Drug Administration (FDA) in the USA or the National Institute for Clinical Excellence (NICE) in the UK, the local doctor might not want to get involved.

A final comment would be this. Perception can distort the assessment. The newspapers report the things that go wrong. They do not write about the far more common things that go right. Even in rich countries surgery can fail. Even in rich countries there is an element of *caveat emptor*. Even in poor countries people can sue. And in both rich and poor countries there is the supervisory function of the professional bodies and of the media. Irrespective of the outcome of a court case, a doctor does not want to lose his good name or be struck off the roll. A hospital does not want to become known for employing underqualified doctors who inflate the statistics on post-operative complications and are behind avoidable deaths in theatre.

4.3   INFORMATION

Any assessment of quality, before or after a service is purchased, presupposes reliable intelligence on prices, waits, amenities and outcomes. It is one of the attractive features of the information age that more is in the public domain than ever before. Asked in a survey how they found out about medical tourism, 49 per cent of respondents said the Internet, and only 2 per cent said their doctor. Asked how they researched the alternative destinations and hospitals, 73 per cent said the Internet, 5 per cent said a friend, and 5 per cent said a facilitator. Books were not mentioned. The clued-up nowadays are all online (Medical Tourism Association, 2009: 34).

Some of the information is made available by the suppliers. Foreign hospitals have their own websites. Where these are in their own language, many will either add a parallel website in a target language (English, Japanese, Arabic, Chinese and Russian are commercially-attractive choices) or register with multilingual portals such as ONMEDIX in Germany. Treatment Abroad, the leading information portal for medical tourism, offers a 'Perfect English' editing service: its English-speaking copywriters will review a foreign website, correct the grammar and make it easy to understand. First impressions count. The website is often the first contact the client will have with a potential provider. Most hospital websites in Japan are available in Japanese only.

Suppliers open offices in key overseas markets. They employ foreign middlemen to represent their interests. They go direct to the doctors, the travel agencies and the insurance companies in the importing nations. They indulge in salesmanship through joint packages that include accommodation and tourism. They offer discounts for repeat business. They make use of in-flight magazines to attract customers who are already en route for business or pleasure. A service is not of any use to its clients if they do not know it exists.

Suppliers also advertise in newspapers and journals targeted at international patients. They are sometimes allowed to do this even where direct advertising of medical services is deemed unethical and (as in Japan) not permitted at home. In some countries the publicity will include glossy photographs and testimonials from satisfied customers. In other countries there will be little more than a description of the services, the qualifications of the doctor, the address of the clinic and a small photograph. In Malaysia, where advertising of local (but not foreign) hospitals was legalised in 2006, the Ministry of Health's Medical Advertisements Board (MAB) must approve all medical advertisements. Superlatives like 'world class' and exaggerated promises are not allowed. In Thailand private hospitals often ask the Thai Medical Council to review the materials they have drafted for branding and promotion. Guidelines steer a middle course between rigid prohibition and unrestricted licence. Loosened regulation gives the providers the freedom to cry their wares. How many tourists in Vietnam have been made aware of the Kim Boi Mineral Waters at Hoa Binh or the Thap Ba Hot Spring Centre at Nha Trang?

Hospital websites post information on linguistic competence, security, confidentiality, food, bed availability. Those seeking to attract international business are under real pressure to make their quality indicators known. They are likely to reveal the prices, tabulate past outcomes and state the number of times a given procedure has been performed. They may make available the CVs, the credentials and the track records of the individual doctors: 'Many medical travellers know more about their doctors overseas than about their doctors at home' (Ehrbeck et al., 2008). Sometimes they post before-and-after photographs. Sometimes they post testimonials from satisfied customers. Sometimes they make use of the video function to offer a virtual tour. Sometimes they have a 24-hour inquiry line so that sufferers in the time zones can ask what they need to know.

Foreign hospitals on demand will normally provide selected names of past patients. Such disclosure allows potential clients to consult the 'alumni' on the nature of the experience. They can ask about the courtesy of the staff and their bedside manner. Patients may also post their ratings and reviews (suitably vetted for libel, obvious falsehood or crass commercialism) on social networking sites. Sites such as these provide an insider's perspective not just on the treatment centre but on the treatment itself. Information can be posted on possible side-effects, post-operative discomfort and the rigours of the long journey home.

Computers enable consumers to enlighten one another. So, however, do direct contacts. Personal recommendations and word-of-mouth provide guidance to would-be patients who want to make a rational choice. Hospital visits enable the expatriate already living in a country to tour the facilities and speak to the staff. Interactive video and telephone conversations give the foreign patient and the foreign doctor a chance to exchange information on the service that is demanded and supplied.

Professional bodies provide information. The Medical Tourism Association, representing United States hospitals, medical facilitators and insurers, is prepared to share information on quality indicators, costs, safety and hygiene. There are also the specialised sites. Treatment Abroad, neither a provider nor an agency, is the most frequently accessed of these infomediaries. Established in 2005, www.treatmentabroad.com within five years was attracting 70,000 visitors a month. About 1500 of those visitors were making inquiries about a specific procedure. They were going online cheaply and quickly to source a clinic for their eyelift, their tooth implant and even their heart.

There are general search engines such as www.RevaHealth.com, based in Dublin: it compares prices and offerings from a database of over 60,000 providers in England, Ireland and a further 50 countries (only 1000 of which actually pay for their listing). There are country-specific websites such as www.treatmentindia.com and www.IndiaCares.com (for India) or www.treatmentincyprus.com (for Cyprus): they bring the rest of the world up to date on the state of play in a single country. There are regional portals such as www.ArabMedicine.com and www.arabmedicaltourist. com: they cater to the 3 million Arabs who go abroad for medical care.

Some websites are unsponsored: Cosmetic Miracles at www.cosmetic miracles.com provides a league table for plastic surgery in various countries and does so without support from the industry that could call its impartiality into question. Most, being privately owned, have to raise their money through advertisements from clinics and travel agencies.

Some travel agencies nonetheless have reservations about information being provided directly in this way. If the consumer can make up his own mind, the middleman might not be required. The direct route keeps the transaction costs down. An agent, of course, reduces the opportunity costs of search. Time is money. Busy people on high incomes may therefore prefer to employ a facilitator. So might people on low incomes who do not have the education for the Internet. Either way, delegation to an insider may be the more economical choice.

Additional information is available through the media. Newspaper articles describe what the patient has seen. Television programmes and satellite channels showcase the choices. Then there are *Complete Medical Tourist, Medical Tourism in India, Medical Tourism: A Bangalore Perspective, Mexico: Health and Safety Travel Guide* and a number of other guidebooks. The most widely consulted is Josef Woodman's *Patients Beyond Borders: Everybody's Guide to Affordable, World-Class Medical Tourism.* First published as a general survey in 2007, it is now also available in country-specific editions (for Singapore, Korea, Turkey, Taiwan, Malaysia and India). In some cases there has been collaboration from local players. In the case of Malaysia, for example, there was input from the Ministry of Health and the Association of Private Hospitals of Malaysia (APHM). In the case of Turkey, advice was received from the Accredited Hospitals Association of Turkey (AHAT). A website for patient feedback and updates complements the book. There is a special orthopaedic edition. In future there will probably be editions devoted to other medical conditions as well.

There is a great deal of information in the market for care. Too much is as bad as too little. Overwhelmed by overload, there is a possibility that confused patients will fall back on heuristics and rules of thumb. Hospitals and countries will be treated as synonymous with success. Patients who know they are buying trustworthiness and peace of mind will buy what looks and sounds right. Reputation is capital. The Bumrungrad or the Singapore brand name puts patients in beds. Groote Schuur in Cape Town is famous for its heart surgery. The Portland image is swish and modern. West is best.

A well-publicised failure or a recent court case can have the opposite effect. Foreigners might desert the hospital and even the country if they hear that a patient was dropped in theatre or an out-of-date drug sold on as new. Presentation counts. Much is in the mind. Selective recall can drive business away rather than attracting it in. As valuable as objective indicators will be, decrepit buildings must give way to marble columns and the staff must be given a clothing allowance.

Consulting the league tables, admiring the marble columns, what is clear is that patients are increasingly taking matters into their own hands. They are obliged to do so: 'Medical systems are under stress as demand for physician time exceeds supply. As a result, patients are researching their illnesses and suggesting treatment options to the doctors in a bizarre form of reverse doctoring. Such active participation by patients has been simultaneously called a doctor's best dream and worst nightmare' (Bookman and Bookman, 2008: 60). Education and computer literacy mean that patients are in a better position to collect the evidence and compare the alternatives. Co-payment gives the consumer an incentive to shop around. Many helping hands help. The consequence is that patients are better placed than ever before to exercise their freedom to choose.

4.4 PRINCIPAL AND AGENT

Consumers can make their choice on their own. In doing so, they will be doing no more than what is described in the economics textbook when it explains how rational shoppers proportion the price to the marginal utility. Yet health care is different. General knowledge might not be enough. The wrong decision might be irreversible. Free to choose as they are, rational shoppers therefore fall back on authority because they do not want to make a mistake. They frequently employ an agent because they do not want to damage their health.

The treatment episode almost always begins in an agent's office. The first point of contact for a patient who doesn't feel well will usually be a general practitioner in his or her home territory. The doctor will provide an initial diagnosis, explain the options, estimate the costs. The doctor will if requested provide advice on the availability and quality of service alternatives abroad. Discounting as appropriate for embellishment and concealment, the doctor will bring information on foreign treatment-centres to the attention of the client.

Often the doctor in the importing country will have an established link with a doctor abroad. As in all industries, networking shares information and uncovers opportunities. It is a warranty that, like a consumer protection law, corrects a market failure. It may cost money. If so, it may be money well spent:

Economists have been puzzled by the degree of price heterogeneity in markets for consumer goods and services. . . . Research on the role of social networks suggests that some price variation may reflect not only interpersonal variation in the possession of information, but also heterogeneity across transactions in buyer–seller relationships. Presumably, under conditions that have yet to be specified, apparent deviations from equilibrium prices may represent either quasi-insurance costs to buyers, investments in long-term relationships by either party, or other moves in systems of dyadic or generalized reciprocity (DiMaggio and Louch, 1998: 636).

Doctors at a distance will be able to turn to their counterparts on the spot for advice and good counsel. Primary-care practitioners will send patients to an out-of-country professional in the same way that they would make a considered referral to a tried-and-tested contact at home. Repeat business keeps the standards up. Sequential contracting fosters trust and reduces uncertainty. The treatment centre knows that the referring doctor will not send it further business if it has padded its invoices or been shamed in a CNN tell-all. Embeddedness promotes cooperation. Short-run self-denial is an investment in long-term self-interest.

The doctor in the country of origin will screen the patient pre-departure to make sure he or she is well enough to travel. A quote will be obtained from an overseas surgeon. Medical findings may be faxed across. A tele-conference may be held. In some cases the patient will have a preliminary consultation with the designated surgeon before he actually goes abroad. This is the case where the initial referral is to the John Radcliffe Hospital in Oxford but the actual operation is performed at the Durdans Hospital in Colombo. The British specialist flies out to serve as the lead surgeon in Sri Lanka. The package (including a stay in a four-star hotel) costs the patient half what it would have done in the UK.

Later on, once the patient has returned home, the referring doctor is able to provide post-discharge follow-up. This is a guarantee that performance will be audited and standards monitored. It answers the objection that treatment abroad is of inferior quality because it does not allow for continuity of care. Information technology ensures the instantaneous transfer of files in both directions. The general practitioner at home will have a complete record of the procedures and drugs that were administered to the patient overseas.

The referring doctors exercise an active check. Their efforts are reinforced by those of the insurance agencies. Since it is the insurers who will have to pay, it is in their financial interest to ensure that an operation is value for money. Blue Cross has made its own arrangements with named hospitals in Asia, Europe and Latin America. Its senior executives have flown out to conduct site visits and consolidate personal contacts. Nurses inspect the safety facilities and assess the level of comfort. Screening in this way, the insurer is able to see what it is buying. It is able to reassure itself that the quality will be sound. Insurers' visits can complement JCI accreditation. They help to keep the unit cost within bounds.

Quality can be controlled by an insuring agency. If the insurer serves as the representative, and if there is an established tie-in, the principal has a reasonable expectation that the foreign clinic will not let the side down. Similar reassurance is provided by specialist facilitators. Medical facilitators are factotum businesses that walk the patient through all the steps:

> Medical facilitators are companies that guide the use of medical tourism for patients and providers. Many patients find using facilitators to be more convenient and expedient than looking for a program on their own. Facilitators have experience in the medical tourism process and are able to address any concerns or questions that patients might have. They can advise on cleanliness, waiting lists and MRSA. They often provide assistance with logistics, travel arrangements, translators, scheduling of appointments, coordinating follow-up, the transfer of medical records, airport pickup, accommodation before and after the hospital stay, travel insurance. Some promise a personal coordinator on call 24 hours a day. Patients may even be able to get lower rates from medical facilitators than directly from clinical programs abroad (Deloitte Center for Health Solutions, 2008: 12).

It is believed that there are almost 1000 niche facilitators in the market. Most target Americans. Agents are not free. They charge a commission that can be 20 per cent of the medical bill.

Some facilitators are hotel chains: the ITC-Welcome Group links up the patient with the provider. Some are travel agencies: Commonwealth Travel in Singapore acts as a one-stop shop for planning and logistics. Some are specialist brokers that do nothing but arrange medical trips. Leading names in this field include PlanetHospital, MedRetreat, IndUShealth, MedSolution, Global Choice Healthcare, Med Journeys, Companion Global Healthcare, BridgeHealth International, Operations Abroad, Medical Tours International, Surgical Tourism Canada and the Medical Tourist Co.

Some facilitators have an established relationship with named foreign centres. Thus Medical Tourism Partners in New York specialises in sending Americans without health insurance to Bangkok Hospital Medical Center or Samitivej Hospital, also in Bangkok. Both have JCI status. SM Tours in Myanmar sends local patients to Phyathai in Bangkok. Vertex in Myanmar is an authorised agent for AMRI in Kolkatta. Tam Tam Tours in Mauritius and Cloud Web Travel in Ethiopia are global agents for Apollo. American-owned Meddent refers only to the Orthodent clinic in Serbia. Serbian-owned Medical-Tourism-in-Belgrade is a fully owned subsidiary of the only clinic it recommends, the Dr Kuljaca Clinic in Belgrade. Renaissance has a continuing relationship for cosmetic surgery with the San Lucas Clinic in Buenos Aires. Restored Beauty Gateways sends patients to Bangkok Hospital Pattaya and Bangkok Hospital Phuket. The Akbar Group in Pakistan represents HCA International Hospitals in the UK. The HCA network, the largest private hospital group in Britain, musters the Wellington, Lister, Princess Grace, Portland, the London Bridge Hospitals, the Harley Street Clinic and others. Apart from Pakistan, HCA has representatives in Nigeria, Kuwait, United Arab Emirates, Greece, Cyprus, Libya and Egypt.

Some facilitators represent a named supplier. Others specialise in a single country. New Medical Horizons brings medical tourists to the United States. There are over 70 medical travel agencies in the US that send patients to India. Doctour brings patients to Korea. MedTral funnels surgical cases to New Zealand. Destination Health Greece sends patients to Greece. Dental Travel Romania sends patients to Romania. Beautiphil Holidays has an unrestricted list of specialists in the Philippines. Medical Tourism in Panama uses a call centre in Sydney to market Panama to clients in Australia and New Zealand. Surgical centres in Panama are recommended to it by its local partner, South Seas Pharmaceuticals S.A. The website of South Seas Pharmaceuticals S.A. well encapsulates the nature of its business: www.nipandtuckpanama.com.

Just as some facilitators specialise on a single provider or region, so others are non-exclusive and untied. They make clear that their contract lies solely with the patient. One example would be the Jeddah office of California-based PlanetHospital: its aim is to advise outbound medical tourists from Saudi Arabia and the Gulf on the medical centre that would best meet their requirements. Another example would be Star Hospitals, owned privately in India, which operates a call centre staffed by medical professionals. A clinical recommendation is made by a doctor or trained assistant. After that the caller is given information on accredited centres in India, Singapore and Thailand.

Facilitators differ greatly in the personal service they provide. Some make appointments and little else. Others, like Beautiphil, offer a concierge service and operate a 24-hour helpline. Restored Beauty Gateways not only sends its Australian customers to trusted Asian clinics, it arranges for its groups to be escorted by an Australian trouble-shooter who personally deals with problems on the ground. MedToGo in the United States, run by medical doctors in Arizona, inspects premises in Mexico, interviews professionals and does background checks. Where required, its representatives go with the patient to Mexico.

Medical facilitators can arrange for the patient to be accompanied by road or air. They often employ representatives to meet-and-greet their clients at the airport and befriend them while they are in the country. Health care aside, facilitators can provide the normal services of a non-medical travel agent. They procure tickets and visas, reserve hotel rooms, smooth the transfers from hotel to treatment centre, pass on dietary arrangements. They make it their business to know about unusual deals such as a package combining full-body screening with Botox injections and sightseeing or the beach. ALLO Holidays advises British people not just on cosmetic and dental tourism in Poland but on skiing holidays and winter sports as well. Absolutely Thailand Dental Makeover Vacations arranges for New Zealanders to be treated in Chiang Mai by dentists trained in the USA or Germany. After their teeth are straight it whisks them off to see the elephants, the hill tribes and the night bazaar.

Facilitators market in territories where they feel there is an untapped need. It makes sense for the agency to be in the same country as its patients. An agency on the spot can use local knowledge to focus its appeal. It is probable as well that the uninitiated will feel more comfortable dealing with their own countrymen than they would with foreigners based abroad. A halfway-house would be the franchise. Thus Beauty Gateways, headquartered in Perth, has franchised its name and business model to investors in New Zealand and the UK. The initial period of the franchise is two years. The upfront cost is £40,000.

Facilitators, like the referring doctor and the insurer who pays, make a useful contribution to the quality of care. They are led by pursuit of their own profits and their own market share to scrutinise the qualifications of foreign surgeons. They verify that professional memberships are up to date. They perform due diligence to confirm that medical equipment is best-practice. They visit the laundry and the stores to ensure that hotel and catering facilities are up to scratch. It is in the economic interest of the providers to ensure that good standards are maintained at all times. Hernias come and go but facilitators go on and on. Doctors and hospital want to be retained in the portfolio.

Facilitators form networks of their own to share knowledge of trustworthy professionals and gold-standard institutions. Regular conferences are held which allow them to refresh their contacts. Trade publications and postings give participants an overview of the market. Because they are a community, the facilitators are in a better position to exercise countervailing power than if they were isolated contractors who had to assess each provider *ab initio*. The problem is that the facilitators themselves may be a new Wild West. The facilitators limit the power of the providers. No one, however, seems to be enforcing the transparency and the accountability that would keep the power of the facilitators in check.

Dedicated trade bodies such as the Medical Travel Association, the International Medical Travel Association (collaborating with the Pacific Asia Travel Association), the Asian Association of Medical Tourism, the European Medical Tourism Alliance and HealthCare Tourism International are attempting to fill the gap. Their watching brief is especially useful in view of the fact that facilitators have not had medical training. Industrial self-regulation is, however, still in its infancy. Different home countries, different medical destinations and different kinds of treatment make the industry by its very nature complex and heterogeneous. Besides that, the seal of approval is not obligatory. Travel agents are understandably reluctant to pay for a certificate so long as it is not required. Perhaps the solution lies in the hands of the patients. If the sick demand memberships and certificates before they part with their money, there will be an economic incentive for the health-travel agents to agree to inspection in order to secure the lucrative letters after their name.

On the one hand there are the strict standards of the medical professionals. The Singapore Medical Council's Ethical Code states explicitly that Singapore doctors should not share fees with agents or receive commissions for referring clients. On the other hand there are the guidelines and recommendations of the business practitioners. Travel Abroad gives advice on business dealings in its *Code of Practice for Medical Tourism*. The Singapore Ethical Code is enforced by the Singapore Medical Association. Doctors who go in for fee-splitting can be suspended. The Treatment Abroad Code is enforced mainly by the Kantian Categorical Imperative. Agents who offer credit at extortionate interest or pocket membership fees without delivering quality advice, so long as they do not abscond with their client's money or otherwise break the law, are subject to no real sanctions save for spoiled self-image and the bite of conscience. It might not be enough.

As in all industries, there are going to be cowboys and scoundrels. Entry is easy, even for players with no background in travel or medicine. Often the facilitators are too small or too new for a bank to back them up with a financial bond. Sometimes the agents will evade controls by situating their physical premises outside a tightly regulated market or by trading through a virtual agency that is not compelled to carry insurance. There would seem to be a good case not just for national regulation and professional associations but for multinational benchmarks and cross-border licences as well.

Facilitators would submit a portfolio documenting their experience, insurance status, and possibly even general knowledge. They would include references both from the supply and the demand side of the business. A peer review panel would confirm that their track record was of a reasonable standard in areas such as hotel bookings, airline reservations, lost luggage and the specific problems of travellers with disabilities. The business is global. The rule of rules ought to become global as well.

4.5   INTERNATIONAL COLLABORATION

Heuristics abound. The brand name of an established corporation is a proxy guarantee that its drugs are safe. Commercial blood banks are trusted because the Ministry spot-checks for contamination and date-stamps. And then there is the international affiliation. A memorandum of understanding with a foreign medical school or a foreign treatment centre is an unspoken promise that quality will be upgraded until it reflects well on the international name. It is a way of saying that local hospitals will have access to the latest in medical thinking and managerial technique. Local hospitals will not have to make their own mistakes.

Wockhardt Hospital in India and the Healthcare City in Dubai have a connection with Harvard Medical International. HMI is the global arm of Harvard Medical School. Wockhardt itself is providing expertise in setting up and operating a best-practice hospital in Abu Dhabi. Apollo in India, like Hospital Punta Pacifica in Panama, has a link with Johns Hopkins International. Clinica Hospital San Fernando and Centro Medico Paitilla, also in Panama, have tie-ups with the Cleveland Clinic, Tulane University Medical Center, Baptist Hospital South Florida and Miami Children's Hospital.

St Luke's Medical Center in Manila has links with the Columbia University College of Physicians and Surgeons, the Weill Cornell Medical College and the Memorial Sloan-Kettering Cancer Center. The Columbia University College of Physicians and Surgeons has further arrangements with hospitals in Paris, Beersheba and Istanbul. The Memorial Sloan-Kettering Cancer Center has relationships with institutions in Hong Kong, Barcelona, Geneva, Athens, São Paulo, Istanbul and Singapore.

The international connection gives the patient confidence that the quality of the service will approach that in the foreign partner's country of origin. Everyone trusts Johns Hopkins. Clinica las Condes in Chile is not yet a household name. Its 10-year affiliation with Johns Hopkins and its JCI status will help the Clinica to attract more international as well as more domestic patients.

In some cases the partnership is loose: the foreign partner is only con-firming that germs are under control, data stored securely, medical staff doing a reasonable job. In other cases there will be an element of vertical integration: patients being diagnosed or treated abroad will be referred back to the metropolitan hospital if a higher standard of expertise is required. The collaboration is in this sense a two-way street. Not only do American patients have the reassurance they need to go abroad, foreign clients learn from the international partner about the treatment opportunities on offer in the United States. US hospitals in this way gain a foothold in the business. Sometimes foreign doctors, trained in the United States, will have retained their contacts. Sometimes American doctors will be sent on secondment to support the foreign team. Either way, the level of expertise will be raised. The local hospital will stand out in the crowd.

International arrangements can involve provision as well as validation. The University of Pittsburgh Medical Center not only has partnerships with Palermo, Cyprus, Qatar and Dublin but has also gone into a joint venture with GE Healthcare. GE Healthcare is a British-based company which specialises in diagnostic equipment, radiation therapy and imaging technologies. Together they are planning to establish 25 specialist cancer centres in Europe, the Middle East and Asia. Their project stops only one step short of the fully-owned subsidiary that dispenses altogether with international collaboration. The Cleveland Clinic has outstation facilities in Canada. It is operating a 360-bed hospital in the large multi-clinic Sheikh Khalifa Medical City in Abu Dhabi. It is doing this on its own rather than playing the role of big brother to an infant hospital trying quickly to create a reputation for itself.

Partnering can extend beyond treatment to training. Cornell Medical School is collaborating in medical education in Qatar. It is operating an advisory centre in Seoul. Duke is partnering the National University of Singapore in the creation of a Graduate Medical School. The presence of foreign (mainly American) institutions such as these protects medical standards, increases the supply of doctors and retains local professionals in the country. Some would have been reluctant to remain in a less-developed region if they had not had access to high-quality institutions that provide in-service training and offer an opportunity for research.

4.6 ACCREDITATION AND CERTIFICATION

A manufacture can be inspected before it is bought. A service cannot be, and the delivery can be irreversible. Certification of the supplier is the standard way in which expected quality can be estimated even before the artist turns to the blank canvas and begins to work. About 59 per cent of patients surveyed in 2008 stated that hospital accreditation was 'very important', 22 per cent that it was 'important'. Only 7 per cent said it was not important at all (Medical Tourism Association, 2009: 36).

4.6.1 Doctors

The educational background of professional staff is frequently used as an indicator of quality. Where and when they studied, where and when they have worked, what experience (if any) they have had in foreign countries, how many times they have successfully performed a named intervention are all taken as proxies for competence. So are licences granted by the Ministry of Health or by professional associations. Periodic renewals add supplementary value. In Japan the doctors are licensed for life. Continuing education is not mandatory.

Many doctors have trained or worked abroad. As there are no medical schools in Cyprus (the first is planned for 2013, but with an annual intake of only 70), all doctors on the island have been trained in Greece, the UK, the US or continental Europe. One consequence is that they will often remain members of leading professional associations abroad. The foreign patient will be reassured where these bodies are based in the patient's own country. All surgeons in Malta are registered with Britain's General Medical Council. Cosmetic surgeons may be members of the British Association of Plastic, Reconstructive and Aesthetic Surgeons (BAPRAS) or the American Society of Plastic Surgeons (ASPS). Dentists may be registered with the General Dental Council (GDC) or may be members of the British Academy of Cosmetic Dentistry (BACD). The American Board of Medical Specialities (ABMS) has member panels that certify standards in 24 of the 26 main areas of medicine.

Other countries have their own professional bodies. These are listed on the website of Treatment Abroad. An illustration would be the Brazilian Society of Plastic Surgery. It tests new entrants for background and skill. All candidates are expected to have had three years of specialist training over and above their basic medical education. While there are no certainties in the operating theatre, professional certification from the Brazilian Society is nonetheless a respected shadow on the wall.

There are international memberships as well. These include the International Society of Aesthetic Plastic Surgery (ISAPS) and the European Association of Plastic Surgeons (EURAPS). The names of professionals can be checked with the relevant body. In some cases the list may be obtained online. Crucially, however, these memberships do not carry any rights. Although there is an international driving licence, there is no borderless permit to practise as a doctor. Practitioners must usually be retested and recredentialled in each new country.

Licensing can be done at the level of the nation or it can be factored down to the province or state. Professionals who have trained or worked in a medically-advanced country like the US or the UK will have a head start. International doctors wishing to bring in American patients often take the American examinations on a voluntary basis in order to prove that they have reached the same standard as their American counterparts. At Bumrungrad all the surgeons have secured foreign (mainly American) certification.

Sometimes medical education abroad will itself have been accredited. Metropolitan medical schools often work with foreign medical schools to upgrade their standards. It makes medical travel to India more attractive to an American to know that the local medical schools have had advice from Harvard or Duke. Even the draft curriculum of the Medical Council of India was submitted to, and approved by, the National Committee on Foreign Medical Education and Accreditation (NCFMEA) of the United States Department of Education. This does not mean that the medical schools in India are as good as those in the United States, only that there is agreement on the baseline standard of workmanship. America seems to be the gold standard and the vanguard. While there may be overtones of stereotyping and ethnocentricity, the fact is that there has to be a benchmark of some description. The majority of international patients in any case are American.

As for skills that are not normally tested in America, a local examination (accompanied where necessary by local cross-training) can serve as an indicator of competence. In Singapore TCM practitioners such as acupuncturists must have a diploma from an approved body such as the Singapore College of Traditional Chinese Medicine or the Beijing TCM University. In India practitioners of ayurveda have the option to become certified but are allowed to practise without it. Appropriate bodies have yet to be created that would certify standards in yoga, hypnotherapy, foot massage, stress management, thermal spas, reflexology and the cessation of smoking.

4.6.2 Hospitals

Hospitals, like practitioners, are certified in the first instance by their own Governments and their parastatal authorities. Whether the Ministry of Health in the United Kingdom, the Malaysian Society for Quality in Health (MSQH), the Philippine Council on Accreditation of Health Organizations (PCAHO), the Institute of Hospital Quality Improvement and Accreditation (HA-Thailand) in Thailand or the Consejo General de Salud in Mexico (CGS), the host Government sees to it that a minimum is set and that standards are enforced. Some bureaucratic red tape is the price of market freedom. It is also a sound business investment. Health tourists are more likely to trust a country if its Government is accrediting hospitals on a triennial rota or refusing a licence to a hospital that has failed to achieve a stamp.

Trade associations also perform a quality audit. In India both the Indian Healthcare Federation (IHF) and the National Accreditation Board for Hospitals and Healthcare Providers (NABH) defend the integrity of the product. The NABH is a subsidiary of the Quality Council of India (QCI), an autonomous public-sector body which plays a key role in inspection and enforcement. The indicators they adopt closely resemble those of the JCI. The Confederation of Indian Industry stands behind the attempt of the IHF and the NABH to put quality on a sound business basis.

Jordan is targeting equivalent standards through its Health Care Accreditation Council (HCAC). This is a joint project between its Ministry of Health and the United States Agency for International Development (USAID). Accreditation Canada has been involved in a similar exercise in Kuwait, Serbia, Costa Rica and Brazil. It has even advised highly developed countries such as Italy and France.

The World Health Organization recommends that every country should have its own accreditation board. These should themselves have been accredited by the International Accreditation Federation Council (IAFC). The IAFC is an arm of the International Society for Quality in Health Care (ISQua). The ISQua is an independent, non-profit body which has accredited national accrediting organisations in over 70 countries. It is also the body which, with the recognition of the WHO, accredits supra-national agencies such as the JCI.

The JCI is the most prominent of the cross-border accrediting bodies. The Joint Commission International is a not-for-profit agency that audits hospital success indicators. Based in the US, it has regional offices in France, Dubai and Singapore. JCI is the international arm of the Joint Accreditation Commission for Healthcare Organizations (JACHO) in the United States. The JACHO accredits 5000 American hospitals. This accounts for 96 per cent of the United States bedstock.

JCI by 2009 had validated 242 health care providers (both public and private) in 35 countries. It publishes its benchmarks in a handbook, the *International Accreditation Standards for Hospitals*. The manual is available in several languages, including Korean but (for lack of interest) not Japanese. Hospitals which want the seal will first request advice from the JCI on the specific improvements that will be required. When the hospital is prepared for a visit, an onsite inspection will be conducted. Certification is based on peer review: three to four experts spend a week in the hospital, interview staff on a random as well as a structured basis and write a report. Sometimes the accreditation will be limited to one year, pending further improvements that have to be made. The full accreditation lasts for three years. Standards can deteriorate between one survey and the next. The JCI does not train local monitors or conduct follow-up tracking to ensure that the hospital remains worthy of its certificate.

Institutions have to pay both for advice and for accreditation. The fee is in the region of US$30,000 to US$50,000. There is an additional cost in terms of the time committed to preparing for the assessment. The burden can be a deterrent to new or smaller hospitals. While some insurers and employers insist upon the JCI name, others are prepared to send patients to hospitals that have been accredited by the numerous other international bodies that have ISQua status. They are based in a range of countries. It is not only the United States that can identify First World standards in health.

The list includes the Trent Accreditation Scheme (TAS) in the UK (an outgrowth of a project begun in 1993 to assess hospitals in the Trent Region of the NHS), the Health Service Quality Accreditation (HSQA) in the UK, Accreditation Canada International (ACI), Irish Health Services Accreditation Board (HIQA), Quality Health New Zealand (QHNZ), the Australian Council on Healthcare Standards International (ACHSI), the Netherlands Institute for Accreditation of Hospitals (NIAZ), the Council for Health Service Accreditation of Southern Africa (COHSASA), the European Society for Quality in Healthcare (ESQH), the National Committee for Quality Assurance (NCQA) in the US and the Haute Authorité de Santé (HAS) in France. There is also the International Organization for Standardization (ISO) in Switzerland. It offers ISO 9002 certification but it does not accredit. ISO only confirms that hospitals have met the more relevant of its 17,000 standards of excellence. Many consumers believe that this is more than enough.

Rather than a single accrediting body, the fact is that there is a plethora of associations. It might be too much of a good thing. The sheer range of choice is bound to confuse would-be clients. Also, the certificates are not perfect substitutes. Each body employs a slightly different set of criteria. In a sense some dispersion is inevitable. While there might be consensus on qualifications of staff and hygiene in the wards, it is much harder to quantify characteristics such as communication, ethics and privacy. Although subjective feedback should ideally be incorporated, there is no agreement on how to measure what the median patient actually thinks. Culture too is a problem. Success indicators should be flexible enough to allow for differences in laws and lifestyles. Accrediting bodies have been slow to adapt their criteria to local practices, attitudes and conventions.

Quality audit costs money. While some of the alternatives are less expensive than the JCI, the fact remains that the time devoted to the documentation plus the fees paid to the accreditors could just as easily have been committed to the treatment of patients. In Malaysia, where 77 hospitals have been accredited by the MSQH, a large number of unaccredited hospitals have been deemed respectable enough to ply their trade. A licence to operate is *sine qua non*. Accreditation, some would say, is merely icing on the cake. Rather than bringing in costly teams of assessors, a hospital might simply invite the insuring agencies to examine audited data on staffing and outcomes. Insurers regularly send patients to a hospital. They are in a strong position to know if it is good.

Illness cured and wellness promoted are closely connected. It is a link which will not have escaped the pigeonholing mind. Accreditation, it will be argued, ought logically to extend to the skin care and the sun beds rather than stopping short at the scalpels and the anaesthetics. This is especially so since treatment centres may well be packaged in with a golf course and a gourmet restaurant. A step in the direction of more general regulation has been taken by the European Spa Association which delivers the EUROPESPA Seal of Approval to health resorts that meet its exacting standards of hygiene, safety and comfort. It is not only the hospitals that might have to be accredited, at a cost.

Money is not the only cost. A hospital determined to obtain its certificate will have an incentive to concentrate on those aspects of its work which are the most likely to be assessed. It will neglect other parts of the medical experience which are not likely to come up in the examination. These will include a friendly and supportive bedside manner, patient-led innovation or *pro bono* outreach for charities in the slums. Quality narrowly defined drives out quality broadly defined. What is lost is a cost. A smile or a helping hand is therapeutic even if it does not pay real dividends in the audit.

5. Differentiation

The third reason is differentiation. Some patients go abroad for a lower price or a shorter wait. Some patients go abroad because the foreign option means a better standard of care. Patients from rich countries are more likely to be attracted by the cost. Patients from developing areas are more likely to be attracted by the quality. Yet there is a third reason. Patients also go abroad because the foreign alternative is quite unlike anything that they can experience at home.

The subject of this chapter is the foreign alternative that is unique enough to warrant a visit. Section 1 describes the clinical characteristics. Section 2 explains the pull of a convenient location. Section 3 assesses the attraction of a common culture. Section 4 relates health tourism to recreational tourism. It argues that tourism is tourism. The differences, real as they are, should not blot out the overlap.

5.1 PROCEDURES AND POSSIBILITIES

The Sistine Chapel does not travel. The tourist who wants to see its famous frescoes has no choice but to remove himself to Rome. Its counterpart in the field of health would be the Mövenpick Resort or the Anantara Spa at the Kempinski Hotel Ishtar on the Dead Sea in Jordan. They promise rejuvenating solar rays without the danger of ultraviolet radiation. They offer a relaxing Dead Sea Mud Wrap which would not be possible without access to health-giving dry flotation.

In Cuba the Clinica Cira Garcia is able to treat night blindness and skin diseases that other clinics dismiss as incurable. In Poland the Wieliczka salt mine welcomes a million tourists a year: they come to breathe in its unique oxygen supplies. In Tunisia over 150,000 visitors annually enjoy thalassotherapy: it involves the application of seaweed to enhance their health and beauty. Chale Island in Kenya has sulphur-rich muddy swamps that rejuvenate the skin. In Scandinavia there are clinics with the lowest rates of MRSA in the world. At the Matilda International Hospital in Hong Kong there is a keyhole procedure for lumbar disc degenerative disease that is hard to find outside. In India there is a unique method of hip resurfacing not available in the United States that, involving less trauma than total replacement, facilitates speedy recovery. In other words: 'For some rare invasive or diagnostic procedures, there are specialities that are simply not available elsewhere' (Bookman and Bookman, 2008: 59).

Traditional Chinese medicine (TCM) in forms such as acupuncture, chi gung or herbal medication has critical mass in Chinese communities like Hong Kong. Guangxi Autonomous Region, with its high incidence of centenarians, offers longevity tourism: apart from the pure spring water and the coiled snakes in a bottle of alcohol, the fresh air in Bama County is a draw. The World Health Organization, through its 'Beijing Declaration', has called for traditional medication and naturopathy to be regulated and accredited but also to be better integrated with mainstream health care. Steps to do this have been taken in China, North Korea and Vietnam. Advances have also been made, albeit to a lesser extent, in multiethnic societies like Singapore and the UK. Examples would be Raffles Hospital in Singapore and the NHS South Western Clinic in Brixton. Both use traditional Chinese medicine for pain, drug dependence and strokes.

In Africa about 80 per cent of the population uses non-Western medication. The Philippines relies extensively upon indigenous therapies such as hilot (chiropractic manipulation) and dagdagay (foot massage). Asian spas market reiki and shiatsu. India has well-known strengths in homeopathy, meditation, naturopathy, unani and ayurveda. Kerala is especially prominent in this. Foreigners interested in Indian therapies can go to Kerala for treatments that incorporate the accumulated wisdom and excellence of handed-on experience.

Isolated practitioners may, of course, be found worldwide. It is not just in India that one can learn yoga or receive panchkarma. Philippino hilot is available in Germany and Japan. Yet the holistic perspective emphasises that a single symptom cannot meaningfully be treated without regard to the living patient as an organic whole. Precisely the same may be said about the surrounding context in which a single service is provided: 'By definition, traditional knowledge is produced within communities and based on tradition and historical legacy. . . . Traditional knowledge is typically tacit, non-codified, and not clearly articulated. . . . It tends to be embedded in the experiences of communities, handed down across generations, and often involves intangible factors' (Ghosh, 2003: 127). Kerala is vegetarian food, sitar ragas, de-stressing sunshine and a palm-fringed ashram. Yoga in Dumfries is not the same.

Germany has an established position in spas. Names like Baden, Baden-Baden and Baden-Württemberg demonstrate that it has a history of wellness tourism dating back to Roman times. Japan can offer *onsen* thermal baths in hot springs fed from the volcanic ring of fire. Serbia has over 300 mineral water springs. Turkey has hot mineral water, hot sea water and *hammam*. Thailand has massage performed by blind monks in a *wat*.

Korea is planning an Oriental-Western medical service in a single hospital. Western medicine will be married up with its Eastern equivalent. Korea also offers beauty tours: cosmetic surgery is enlisted to match the flawless looks of Korean actors and actresses. Sometimes the patients arrive with photographs of their favourite stars. About three-quarters of medical tourists to Korea come for aesthetic procedures. Korean clinics claim they know the Asian face even as the Westerners know the Caucasians. Asians, it is argued, can provide better advice on make-up, fashion, hair and other complements to plastic surgery that will make their fellow Asians look good. Foreign women who want to look American would be better off going to the United States for their cheekbones, their skin whitening and their double eyelids.

In a minority of cases the suppliers will establish a physical presence abroad. Some Korean surgeons have set up clinics in Shanghai. More usually, it is the patients who make their way to the doctor. About 10,000 patients from Japan and China are going to Korea each year for aesthetic surgery. There are 1300 plastic surgeons in Seoul alone. The doctors have ten years of formal training behind them. The hospitals have well-honed know-how that has been refined through long production runs into a corporate drill. It is believed that as many as half of South Korean women in their 20s have had some sort of cosmetic operation. As for South Korean men, they now account for 15 per cent of plastic surgery performed in the country. In the US it is 9 per cent. Since men have more purchasing power than women, the male market is likely to have a considerable upside. Plastic surgery is believed in Korea to be a good investment. It is believed to have a tangible effect on social and occupational prospects.

The niche is the look. At Yanhee Hospital in Bangkok patients' files are delivered by mini-skirted young women on roller skates. An annual Miss Yanhee Beauty Contest is held. Yanhee performs the largest number of plastic surgeries in Asia. Brazil has a high profile in the South American market. About 600,000 aesthetic interventions are performed each year in Brazil. This is more than in all the countries in Western Europe combined. Ipanema is synonymous with the body beautiful. Foreigners who seek surgery in Brazil know that they are doing business with a going concern.

Sometimes the competitive advantage is as fixed as the natural endowment. Sometimes it is as place-specific as the Korean look. Sometimes, however, it is as mutable as laws and institutions. A baby born on American soil is automatically entitled to American citizenship. A patient registered with the NHS knows that the price will be the wait. In both cases the policymakers made a conscious decision that altered the relative attractiveness of local versus foreign care. While the Dead Sea does not travel and Kerala will keep its head start, man-made policies at least can be reversed and rethought. Negatively speaking, the Americans could emulate the Singaporeans and withdraw the right to stay. Positively speaking, the NHS could match the foreigners and shorten the queues. Investing in hospital infrastructure to reduce the delay, Britain would in that way be trimming the incentive for the patient to pay extra for a shorter turn-round abroad.

Patients will travel to the source for a single procedure. They will also do so for comprehensive immersion. Dubai, Korea, Bahrain and other territories are constructing health care cities. These communities will be wrap-around conglomerations offering commercial and residential premises, hotels, spas, nutritionists, physiotherapists, sports medicine, beauty shops, leisure centres, wellness counsellors as well as core diagnostic and surgical facilities in well-equipped modern hospitals. An example would be the Dilmunia Health Island that is being planned in Bahrain by the development arm of the Ithmaar banking group. It is a business proposition. If it succeeds, similar projects will be undertaken by Ithmaar in Malaysia, Morocco and further afield.

Practice variation is a further reason why patients go abroad. Like the British National Health or the Dilmunia Health Island, it is a manufacture and not a constant. A procedure might be offered as same-day surgery in Singapore which would require a lengthy hospital stay in Japan. A new drug might be licensed in Britain which is still being trialled in Hong Kong. An MRI might be possible in Bahrain which would be rejected as unnecessary in the NHS. Robots and guided lasers might be available in Costa Rica which domestic hospitals in Trinidad might not yet have secured. Clinical differences in forms such as these are a good reason to travel for care. So is the opportunity to consult the leading specialist in a minority area of care.

Patients also go abroad for procedures which are not encouraged and that are possibly illegal at home. They go to foreign jurisdictions for abortion, contraception, sterilisation, sex-change operations, stem-cell therapeutics and in-vitro fertilisation. Some countries do not allow couples pursuing artificial insemination to select the genes that will engineer their ideal. Other countries, more in sympathy with the consumer's desire for a designer baby, do permit parents to shop proactively for donors who are healthy, educated, intelligent, attractive and tall. Some jurisdictions screen embryos pre-implantation to facilitate the choice of gender. Some jurisdictions are rumoured – there is no proof – to turn a blind eye to human cloning.

Patients travel overseas ('death tourism') for medically-validated suicide. Dignitas in Zurich is one of several organisations that legally offer voluntary euthanasia, albeit only to the severely disabled or the terminally ill. Over 80 per cent of its clients (each paying a membership fee of about US$10,000) are foreigners. They come mainly from Germany, France and the UK. Oregon, Washington, Belgium, the Netherlands and Exit Switzerland also permit or facilitate assisted suicide. They do so, however, only to the resident population. Sick people who go abroad to die have fewer options than healthy people who go abroad to live.

Medical travellers go abroad for confidential treatment of alcoholism or drug addiction. They go abroad for managed detox where the paparazzi cannot find them. They go abroad for placental stem-cell treatment, not always of proven efficacy, as an alternative to a transplant. They also go abroad for adult stem-cell therapy. Difficult to access in the United States save for participants in a clinical trial, adult stem-cell therapy is available without restriction at Asian centres such as the Bangkok Heart Hospital and the Parkway hospitals in Singapore.

International customers pay surrogate mothers in India (where commercial surrogacy has been legal since 2002) because *de jure* womb rental is not permitted at home. As for eggs, a graduate woman can ask 40,000 Rs, an uneducated woman 5500 Rs. International customers also visit twilight zones to buy a kidney from a living foreigner who needs the cash. They do this because the queue in their own country might be too long; or because they know they are too old or too ill to be given a high priority. They might think that their condition will deteriorate if they have to wait. They might fear that they will die before they get their transplant. They might know that a metropolitan kidney will cost them more than they can afford.

The traffic in for-profit organs (legal or black market) is driven by demand from the richer countries. Ethically speaking, it might not feel quite right. Poor people in poor countries are being encouraged to auction off their body parts. Rich people visiting poor countries are paying many times the local price for an organ. Around two million Chinese need transplants each year. Only 20,000 operations can be conducted because of the supply constraint. Reservations have been expressed about queue-jumping on the part of foreigners who end up with additional life-years because they can afford to pay.

The Declaration of Istanbul on Organ Trafficking and Transplant Tourism, issued in 2008 by authoritative associations such as the World Health Organization and the Transplantation Society, expressly condemned the cross-border commercialisation of organs from living donors. China, Pakistan, the Philippines and other countries have now limited or outlawed the supply of transplants to foreign nationals. Hospitals may not advertise their transplants in foreign countries. Domestic transplants must be confined to a small number of hospitals in order that the organ flow might be monitored. In China in 2009 only 164 hospitals had been licensed to conduct such operations.

The laws are there. Enforcement is more difficult. So long as the supply of cadaveric organs is limited by law or taboo, so long as family members are not making the requisite gift, it is only to be expected that the economic ('black') market will match the supply to the demand. Papers are falsified to make it seem that the donor is a blood relative. Sham marriages are registered to circumvent the prohibition on non-related transfers. Compensated donors are told to plead that their motivation is altruistic. Officials are bribed to look the other way. Potential donors are trafficked abroad. Private arrangements are made for unrecorded harvests. The World Health Organization believes that at least 20,000 illegal transplants are taking place each year. Cross-border criminal prosecutions are rare. Once the patient has left the country, there is not much that the legal system can do. Local brokers and local doctors are more exposed.

The recipient might pay as much as US$8500 for a kidney: he or she will be tracked conscientiously for signs of rejection. The donor might be paid as little as US$300 to US$1000 for the organ: he or she will seldom be given follow-up medication or regular check-ups. One view would be that the bargain is a Hobson's choice. It is piecemeal enslavement, the deplorable exploitation of the defenceless and the desperate by the rich who have more money than they need. An alternative view would, however, be that the sale of an organ is no more than the commutation of superfluities that is the broadly-accepted lesson from Adam Smith's *quid pro quo* economics. The typical kidney donor in the Philippines, male, 29, earns US$114 per month. He is paid on average US$2357 for a kidney (McIndoe, 2009: A10). It is not much less than two years' earnings. So long as the exchange is 'bi-laterally voluntary and informed' (Friedman, 1962: 13), so long as both parties expect to feel better off in their own estimation, the advocates of the business deal would say that the sum total of social well-being goes up and that no individual member of the community actually makes a self-perceived loss.

Hindsight is, of course, not the same as expectation: 'Many Indian citizens who have participated as living donors have experienced medical complications such that 79 per cent would not recommend the procedure to others' (Bramstedt and Xu, 2007: 1699). Four-fifths of Indian donors felt that they had made the wrong choice. It was too late. Decision-making is always prospective, never historical. Freedom of choice offers no refunds for regret. The crucial point is that fresh, new Indians were joining the queue. Perhaps more would do so if the living donors were given the option of travelling to America or Britain for the operation.

There is no reason to think that transplant tourism requires the recipient to go abroad.

There is something else. In 2007 there were 17,440 patients on the waiting list for a liver transplant in the United States. There were over 100,000 patients waiting for an organ of some description. The average wait was five years. For a kidney the average wait worldwide is approaching 10 years. One person dies every day in the United Kingdom, 19 die in the US, while waiting in vain. Organ-selling would increase the number of survivals. Transplant tourism would reduce the discomfort and cut short ongoing deterioration. In spite of that the gateway is a narrow one. Only Iran has actually legalised the trade in body parts.

Iran offers one service. Kerala offers another. Health tourism allows them to swap. What this section has shown is that one hand washes the other and that all nations can reap the gains from specialisation as a club. Difference is difference. So long as different countries do not supply an identical suite, there is no reason to think that new nations must inevitably be the new broom that will drive old nations into penury and decline. In the words of Thomas Friedman: '*The Indians and the Chinese are not racing us to the bottom. They are racing us to the top – and that is a good thing!* . . . . The more they have, the more they spend, the more diverse product markets become, and the more niches for specialization are created as well' (Friedman, 2007: 274).

Differentiation is niches. Health tourism is niches. Core competencies protect producers and their countries so long as they have something unique to sell. After a time the kaleidoscope will be shaken again and a new uniqueness will emerge. Albert Einstein said that 'imagination is more important than knowledge'. Citing Einstein, Friedman concludes that the future is not about shares in a fixed pie but rather about an infinity of unforeseeable opportunities: '*The most important competition is now with yourself* – making sure that you are always striving to get the most out of your own imagination, and then acting on it' (Friedman, 2007: 635).

5.2 LOCATION

Sometimes the differentiating feature will be geographical proximity. Domestic travel can be a serious deterrent if medical care in the patient's home country is only available at a distance. International travel cuts down on the time, cost, risk and discomfort. Cross-border can be a synonym for local. Where it is, the patient will choose the foreign centre because it is the more convenient centre, just down the road.

Proximity makes medical travel quite literally a borderline case.

McKinsey excluded short-hop attention from their study of health tourism expressly because the lines on the map do not always have economic or medical significance: 'We. . . . excluded patients who travel in largely contiguous geographies to the closest available care, for they don't consider other medical-travel destinations and the financial burden is minimal' (Ehrbeck et al., 2008). The McKinsey estimate of fewer than 50,000 Americans going overseas was made after netting out neighbouring Mexico and Canada that were local in all but law. It is an artificial distinction. Proximity is nonetheless a selling point for being an easy sell. The near-neighbour is a quasi-monopoly because it is near. Even so, its market power is not absolute. Alternatives exist. It is misleading to say that patients do not consider rival destinations. They would do so if near became dear and they had to reopen their search.

In some cases geography will be the deciding feature. The nearest hospital to jungle Borneo is in East Malaysia or Brunei. In most cases proximity is a supporting characteristic. Consider the Americans who cross to Canada because drugs and doctors cost so much less in Vancouver or Windsor. The attraction is the price but it is also the location. That is why the Americans do not go to India instead. Consider the Canadians who cross to America because named specialists there are seen as top-of-the-range. The price may be higher but the standard is higher too – and America is only a few hours away. The Mayo Clinic attracts 10,000 international patients a year. One reason is that Minnesota is on the Canadian border.

As with the North, so with the South. In Florida the Jackson Memorial Hospital and the Cedars Medical Center have been active in recruiting international patients from Latin America and the Caribbean. The region is only two hours from Miami by plane. Seamless follow-up is not a problem. The patient can travel in for the appointment.

In Texas Mexicans living in Ciudad Juarez often find it easier to obtain specialist care in their twin city of El Paso than in their own national capital. Mexico City is 2197 kilometres away. El Paso is a short trip across a bridge. In California Mexicans living in Baja often cross the border to San Diego or even Los Angeles. The primary reason why they travel is to enjoy a superior standard of service. Crucially, however, it is to America and not further afield that they decide to go. So far from Bangkok, so near to the United States, location is a supporting characteristic which helps to swing their vote.

Americans think in precisely the same way when they go to Mexico and not to Bangkok for cost-effective care. Dentistry just over the border at Nuevo Progresso (population: 9125, dentists: 70) or Los Algodones (population: 15,000, doctors and dentists: 250) costs only 20 per cent of the price being charged a few miles north: 'People from Minnesota and California arrive in chartered planes to get their teeth fixed in these dental oases' (Kher, 2006). Retired people go on organised coach tours for their fillings. Some American dentists have opened subsidiary clinics in northern Mexico to save on costs.

Drugs, tests and treatments are cheaper in Mexico. A hip replacement in Mexico costs US$12,000. It costs US$43,000–US$63,000 in the United States. Angioplasty costs US$10,000 and US$57,000–US$82,000 respectively. Bariatric surgery for the obese costs US$7500 in Mexico, US$20,000–US$35,000 in the USA. Insured or uninsured, Americans prefer not to pay over the odds. Lower quality is not a cause for concern. There are clinics near the border where the standards have been validated as equivalent by bodies such as the California State Department of Managed Care.

At Hospital Angeles Tijuana about 40 per cent of the patients are American medical tourists. At Hospital Angeles Ciudad Juarez the proportion is 70 per cent. The hospitals are members of Grupo Empressarial Angeles, Mexico's largest private hospital and hotel chain. Initially concentrating on cosmetic surgery and dentistry, the group has expanded into heart surgery and oncology. Hotel and catering services are five-star. Employees are fluent in both English and Spanish. Middle-class Mexicans who would otherwise have crossed to the United States are able to enjoy top-quality care in Mexico at an affordable price.

Americans wishing to be treated in Mexico in an American-owned hospital can turn to the Grupo StarMedica (eight hospitals), International Hospital Corporation (eight hospitals) or AmeriMed Hospitals (ten hospitals). Christus Health, which operates 40 hospitals in the United States, is the joint proprietor of seven hospitals in northern Mexico through its partnership with the Mexican-run Muguerza group. Grupo Christus Muguerza is planning to have at least 20 hospitals, all with JCI certification. Its flagship, Christus Muguerza Alta Especialidad in Monterrey, already has this distinction.

The International Hospital Corporation, also from Texas, owns and operates three American-style hospitals just over the border. It has further hospitals in Mexico City, Brazil and Costa Rica. About 11 per cent of its patients are international (two-thirds of them from the United States). At its Costa Rica centre about 25 per cent of its patients are foreigners.

A cross-border location opens up a range of possibilities. In the United States 70 per cent of surgery is now day-case: Americans wishing to be treated on an ambulatory basis do not even need to stay the night. Also, patients found post-admission to be in need of specialist care can be referred across the border without delay. Christus Health has its own hospitals in Texas to which a sick patient can be transferred. This network effect would not be possible if the patient were receiving treatment in Bangalore or Kolkata.

Proximity pays. Although accurate data is not collected, it is likely that over 1 million US residents travel to Mexico each year for medical or dental attention. The Indians know this. The Narayana Hrudayalaya hospital chain is planning to build a 3000–5000-bed health city in northern Mexico. It is hoping to enlist the support of American hospitals and other investors to do this. At present Americans must make a 20-hour journey to India to be treated in a Narayana hospital. A Narayana hospital in northern Mexico would plant India on the Americans' own doorstep. India is cheap. Texas is dear. Mexico is near. One way or another, location does count.

This is certainly the case with the Jeju Healthcare Centre in Korea. Apart from Korean medical excellence and the natural attractions of the tourist island itself, Jeju is only a two-hour flight from five major urban concentrations: Seoul, Shanghai, Beijing, Hong Kong and Tokyo. It is near to Mongolia and eastern Russia. These territories are already sending dental patients to Korea because Korean dentistry is convenient and good.

The Baltic states are seeking to attract wealthy patients from western Russia. They have done well with the Scandinavians. One in ten Swedes or Finns has visited a doctor or a dentist in Latvia, Lithuania or Estonia. The cost can be 60 per cent less than in northern Europe. The safety standards conform to the EU norms. The location is ideal. The shortest flight from Stockholm to Riga takes one hour. The cheapest ticket costs 46 euros.

Mauritius, already a world-class tourist destination with a multilingual population, is targeting clients from nearby Africa, Asia and the Middle East. Turkey, strategically situated between East and West, has the World Eye Hospital, the Anadolou Medical Center and the Memorial Hospital: medical fees are from 20 per cent to 50 per cent of the fees in Western Europe. The Czech Republic is marketing cosmetic surgery in Austria and Germany. Hungary is offering dentistry and refraction. Sopron (population 20,000; dentists and optometrists: 200) is situated less than an hour's drive from Vienna. It is believed that up to a third of Austrians now travel to Hungary for their dental treatment.

Tunisia, only a short flight from Europe, offers breast enlargement by French-trained professionals at half the price that would be charged in France. Libyans and Algerians go to Tunisia. Approximately four-fifths of foreign customers in Tunisia come from neighbouring countries.

In Singapore 84 per cent of foreign patients come from Malaysia and Indonesia. In Thailand about 89 per cent of foreign patients are local expatriates or Asian nationals (Lautier, 2008: 108). Because there are few good-quality hospitals in rural Laos, Cambodia or Myanmar, patients often cross to neighbouring Thailand. The nearest good-quality hospital for them will not be in Taunggyi or Savannakhet but in Udon Thani, Khon Kaen, Rayong or Chiang Rai.

Singaporeans cross the Causeway to see dentists in Johore. Jamaicans travel to Puerto Rico. The Taiwanese go to southern China. The Japanese go to Taiwan. The National Taiwan University Hospital and the Municipal Wan Fang Hospital have international inpatient and outpatient facilities that offer an entry to exit service. As well as medical care, they arrange for visas, transfers and accommodation. The 1000-bed Chang-Bing Show Chwean Health Park will provide a full range of medical specialities. It will be targeting clients from Japan, the People's Republic and other countries in the region. As direct air links open up between Taiwan and the mainland, medical tourists will discover what the military strategists have known all along. There is barely time to drink a cup of coffee before a plane from Fujian is hovering low over Taipei. The world is flat. America is near to Cuba. Seoul is near to Pyongyang. As the prohibitions are relaxed and travel takes off, nearby destinations will attract the pent-up demand that has been there all along.

Location counts. Middle Easterners go to Dubai because it is conveniently situated in the Arab world. Europeans working in Indonesia are prepared to be treated in Singapore because Parkway is close. Even if Europe is their first choice, still the distances will often cause them to opt for the regional centre instead. The most that can be said is that nothing is set in stone. A no-frills airline from Indonesia to Europe might undermine the situational rent of treatment near at hand.

5.3 CULTURE

Culture too can differentiate the product. Mexican-Americans will be familiar with the Mexican way of life. Americans of Irish descent will share a hidden curriculum with an Irish doctor or nurse. Britons or Kenyans who have an Indian heritage might feel at home in an Indian clinic. Syrians might be comfortable in Jordan because fellow Arabs are easier to read. The world is flat. People, however, are not.

In some cultures the doctors listen and explain, the staple food is rice and the language in the corridors is English. In other cultures the trained paternalists get on with the job, the staple food is chips and the nurse giggles unless she is spoken to in Chinese. Price matters and the quality must be good. Even so, culture is not always and everywhere the same. Pain thresholds are learned and not innate. The way we live is a differentiating characteristic. Tourists take culture into account when they are deciding where to go for care.

Migrants in the global economy are crossing frontiers as never before. One implication for medical tourism is that there might be the unprecedented phenomenon of patient reflux. It might be that some of the incomers will want, when ill, to return to their country of origin. South Asians in America will have less anxiety about a good-class Indian facility. The overseas Philippinos ('balikbayan'), overseas Koreans ('gyopo') and overseas Vietnamese ('Viet khieu') will see the attraction of an executive checkup or even elective laparoscopy in a culture that embodies their unspoken customs. The uprooted who go back will be seeking treatment abroad. Their foreign treatment will, however, not be all that foreign in terms of their deep socialisation.

Where extended families are divided, relatives in the destination country will be on hand to allay the isolation. The primary objective might even be the social visit. Opportunistic medical attention might be something that is casually slotted in. Seeing a doctor for asthma or buying a new pair of glasses might be a secondary consequence of going to Amritsar primarily for a wedding. Dual nationals will often pay concessionary fees at local rates. They will sometimes retain their entitlement to free medical services in the country of their birth.

Culture does have an impact on choice. Orthodox Jews feel at ease on El Al. Koreans get kimche with their bulgogi when they go by Korean Air. As with the airlines, so with the hospitals. Muslim patients may prefer to have their medical treatment in a Muslim country. They may want to ensure that their prayer times will be respected, the Ramadan fast understood and a halal diet prepared for them in a dedicated kitchen.

Communication itself can be a problem. Not all hospital websites are fully translated into English. Not all medical tourists are fluent enough to speak English with their surgeon. Some patients prefer to discuss tummy tucks, breast reconstruction or a double bypass in their own language. Low cost is not sufficient where the operation is a complicated one and the patient lacks the vocabulary to ask the big questions. The Taiwanese patient in Guangdong or the People's Republic patient in Hong Kong is at least in a position to get his message across.

El Al and Korean Air capitalise on the cultural baggage. Yet other airlines too provide kosher food and marinated beef. They do so precisely because differentiation sells and they have to compete. Patient-pleasing medicine is no more than more of the same. Hospitals in Thailand have special wings for Muslim patients. Hospitals in Germany offer Japanese food. Hospitals in London employ Madrileños who can speak Spanish. Hospitals all over the world have medical interpreters who can translate words like aorta and spleen. This is not to underestimate the significance of cultural factors, only to say that the same tastes can adequately be met in a variety of destinations. The proviso is that treatment centres will become sensitive to the social differences and deliver what the client demands.

5.4   TOURISM AND HEALTH TOURISM

In 1950 25 million tourists took an overseas holiday. In 2005 it was 803 million. By 2030 some forecasts suggest that the world total will be 2 billion. Travellers will be spending US$2 trillion. In Asia alone more than US$1.5 billion will be spent every day by international tourists (Yeoman, 2008: 41). The United Nations World Tourism Organization forecasts that tourism will grow at an average annual rate of 4.1 per cent between 1995 and 2020. This outpaces the growth in the world GDP. Tourism to East Asia and the Pacific will grow at 6.5 per cent. Total international arrivals were 694 million in 2005. They will be 1.65 billion in 2020 (www.unwto.org/facts).

Tourism is not one market but many. There are battlefield tours and Bible tours. There are Dracula tours and space satellite tours. There are gastronomic tours and find-your-roots tours. Health tourism is just another niche within the broad genus of travel.

Product differentiation goes beyond the medical encounter, narrowly defined. Treatment abroad gives the patients the option to package in a foreign holiday with their varicose veins. Not all will want to do so: health travel and health tourism are not synonyms. Many patients will separate the tourism from the surgery rather than consuming both in a single trip. Especially if they have gone abroad for a serious and life-threatening condition, they might prefer to return home to rest as soon as the doctors and the hospitals permit. Other patients, however, will reason that a straighter nose is no reason not to see new places and do new things. This section is concerned with the latter class of patients. They are the ones who want to complement their medical treatment with a non-medical component abroad.

5.4.1   Illness Tourism

In the case of illness tourism the patient goes abroad to put right an existing shortfall. Once abroad, however, the patient decides to make the most of the opportunity. Bundling and add-ons make the combination more cost-effective as well as more satisfying to the consumer. The health tourist is effectively buying a package for not one but two of the host country's invisible exports.

Tie-ins mean that the medical element becomes a part of a joint product. South Africa offers 'scalpel and safari' tours: as well as their neurology, their cardiology or their liposuction, patients have a chance by land-rover at the African 'Big Five'. Bulgaria has more than dentistry at 40 per cent what it would cost in the older EU: it also has the Black Sea at Varna and the wild Rodopi valleys that are best seen on a bike. Argentina promises both snow-capped mountains and nip-and-tuck treatments: *The Guardian*, writing on 'Buenos Aires or bust', describes this as 'the tango-and-boob-job break' (Balch, 2006). The equivalent phrase in Malaysia is 'sea, sand and silicon'.

The hospitals as well as the tour operators have a presence in the market. Cebu Doctors' University Hospital offers a resort stay in the Philippines along with its heart bypass surgery. Wockhardt is prepared to facilitate a trip to the Taj Mahal. Apollo offers medical treatment followed by post-operative convalescence at its own hotel in Goa. In Ecuador it is possible to enjoy dentistry at 15 per cent of the cost in the United States accompanied by a good view of a rain forest and a smoking volcano.

The hotels themselves are active in the market. The Palace of the Golden Horses near Kuala Lumpur packages rest with a full medical examination. Its in-house medical centre delivers the results of all diagnostic tests in less than five hours. The Shangri-La Bangkok takes pride in its Chi Sen treatment. Relying on traditional Taoist healing the aim is to relieve tension by unblocking energy lines in the abdominal area. The Kempinski Grand Hotel in St Moritz is in partnership with the top-end Diagnostic and Prevention Center. Two-day check-ups are combined with five-star comfort. The hotel has its own fitness facilities.

The Ritz-Carlton Tokyo has a link with the Tokyo Midtown Medical Center (which itself has a link with Johns Hopkins Medicine International). Although the Medical Centre is not situated in the hotel itself, both the Centre and the hotel are located in the same building, the Tokyo Midtown Tower. They are only 41 storeys apart. The hotel element is useful since a full screening package can extend over several days. It takes time for the Centre to arrange the bone density scans, blood and urine checks, X-rays, electrocardiograms, ultrasound, pulmonary tests, or to schedule the renewal of immunisation for hepatitis and tetanus. Meanwhile, when the patients are not seeing the doctors, they have the chance to see the sights.

Hotels and hospitals have much in common. Acknowledging the overlap, Apollo Hospitals has actually set up a specialist subsidiary of its own to deal with the non-clinical needs of its medical tourists. Apollo Sindoori Hotels Ltd operates a three-star hotel in Chennai for patients and relatives. It runs a travel agency. It provides concierge services such as car rental. There is an obvious symbiosis. Whether the hospitals themselves should branch out in this way is less certain. Rather than becoming a multiproduct jack-of-all-trades, there is an argument for saying that hospitals should concentrate on their medical skill-set but that hotels and travel agencies should be encouraged to establish a presence on the same or an adjacent site.

5.4.2 Wellness Tourism

Illness tourism is diagnosis and treatment. Wellness tourism is refreshment and renewal. Illness tourism is *ex post*: the sick person goes abroad to bend back the bent rod. Wellness tourism is *ex ante*: the fit person invests in health capital because a stitch in time saves nine.

Wellness tourism can be sleeping late, luxuriating in a jacuzzi, being pampered in a honey wine wrap, going on a personalised diet, enjoying garlic-rich organic food, having a massage or a facial, taking time for a swim or a sauna, going to a fitness centre. Wellness tourism can be hydrotherapy, homeopathy, naturopathy, colonic irrigation, cellulite control, stress management, weight management. Wellness tourism can be lifestyle coaching that puts backbone into smokers, drug-addicts and alcoholics before they need curative treatment in a bed. Wellness tourism can be anti-ageing beauty treatments that would be called medical if *ex post* they had to be a facelift or a chemical peel. The quest for eternal youth does not necessarily mean the surgeon's knife. It can also mean a two-week visit to a balneal resort in western Bohemia.

The demand for spas has grown exponentially. In 2007 there were more spas in the United States (15,699) than there were Starbucks coffee shops (13,728) in the world. Narcissism is in the air. At the VinoSense Spa in Hungary tourists, aware of the anti-ageing properties of grapes, bathe in wine in a barrel and afterwards have a soothing massage. At the Hotel Fortuna Spa Resort in Malta there are magnetic mattresses, anti-bacterial bedding, air purifiers, a hot tub, a sauna, five swimming pools, physiotherapists and a Power Plate that gives the equivalent of a full body workout in only 15 minutes. At the Venetian Macao Resort Hotel visitors who have come for the gambling may enjoy the services of a high-profit spa and fitness centre. None of these facilities is curative, narrowly defined. Through prevention, however, all make a positive contribution to health. People do not want merely to escape illness. They also want to feel good and look good. Holistic wellness gives them what they need.

There is a real sense in which it would be true to say that all tourism is wellness tourism. A complete break with none of the distractions of home is therapeutic in itself. A good income is not enough if one has little leisure in which to enjoy it. Psychological illness costs more working days in developed countries than do the accidents and the germs combined. Not just the mentally besieged but their profit-seeking bosses would reap a worthwhile gain from restful leave that stops sapping depression in its tracks.

Physical illness too can be kept at bay through exercise, peace and a contemplative retreat. Philippa Hunter-Jones has made a study of cancer patients. Her thesis is that they were contributing to their own recovery through ecotourism and art galleries, sun and sand, anonymity and privacy. She concludes that holiday-taking per se is 'a vehicle for coping with the problems associated with illness':

> Travel can help in the rediscovery of self and the identity of self in everyday life. For many informants the planning and preparation of a holiday proved significant not only in returning a sense of control back to the individual but also in giving them something to plan and look forward to. Effectively the holiday represented a vehicle that enabled them to transcend illness (Hunter-Jones, 2003: 193, 194).

Tourism and not just health tourism is good for your health. That being the case, the net burden even of illness tourism might be less than the gross cost that makes no allowance for the beach volleyball, the beauty sleep, the Jurong Birdpark, the art galleries, the unscripted interaction with the locals. It affects the way in which the statistics are presented. Of 200,000 health tourists in Turkey in 2008, it is estimated that 180,000 were wellness tourists. Only 20,000 had come for surgery, dentistry and general medical care.

5.4.3   The Paths Converge

It is misleading to make too sharp a distinction between illness tourism and wellness tourism. A patient who goes abroad for a hernia can invest in his complexion through a steaming mud bath and his digestion through a nutritious vegetarian *nibitashi*. It is no less misleading to say that health tourism and recreational tourism are as different as the tiger and the horse. Building sandcastles on the beach helps the overworked to recharge their batteries. Sightseeing in the interior exposes the stuck-in-a-rut to something new. Illness tourism, wellness tourism, health tourism, recreational tourism – they are not the same but still the experiences overlap. The ancient Romans knew this. The term spa is sometimes said to come from the Latin *sanitas per aquam* – health through water. Other people say that the generic term for medicinal bathing is derived from the town of Spa in Belgium. Since Spa, then called Aquae Spadanae, was known to the ancient Romans, it is possible that both versions are correct.

Both health tourism and recreational tourism have a high income elasticity of demand. The World Health Organization predicts that health care will represent 12 per cent of world GDP by 2022, tourism another 11 per cent (Yeoman, 2008: 66). As affluence becomes more general and the long-haul flight is financially less daunting, so there will be a trickle down from the milord to the taxi-driver in the chance to tap into the world. The middle classes from mainland China will go abroad for high-end medical procedures. The middle classes from Costa Rica will journey to Nepal to see Kathmandu. In both cases, higher incomes, more savings, easier access to insurance all mean that there is less of a need to stay at home. Recreational tourism comes first. It is a platform on which health tourism can build. Health tourism can repay the favour by bringing in additional foreigners who might want a rest before or after their jab.

Education, television and cinema have at the same time made people more familiar with far-off places. They are less frightened of the world outside. Travel itself is a cause of further travel. The more people have holidayed in foreign countries, they more they will be prepared to trust a foreign doctor to deliver reliable care.

Literacy and computer literacy are favourable to the global market. Both health tourism and recreational tourism benefit from the new transparency. Consumers are able to find out quickly what is available and what it will cost. They can use Internet sites to book the flight, the hotel and the medical procedure as a single package. They know how to turn information and competition to their own advantage. Rising costs in richer countries have created new openings in the Third World. Education and electronics make it easier for shoppers to buy their treatment as they buy their hospitality by making full use of supply and demand.

There is a growing interest in health. Total expenditure on health went up in the UK from 5 per cent of the GDP in 1999 to 8 per cent in 2009. People are smoking less and going to the gym. They are concerned about their appearance and sensitive about their age. Health tourism and recreational tourism alike benefit from the discretionary element that may be illustrated in the former case by weight-loss surgery and in the latter case by a temple stay. About 50,000 people in Britain have cosmetic surgery: the market is growing by 40 per cent a year. Health tourism can be as narrowly medical as invasive surgery for cancer of the colon. Increasingly, however, it is much else as well. Yeoman says that health tourism is not just about cut-price surgery, tattoo removal and hair replacement but also about self-presentation, comfortable surrounding and the search for fulfilment: 'No longer happy to be viewed as bodies that occasionally need fixing, more and more people are demanding to be viewed as a "whole person". . . . Demand for wellness will soar as the consumer's perception of health changes into a concept of a combination of mind, body and spirit' (Yeoman, 2008: 75, 90). A luxury hotel or a straighter nose, the niche is non-essential and all but the same.

Sometimes the recreational element will be a joined-up continuation of the medical intervention. Rehabilitation, recovery, follow-up observation all take time. Patients while they are waiting for their next appointment will need long-stay apartments and something to do. Namibia Wildlife Resorts runs a wellness centre and health spa in a game park. Renaissance Cruises offers post-operative recovery on board ship. Gleneagles Penang allows for convalescence on the beach at Batu Ferringhi. Even if the surgery is day-case, the overseas patient will still require a hotel room for the night. The wellness and the tourism work hand in glove. Beds and meals become a part of the healing process. Accompanying relatives have to be sheltered and fed.

The mass market in both health and recreation will expand because of the silvering population. Age and retirement give older people more leisure time. They are free to travel out of season for discounted rooms in hotels which would otherwise have slack. They are forced to explore cost-effective options by the drop in their income and the decay in their extended family. Yet there is something else. Older people are often *active* older people. If they go abroad for their health, they will often stay abroad for a break. Older people may be the harbingers of what is to come. Illness, wellness, medicine, sightseeing, the bandwagon and the momentum suggest that the paths are converging and that all the beacons point up.

6. Health tourism: the benefits

International trade delivers the goods. The American patient is importing a service when he travels to Thailand to spend American dollars in a local clinic. The British hospital is exporting a service when it supplies major surgery to a Lebanese who has bought British first. What is true of commodities is just as true of invisibles. International trade makes both parties better off in their own estimation.

This chapter examines the ways in which both the importing and the exporting nation can reap gains from medical trade. The focus is on countries. Generalisation is always a problem where the countries are not all the same. Perhaps the them-and-us should be seen as a first approximation. Singapore, India and the United States are at once inbound and outbound destinations. Developed countries and developing countries have a presence on both sides of the bargain. Often the countries that buy are the same as the countries that sell. It is like that in the market for chocolates and children's toys. It is like that in the market for cosmetic surgery as well.

6.1 THE COUNTRIES THAT BUY

Chapters 3, 4 and 5 set out the stall. The foreign centre quotes a lower price and a shorter wait. Treatment abroad is of the same or a superior standard. A foreign clinic promises an unusual service or a unique specialist. Control, choice and autonomy all improve the patient's well-being, self-perceived. Socially as well as individually, it is a plus-sum game. Ordinary people obtain dental implants in Costa Rica which they would not have been able to afford at home. A compassionate society ought to rejoice in their freedom to import what otherwise they would not have been able to enjoy at all.

The world's first Dental Tourism survey was carried out by RevaHealth. com. in 2007. RevaHealth.com, based in Dublin but with online access worldwide, is the world's largest medical and dental search engine. Its cross-national survey found that patients who had travelled abroad for treatment had an average satisfaction rating of 84 per cent. Satisfaction was highest for treatments in Hungary, Poland and Thailand. The average

99

cost-saving was £3200. Patients spent approximately 40 per cent of what they would have had to pay in their own countries. About 95 per cent of the respondents said that the main reason for going abroad was the cost. Having decided to go abroad, they then used the search engine to find a good-quality clinic.

The survey established that only 50 per cent of the respondents had seen their own dentist before visiting Reva.Health.com. Only 54 per cent knew exactly what kind of dental care they required (Reva.Health.com, 2008). In Britain, about 30 per cent of residents aged between 16 and 64 had not had a dental check-up for at least two years. About 20 per cent had not followed up with the dental work that was recommended. About one in seven people in Britain said that their teeth were in poor or extremely poor condition (Dentale, 2008). The reason given in each case was the cost. Affordability was holding them back. Dental tourism was giving them a chance.

Yet there are other benefits as well. Cross-border competition forces domestic suppliers (who may be State monopolies) to improve their productivity, fine-tune their products and reduce their rates. Doctors in the more developed countries are obliged to match the price and product in India or Thailand. Local people get a better standard of service. They do not need to go abroad to reap the gain.

Patients who do go abroad reduce the pressure on the rest. Availability out-of-country diverts at least some of the demand. In the United States health care expenditures per capita are 2.3 times higher than in other developed countries. They are projected to increase by 83 per cent by 2015 (Adams et al., 2007: 1). Public and private health care expenditure absorbed 17.6 per cent of the GDP in 2008. Americans were then spending $7421 per person. It was the highest figure per capita in the world.

Globalisation may help to contain the burden. Not least will it contain the burden on the overloaded State. The ageing population (combined with the rising cost of new technology and drugs) is a ticking time-bomb that focuses the mind. In Japan, where there are few foreign health workers, there is considerable pressure on medical facilities. It does not cost much more to fly to a Japanese wing in Bangkok than it does to go from provincial Japan to Tokyo for a check-up or elective surgery. Some older people have high net worth and portable insurance. Others have little more than their disproportionate need. As nations age, the option of cheaper medical care abroad will become an increasingly valuable safety valve.

America, experiencing a very rapid rate of health care cost inflation, spends that much less whenever American demand is shunted off to Bangkok. Mattoo and Rathindran (making the optimistic assumption that the space vacated will not immediately be filled up at home) have put a figure on the gain. They estimate that the United States could save as much as US$1.4 billion annually if only one in ten of its home patients underwent treatment for 15 named procedures in a lower-cost country abroad (Mattoo and Rathindran, 2006). Grail Research, finding that the average savings per procedure performed outside the United States is US$15,000, says that the total savings for US payors, employers and patients could be as much as US$10.7 billion (Grail Research, 2009: 4). Jagdish Bhagwati calculates that the offshoring of customer service and claims processing alone would produce savings in the United States of between US$70 and US$75 billion a year (*Economist*, 2008). Outsourcing is in the Americans' interest. Even Mode 1 would keep down the cost to the system and to the consumer.

Just as a debit can go abroad, so a credit can come in. Modes 1 and 2 reduce domestic demand. Modes 3 and 4 increase domestic supply. They are the gain-seeker's response to an import demand that can be satisfied at home. New capital comes in. Foreign-owned hospitals increase the availability of service. More skills come in. Foreign-trained professionals reduce the shortfall in the countries to which they relocate.

Sometimes the foreigners will have superior qualifications: it is not uncommon for a Philippine doctor to work as a nurse. Sometimes they will accept lower pay: local people receive their treatment more cheaply if new immigrants go on an inferior scale. Either way, there is a benefit to the country that brings in the technical know-how. The benefit is that much greater since the host country spent nothing on the formation of human capital. It was Iran and not America that paid for the bedrock education and later for the medical school. It is the Third World that is providing medical aid to the First.

About one-third of Ghanaians with higher education have left the country. In the case of medical doctors, it may be as much as 60 per cent (Eastwood et al., 2005: 1893). About 40 per cent of Nigerian medical graduates are in the US, the UK or Ireland (Ihekweazu et al., 2005: 1847). The 'brain gain' is a considerable plus to the nations where they settle and work. Yet the external economy may also be regarded as a double-edged sword. As the medical sector expands in the Third World, foreign-born doctors who entered the rich countries will be tempted to exit again. Quantity will fall in the rich countries. Price will rise. Importation staved off by foreign manpower will become importation once more.

6.2   THE COUNTRIES THAT SELL

More services mean more fees. A clinic that treats foreign patients augments the income that it receives from its local business. Often it does so at a mark-up. Foreigners pay on the spot. Foreigners do not receive the citizen's subsidy. Price discrimination is tempting when the foreigners are believed to be well-to-do or when the insurance companies are known to reimburse. Often the locals cannot afford to pay for up-market services. Foreigners ensure that the specialists and the capital will be more fully employed.

Foreigners bring in foreign exchange. Admittedly the tourists will often buy a prepaid package in their country of origin. Only a proportion of their spend might actually reach the exporting nation. Also, where a treatment centre is foreign-owned or foreign-staffed, profits will be repatriated and salaries remitted. Money earned in Mexico is money spent in America. Forces such as these reduce the value of the transfer but they do not eliminate it.

A medical tourist may be spending considerably more than a recreational tourist. American recreational tourists spend on average US$144 a day. American health care tourists spend US$362 (Hotel Marketing Newsletter, 2006). In India a medical traveller spends a total of US$7000. A foreign holiday-maker spends only US$3000. Convertible currency is always welcome in a country that has a balance of payments problem. Cuba reports that it is earning US$30 million from 25,000 foreign patients. Israel is earning US$150 million from 20,000 foreigners. The export demand strengthens the nation's reserves. It also increases the pool of public finance. In Thailand hospitals pay corporation tax at 30 per cent.

Import substitution has a similar effect. At least 200,000 well-to-do Indonesians a year seek treatment abroad. The Indonesian Government is hoping to divert a quarter or more of those patients into VIP and VVIP wards at world-class local hospitals such as the Cipto Mangunkusumo General Hospital or the Siloam Hospital Lippo in Jakarta. Siloam Lippo was the first hospital in Indonesia to secure JCI status. Managed by an Australian team, it treats more than 250,000 outpatients and inpatients a year. Recognising the potential, the Health Ministry in Indonesia has offered to make a contribution towards the costs of construction and equipment. The German Government has contributed 40 million euros towards the construction of a world-class hospital in tsunami-torn Aceh, able to match the best in Penang and Singapore. It will be worth it, as is shown by the saving on convertible currency that has been made in the Middle East:

> In Oman, government-funded medical travel for oncology fell by 92 per cent from 2004 to 2005 after an oncology center opened. In Abu Dhabi, government-funded medical travel for cardiology decreased by 55 per cent from 2004 to 2006 after a cardiac-surgery team with significant international experience set up shop in the emirate (Ehrbeck et al., 2008).

Health exports protect reserves. Health exports also create employment. All grades of skill stand to gain.

At the lower levels there will be a need for unskilled and semi-skilled locals, some of them unemployed or under-employed, to serve as builders, gardeners, porters, cooks, orderlies, cleaners and receptionists. Often they will be given on-the-job training in areas such as word-processing, computer spread-sheets and conversational English. Often they will acquire a familiarity with new equipment ranging from a biodiesel centrifuge to an electric dishwasher. Such knowledge will put them on the ladder to a better job in the future. Women will be given new opportunities as nurses and even doctors in countries where cultural barriers exist.

At the higher levels, meanwhile, there will be a demand for skilled practitioners. Citizens of poorer countries, especially if they have trained overseas, know that they have an economic value in the international marketplace. Well-equipped hospitals paying competitive salaries will give them an incentive to return home. While medical professionals will possibly be able to earn more in the First World, they know that the cost of living is lower in the Third. The doctor who is active in health tourism can afford to live well. Foreign patients create jobs for high-end professionals who might otherwise not have come back.

Service exports in that way improve the residents' access to care. Treatment centres that take in foreigners also take in nationals. Facilities catering to international patients will normally have a better reputation and charge higher fees. Even so, the charges might still be within the budget of a middle-class local who knows that it would cost even more to go abroad. Nor will all the beneficiaries be in a position to travel. The emergency case or the chronically disabled must be treated quickly and on the spot. Such patients will be especially appreciative of high-standard hospitals that set up subsidiaries in second-tier and third-tier municipalities. There is no reason to think that all medical tourism has to be funneled through the capital.

Even the very poor might gain from the growth in the export trade. Governments sometimes require upmarket new entrants to deliver medical attention to the absolutely deprived. Where they do so, the nation's own poor are effectively being supported by the incoming foreign demand. There is, however, a caveat. If locals, rich or poor, are obtaining treatment in the glamorous commercial clinics, the State might seize the opportunity to reduce the bedstock and the headcount in the public-sector institutions. New entry could in that way make the bed and the doctor shortage worse. Higher prices could be the result. Higher prices are like a regressive tax. They hit the lower-income groups most.

Assuming, however, that the State sector can resist the temptation to contract, the expansion in the private sector is likely to be a plus-sum gain. Foreign direct funding relieves the pressure on public finance: 'For many, the attraction is debt-free investment. . . . Public sector resources could, in principle, be released to improve health care for the poor if the wealthy pay for care from these new foreign enterprises' (Smith, 2004: 2315). The two sectors could even go forward in step. They could pool information, share expensive capital, jointly sponsor specialist in-service training. It is public–private partnership. Economies of scale become possible even if the domestic economy lacks critical mass. Surgeons refresh their skills through the expanded throughput. Referrals cross the sectoral divide. Patients who cannot find State beds are contracted in to excess capacity in the private hospitals. Assuming that the private sector offers a higher standard of attention, cooperation between the two sectors is likely to have the unintended result of enriching the quality of care.

The domestic sector benefits from the internationalisation of business: 'The Indian government predicts that India's $17-billion-a-year health-care industry could grow 13 per cent in each of the next six years, boosted by medical tourism, which industry watchers say is growing at 30 per cent annually' (Gupta, 2004). Exponential growth is adding up to a considerable wall of money. It is priming the pump.

All trade is aggregate demand. More employment means more income: doctors, nurses, auxiliaries and cleaners spend what they earn in the shops. More foreigners mean more consumption: taxis, restaurants and hotels gain the spillover since patients and their relatives pay for more than medical care alone. Up to 40 per cent of the guests at the Ariyasomvilla and FuramaXclusive hotels in Bangkok, both located near to Bumrungrad, are medical tourists or their family members. G Hotel and Berjaya Georgetown in Penang draw considerable benefit from their proximity to Gleneagles. Medical tourists tend to have an above-average stay. Medical tourists tend not to travel alone. About 83 per cent told a survey that they travelled with a companion. About 95 per cent said that they indulged in non-medical activities such as shopping and sightseeing (Medical Tourism Association, 2009: 34, 35). The incidentals and the knock-ons put up the tourist take.

Construction, communications and transport share in the new demand. So does local industry which churns out the pharmaceuticals and the equipment, previously imported. So does the illiterate fisherman who opens the coconuts for the post-operatives on the beach. Forward and backward linkages create jobs and add value. A regional multiplier is a powerful thing. It is also an investment in the health of the nation. Higher living standards lead to improvements in morbidity and mortality. Health capital in its turn contributes to further economic growth.

Few countries will be able to make health tourism their primary engine of growth. Recreational tourism would be a safer bet. Croatia is fortunate in that it has the Adriatic as well as the plastic surgery. Even a secondary engine, however, can be a welcome antidote to poverty and social exclusion. Especially will this be so if foreign direct investment shocks a backward economy out of a lethargic vicious circle. Foreign capital is not just an injection of savings. It is also an inflow of managerial flair, modern technology, mould-breaking expertise and the entrepreneurial mindset: 'Dynamic gains from trade may have the greatest benefits for economic development as the international tourism sector facilitates the intangible flow of ideas across borders and cultures. In economic terms, this flow of ideas may result in higher productivity and positive intersectoral externalities' (Skerritt and Huybers, 2005: 25). Know-how and innovation are diffused through mimicry. Top-flight entrants have a demonstration effect. New areas of activity are opened up. It is a catalyst and an external economy. Quantity and quality both improve.

More competition will shake up the market in the receiving nation. Complacent oligopolies will be challenged by novelty and difference. Fees and premiums will become more flexible. Foreign medical schools, accompanying foreign-owned hospitals, will expand the pool of well-trained locals. Skills will be transferred and human capital built up. Collaborative research with the foreign parent will adapt general results to local conditions. Membership in a multinational network allows for synergies and exchanges. It also strengthens the bargaining position of local enterprise vis-à-vis the pharmaceutical companies and the equipment majors.

International capital in a receiving country pays for new hospitals that neither the pressured public sector nor start-up local entrepreneurship is in a position to finance. Sometimes a local business that has made money in a related area such as a hotel will want to diversify. Sometimes local people will borrow venture capital from a bank or float a new issue. Options such as these do, however, presuppose a take-off level of national wealth as well as a respectable track-record in business or medicine. Where the launch-pad is lacking, Mode 3 can correct the market void.

There is also Mode 4. Foreigners who come in will fill vacancies. Many of them will pass on learning-by-doing. As incomes rise and populations age, there may be a demand for health workers that local sources cannot meet. The shortfall of nurses may be as great as 35,000 in the UK, 270,000 in the US, 31,000 in Australia, 16,000 in Canada (Smith et al., 2009: 598). Rich-country health workers are themselves going abroad. Some of them will return in the long run with upgraded human capital and a coal-face exposure to different conditions and techniques. The dissemination of knowledge is a considerable plus in itself. Whether the deficit is permanent or temporary, foreigners step in and do the jobs.

Local people who go out for higher remuneration will send money home. Immigrants working in Britain remitted a total of £4 billion in 2008. Such transfers make a great difference to living standards in the recipient states. Remittances in 2008 accounted for 45 per cent of the national income of Tajikistan, 38 per cent in Moldova, 25 per cent in Honduras: 'Over the last decade remittances have soared from $73 billion to a record $283 billion last year, surpassing the volume of foreign aid to many of the poorest countries' (Margolis, 2009: 14). In the Philippines at any one time about 8 million nationals (25 per cent of the working-age population) are employed abroad. A third of them are in the United States. Approximately US$12 billion was remitted to the Philippines in 2008. In Mexico the equivalent figure was $23 billion. It was the second largest source of foreign currency, after oil. Money sent home was approximately 10 per cent of the Philippine GDP in 2008. While some jobs (such as those in construction, oil and shipping) are susceptible to seasonal downturns, Philippinos employed as health-care professionals are less likely than the average to be retrenched.

7.   Health tourism: the costs

Both the importing and the exporting side derive benefits from trade in health. As well as the gains there are also the risks. This chapter shows that it would be a mistake to assume that the balance will necessarily end up in the black.

7.1   THE COUNTRIES THAT BUY

In the importing countries there is a danger that the exit option will put off the solution of the underlying problem. The uninsured and the uninsurable seek treatment abroad because America cannot guarantee them affordable medical care at home. The well-heeled and the anxious buy shorter waits in foreign countries because Britain is not satisfactorily reducing the queues in its National Health. The middle classes who can pay get the prime cut. The poor who cannot pay get what they are given. It is the dual standard all over again.

Globalisation is privatisation. Privatisation is life-chances shaken up. A refuge for the educated and the mainstream, the market creams off some of the most vocal spokesmen for higher standards and better amenities. It is unlikely that the old, the disturbed and the deprived will be able to lobby as effectively for themselves if the middle classes opt out into an apartheid of their own construction. It was precisely this kind of stratified separation, Titmuss writes, that Britain's NHS in 1948 had been created to destroy: 'The middle-classes, invited to enter the Service in 1948, did so and have since largely stayed. . . . Their continuing participation, and their more articulate demands for improvements, have been an important factor in a general rise in standards of service' (Titmuss, 1968: 196).

The import option relieves some of the pressure on underfunded facilities. It is a mixed blessing. India or Thailand, by papering over the cracks, may be standing in the way of much-needed improvements in America or the United Kingdom. The Chief Executive Officer of Bumrungrad, commenting on the 60,000 Americans who were treated at his hospital in 2007, could not have been more candid about the gulf that his hospital was helping to bridge:

> We are not positioning ourselves to be the solution to America's health-care problems. To some degree, we are a symptom of the problem. We are a very glaring example that there is something wrong. Otherwise the American patients wouldn't be coming. They're not coming because they like Thai food; they're coming because they have no other choice (Curtis Schroeder, quoted in Einhorn, 2008).

They are coming because their own system has let them down. It is not a ringing endorsement of the American approach to health. It can get worse: 'By encouraging medical tourism one risks a loss of corresponding service in the US' (Bies and Zacharia, 2007: 1150).

What America needs is not so much a safety valve as a more affordable, more inclusive system. Arnold Milstein, doctor and administrator, has made clear that what some call a success indicator others call a cry for help:

> Since wealthier Americans have not been willing to pay enough more in taxes or income-adjusted health insurance premiums to make access to health care universal, non-wealthy Americans and their employers are actively searching for more affordable solutions. Their interests would be far better served by a U.S. health care system that aggressively and perpetually reengineered its processes to deliver an internationally distinguished level of quality at a much lower cost. . . . 30–40 per cent of current U.S. health care spending is attributable to insufficiently engineered processes of care delivery (Milstein, 2006: 2).

The wealthiest 5 per cent of the American population accounts for 50 per cent of US spending on health. The US is ranked first in the world by share of the GDP devoted to health but only 37th in terms of accessibility and outcome indicators. Many Americans have to choose between financial stringency and an acceptance of the grim alternative. Top-flight care abroad is one way in which the Americans can deal with their health care crisis. It is not the only way. Nor is it necessarily the best.

Yet the UK too has its winners and its residuals. Tooth tourism is the proof that a promise made in 1948 has not been kept. Britain's National Health Service guarantees access to dental care. Despite that undertaking, about 7.4 million Britons in 2008 could not obtain their procedures on the NHS. Some estimates suggest that half of British residents are not registered with an NHS dentist at all. An NHS dentist is not easy to find.

The alternative is to go private. A private dentist in the UK charges approximately three times as much as the State. A private dentist abroad is much cheaper. Dentists charge £199 for a crown in Hungary. The average cost in the UK private sector is £550. Root canal work costs £69 in Hungary, £210 at home. An implant costs, respectively, £550 and £1800. A full set of implants costs £30,000 in Hungary, £70,000 in the UK. Cosmetic dentistry is not in any case available on the NHS.

The Hungarians know the score. They mount roadshows in the UK to help people grasp what is available and what it will cost. They put up inflatable consulting rooms to show what a visit to the dentist is like. Eleven UK airports have direct flights to Hungary. There are budget carriers. Traditionally it has been the Germans and the Austrians who have gone East for dental attention. Now it is the British as well. In 2006 about 55,000 Britons travelled to Poland or Hungary for their teeth (*Weekly Telegraph*, 2008: 37).

The package can be arranged through a specialist agency such as Smile Savers Hungary. Smile Savers makes the dental appointments and organises the transfers. It books the hotel, the airtickets and the sightseeing. The number of customers passing through Smile Savers Hungary is growing annually by 50 per cent. Hungary has more qualified dentists per capita than any other country. Dentists there are required to attend in-service courses throughout their professional career. That is the pull. There is also the push. Dentists in the UK are not easy to find or else are too expensive. Good quality outside is matched by the atrophy within.

Britain is sourcing its dentistry abroad. So is Ireland. The Irish Competition Authority is in no doubt that it is avoidable market imperfections that are forcing patients who can pay to take matters into their own hands:

> The dental profession in Ireland is hindered by numerous layers of unnecessary laws and regulations. Competition is not working well for consumers of dental services, i.e. individual patients and the State. . . . Some consumers have even opted to travel to other countries for certain dental services. This is not surprising when competition is actively discouraged (Competition Authority, 2005: i).

The price of dental treatments in Ireland had gone up by 140 per cent between 1990 and 2004. General health care inflation had been 129 per cent. Consumer price inflation had been only 56 per cent. The reason, the Competition Authority reported, was nothing other than a man-made market failure. Dentists were not allowed to advertise or discount. Dentists faced obstacles when they tried to introduce new services. Dental hygienists were not allowed to work save under the supervision of a dentist. Dental technicians were not allowed to fit and sell dentures unless a dentist was monitoring the mouth. The number of trained dentists had been artificially restricted by profit-seeking collusion. What was needed was price cutting and deregulation that would put the patients first. What was offered was rigid professionalism at home, the safety valve of Budapest abroad. Rather than taking the bull by the horns, the Irish Government simply told its people to get on a plane.

Teeth in Budapest may, of course, be second-rate teeth. The British
Dental Health Federation has warned that dentistry abroad can be shoddy
dentistry, nasty even as it is cheap. Dentists might be inadequately trained.
Qualifying examinations might be less probing. Equipment might be less
sterile. Corners might be cut. Complications might result. Patients are
more likely to go abroad for complex procedures than for a one-off filling.
The more complex the procedure, the greater the likelihood that the
clumsy foreigner will split a neighbouring tooth.

It may be special pleading. Some foreigners have done their training in
the UK. A Cypriot from Guy's is not congenitally more ham-fisted than
an Englishman from Guy's. Also, the foreign standard might actually be
higher: inferior dentistry does not necessarily begin at Calais. If British is
best, then Latvian might be super-best. The evidence is not available to say
if teeth abroad are going to be a risk. If they are, then the sub-standard
workmanship only reinforces the main point, that there are not enough
dentists in the UK to meet the need. Without the chance of Budapest,
Britons would have to put pressure on their Members of Parliament to
help them get the drill and fill that they were promised in 1948.

A compromise solution would be for Hungarian dentists to travel to the
UK. It would be health tourism involving the supplier rather than the consumer. The advantage is that the patient would not have to leave home.
The disadvantage is the open door. Where foreign doctors establish short-
term practices without a local registration, they might not have the skills
or the commitment that the patient has a right to expect. International
certification of physicians would reduce but not eliminate the risk.
Meanwhile, there is another option. A local collaborator could do the
initial assessment. Later, when the patient comes back from Budapest, the
on-the-spot partner could provide the follow-up care.

A further cost is the potential displacement of the sitting tenant. If
foreign doctors and nurses enter the high-cost countries, and if health
care budgets are finite, then there is a real possibility that cheap foreigners will take jobs away from the sons of the soil. The hollowing out of the
manpower stock can be the unwelcome downside of the improvements in
quantity and price. The effect can be a snowball. If pay goes down because
foreigners come in, then locals will have less of an incentive to train. This
will exacerbate the shortage of doctors and nurses in an uncertain inter-
regnum when countries are growing old and local professionals are within
sight of their retirement age.

Foreigners might be planning to move on. Temporary rather than permanent, it is therefore uneconomic to offer them on-the-job training even
when they need the know-how to supply a state-of-the-art service. Mode
4 can be passing trade, a stop-gap rather than a long-term solution. It is

a cost. New people have not had time to become familiar with the local culture. They might not speak the local language. Saudi Arabia is one of the largest markets for Philippine nurses. Not all of them can ask their patients in Arabic if they are hungry, thirsty or in pain.

Patients when they go abroad are more vulnerable, more exposed. Unnecessary intervention is an additional cost that the importing nation will have to take into account. Much of cross-border medical care is consumer-led: the patient goes directly to a specialist without the inter-mediation and advice of a family doctor. One consequence can be supplier-induced demand: asymmetrical information can lead to uneco-nomic waste. Another consequence can be consumer-led supply: if the patient demands marginal interventions, there is no one save a doctor with a pecuniary stake to say that the client should re-examine his motives. The shopkeeper is likely to press for a walk-in sale. It may not be in the patient's best interests for the transaction to take place.

Even if the foreign practitioner is qualified and certified, even if the probabilities and the risks are described in a transparent and an intelligible manner, there is nonetheless the complex psychological baggage which a one-off medical encounter will not be able to unpack. It is a cost. The plastic surgeon is unlikely to counsel the latest unhappy body on whether low self-esteem will really be enhanced through breast enlargement. The medical specialist is unlikely to grasp the multifaceted nature of spoiled identity when the forever revolving door states that he needs expensive liposuction to appear in public without shame. Yet health care is about empathy and not simply technique. Not all patients are rational. Some are poorly informed, unfocused, over-emotional or downright disturbed. At home there is more likely to be a general practitioner who has a continu-ing relationship with the patient and who will be prepared to talk things through. In the international marketplace there is not the same set of checks and balances. It is a subjective as well as a paid-out cost.

A final cost to the importing nation is the loss of foreign exchange. Treatment for heart disease costs about 20 times as much in Europe as it does in Nigeria. The Nigerian Government is proposing the construction of cardiovascular centres in six zones within the country. Even if foreign surgeons had to be brought in for the most difficult operations, still the con-tainment of outbound tourism would stem the loss of convertible currency. Dubai in 2008 spent in excess of US$65 million on overseas treatment for its people. The new health care city will keep the money at home.

The financial outflow from America in 2008 was US$2.1 billion. It could be US$21 billion in 2012 (*Economist*, 2008). It could be US$70.2 billion in 2017 (Deloitte Center for Health Solutions, 2008: 14). Had the 750,000 Americans who travelled abroad for elective procedures consumed their dental and medical care at home, the US GDP in 2008 would have been higher to the tune of US$16 billion and the exchange account would have been under less pressure. In that sense health tourism is somewhat of an embarrassment to the American Government. A country with unemployed labour and a balance of payments deficit must think twice before it sends its scarce purchasing power abroad. A country with inadequate provision and an escalating cost of care must, of course, think twice before it fails to do so. The choice is between 'damned if you do' and 'damned if you don't'. It is no surprise that American Presidents age so visibly once they have assumed their high office.

7.2   THE COUNTRIES THAT SELL

In the exporting countries too there is a cost. Medical tourism can make life more difficult for local people. Foreign patients are not a free good.

First of all there is the fiscal welfare. Start-up grants, customs exemptions and tax holidays may be offered to pioneer hospitals that bring in foreign exchange. Scholarships may be promised for locals who fill the gaps in the top-end skills profile. Public money, subsidies plus tax forgone, is paid to prime the pump. That is the problem. It could just as easily have been spent on better schools and clean drinking water instead.

There is also the wasteful overhead of excess and duplication. The private sector in Bangkok has more gamma knife, mammogram and CT-scan capacity than the whole of England and Wales. Competing hospitals active in the market for home and foreign business know that paying customers expect prominent brands and break-through capital. What is attractive in business need not be as attractive in economics. The utilisation rate in Bangkok may be as low as 50 per cent (Janjaroen and Supakankunti, 2002: 97). Quality may be at risk if technicians are only sporadically called upon to use the equipment. Throughput might be inadequate for economies of scale. It is not a long-term solution.

Where suppliers have underexploited potential, desperate rivals might be forced into undignified price-wars. Wages might be held back to absorb the burden of capital. Professionals might be tempted into discretionary tests and unwarranted interventions. Supplier-induced demand, opportunistic and profit-motivated, can in this way undermine trust and raise the cost. Local people as well as foreigners pay more because health tourists will not come unless the hospital can advertise itself as cutting-edge.

Uneconomic average cost is a cause of medical care inflation. The market for medical manpower is another. The unskilled must be paid rises comparable to those in manufacturing. It will be difficult to absorb the rises through an improvement in productivity. Services do not lend themselves to mass production. Then, for the professional grades, globalisation creates an international market. As foreign patients come in, so local professionals must be offered the world rate in order to keep them at home. Health care is labour-intensive. Prices will have to go up. Even the public sector must charge more in order that it can pay more. Otherwise it would only be able to recruit the rejects that the private sector did not want.

New foreign demand on top of unsatisfied local need is itself a cause of care cost inflation. Foreign insurance with first-dollar coverage can lead to unneeded interventions that are not cost-effective. Incomers in a hurry go direct to expensive specialists with a stake in want creation. Locals, following the leader, demand more comfort and fewer generics because they see what the unsubsidised foreigners are being given. Demand-pull is a deterrent. It can price marginal locals out of the market even as more beds and doctors ought to have the opposite effect of improving local people's access to care.

Access is not guaranteed. More beds and doctors do not improve the life of the locals where the facilities are reserved for the high-end niche. Luxury wards are not for residents who cannot afford them: 'The resources used to service one foreigner may be equivalent to those used to service four or five Thais. Thus, the workload may be equivalent to 3 to 4 million Thai patients' (Blouin, 2006: 178). Other things being equal, three or four million Thai patients are not getting proper care because scarce professionals, beds and equipment go where the money is. One consequence of the Thai Government's five-year medical tourism plan in 2003–2008 was that Thai nurses and doctors migrated into the rapidly expanding private sector. At the end of 2008 there were several thousand unfilled vacancies in Thai public health.

The underprovided are priced out in order that the prosperous can eat up their share. The State sector is left to deal with the left-behind as best it can. Poor people with a Health Card are told that there is no cardiologist on call. Rich people with savings and insurance are told that the cardiologist is on his way. Market segmentation can mean major differences in availability and standards. Two-tier in this way chips away at the benefits that an exporting nation has a right to expect. As Chee writes:

> One argument for governments to promote medical tourism is that it retains scarce personnel within a country. It should be pointed out that this is beneficial for the country as a whole only if expertise in the private sector is accessible to the population as a whole, which is not the case in the current dual system of healthcare (Chee, 2008: 2152).

Where the facilities are separate, medical attention goes up for the minority while the majority carries on much as before. Yet the truth is that competition from medical tourists will seldom be serious enough to make a real difference to the locals. In Singapore, even if foreign patients were to number 1 million in 2012, each specialist would still be seeing only two foreign patients a day. It was 0.4 in 2000 (Ministry of Trade and Industry, 2003: Annex 1, 5). In the public sector the crowding out would be even less than that. Upscale facilities will require in-country business as well. This suggests that if there is going to be privatisation by stealth, the cause might be class at least as much as nationality. The patients who are doing the crowding might be the age-old domestic elite.

Yet international patients, foreign and often white, do stand out in the crowd. Non-residents are sometimes resented as carpetbagging queue-jumpers who treat the Third World as a bargain basement where everything is for sale. Xenophobia is an easy way of translating into the language of hatred the fundamental economic proposition that people who pay pipers get to choose their tunes. It is, however, a simplification. The law of effective demand would still hold true even if the health-care imperialists had stayed at home and the top-end facilities had been devoted exclusively to the local nobs. Blouin cites statistics that pre-date health tourism to show that health care distance is as old as social inequality itself:

> In many developing countries, the existing public health system is not offer-ing equal access and services to all citizens. Often, public spending on health concentrates on the richer groups of the population. . . . In Ghana in 1994, the poorest fifth of the population received 12 per cent of public spending on health whereas the richest fifth received 33 per cent. In India in 1995–96, the poorest fifth of the population received 10 per cent of public spending on health whereas the richest fifth received 32 per cent (Blouin, 2006: 183).

It is not the foreigners who can be blamed for that.

Effective demand, foreign and local, has the effect of concentrat-ing provision in the large cities. Remote rural areas might not derive much benefit. The internal brain drain if anything reduces their access to medical care. Salaries in public health lag behind those in prestigious private clinics. It takes great dedication to remain in an under-doctored, under-bedded jungle when the doctors and nurses could more than double their income by relocating to the commercial sector in the towns. It is sometimes suggested that the best are the first to move and that it is principally the 'lemons' who stay behind. If this is true, then it is a cost. It is quality and not just quantity that may be going down as a result of medical tourism. A two-tier system is an unequal system. The imbalance may increase once the prosperous go into the new foreign sector.

Accompanying the internal brain drain is the external brain drain.

Temporary or permanent, it is true by definition that Philippine nurses in the Middle East are not treating Philippine patients in black-spot Mindanao or even in Metro Manila. When bottleneck skills are lost, specialist units might have to close or to rely disproportionately on inexperienced second-raters. Unfilled vacancies, rising workloads and low morale are likely to result in even more rapid turnover. In the end there will be a smaller manpower pool.

Research and development too can have a pro-foreign bias. The fact that pharmaceuticals are being developed and produced in a poor country need not mean that local people are getting the drugs they require. It could mean the opposite if the scientists are being instructed to target their research on bang for the buck:

> Pharmaceutical companies, in the last 20 years. . . . have introduced 12,000 new compounds. Only 11 of those compounds were designed to fight tropical diseases. The World Health Organization reports that global expenditures on health exceed US$56 billion a year. But less than 10 per cent of this money is directed toward the diseases that afflict 90 per cent of humanity (Kierzkowski, 2002: 52).

Laboratories are sited in poorer countries because the labour and the trialling cost less. The drugs being tested are the drugs that pay. They are not necessarily the drugs that will cure sleeping sickness or river blindness. In low-income countries an average of US$22 per capita is spent annually on drugs, doctors and health-related services. About 15 per cent of the world's population accounts for 86 per cent of world expenditure on drugs. Profit-seeking businesses are not motivated to produce for the remaining 85 per cent. The need is there but the effective demand is not: 'Poor people cannot pay for drugs, so there is little research on their diseases' (Stiglitz, 2009: 364). Little money is being devoted to conditions that disproportionately afflict the absolutely deprived in Third World countries. Malaria is the price that poor people pay.

If they are used as test-subjects, it might not be the only price. All drugs have side-effects. Safety standards might be lax. Foreign participants might be exposed to hazards that would not be tolerated at home. Uneducated volunteers might not be aware of the risks. Rich countries' drugs can damage poor countries' health. Meanwhile, the tsetse fly continues to kill 150,000 people a year, mainly in Africa. There is no commercial incentive to wipe it out (Ghosh, 2003: 129).

The critics of medical globalisation point to a further cost. Avoidable dependence on the world market, they say, must amplify the instabilities in total demand. The number of foreign patients coming to Singapore fell by 39 per cent in the 'Asian crisis' that reached Singapore in 1998.

Indonesian patient load went down by 54 per cent (inpatient care) and 57 per cent (day surgery) (Khoo, 2003: 2). Inward travel did not fully recover for five years. The medical shortcomings in the United States are a further threat. The United States will one day close the gaps in its health care net. Compulsory insurance, national coverage, subsidised premiums, generous Medicaid thresholds, medical savings accounts, community rating even for pre-existing conditions, the suppression of annual or lifetime ceilings could mean that fewer Americans will need to go abroad.

Instability is an ever-present consideration. Elective procedures (aesthetic most of all) can be postponed in a cyclical downturn: the mitigating factor might be that bad times would be conducive to medical tourism where patients in a recession were searching for new ways to save money. Specific services can at any time be challenged by a substitute or rival abroad: this is especially the case if a clinic or country has put all its eggs into a small subset of procedures. A joint package with tourism exposes health care both to the seasonal nature and the high price elasticity of its luxury complement. It also means that the joint package can be put at risk by crime on the beaches, well-publicised pollution or a shortage of accommodation in local resorts.

The instability is there but other industries will go up and down as well. There is no evidence to suggest that health tourism is significantly more volatile than the economic alternatives into which a trading nation would move. Self-reliance is the only way to keep out the contagion from abroad. Autarky has the advantage that it insulates local people from trade-borne fluctuations that they never caused. It also reduces living standards. It makes local people materially less well-off. It is in any case too late to turn back the clock.

7.3   COMMODIFICATION AS A MORAL LOSS

Common to both the buying and the receiving countries can be the new nexus of self-interested exchange. Medical tourism can foster a consumerist orientation. The caring professions can become commodified.

Some relationships are mediated through markets: 'It is not from the benevolence of the butcher, the brewer, or the baker that we expect our dinner, but from their regard to their own interest' (Smith, 1961 [1776]: I, 18). Some relationships are a function of right and wrong: the Hippocratic commitment 'to help the sick to the best of my ability and judgment' (Lloyd, 1978: 67) is a reminder that some profit-seeking swaps are precluded by the absolute value of service. Tourism may lend itself to market share and the theology of 'greed is good'. The question must be whether it is equally appropriate to reduce *health* tourism to the same bottom line.

The criticism that may be made of health tourism is that it transforms the service ethos into a business contract: 'Shopping for a surgical procedure could eventually become as routine as trying to find the best deal in airfare' (Newman, 2006: 581). Patients become maximising customers. Health care becomes an economic tradable. FDI is not the same as development aid. Where everything is for sale and medical people work for corporations that work for dividends, there may be a danger that the professional ethic, the merit good and the ideal of disinterested service will give way to an obsession with the return to capital and the year-end bonus.

Hard currency bargains hard. Business is business – but there is more to a nation than business alone. Health tourism is not the sum total of health policy. A country that brings in foreign patients will also want to ensure that it does not lose its soul. Health tourism is no more the road to damnation than any other temptation that morally-minded people are wise enough to resist. So long as the professionals remain balanced and responsible, there is no reason to think that treating a foreigner is any more reprehensible than treating any other human being who is in need of a doctor or a nurse.

8. Health tourism and public policy

The market is prices and choices, supply and demand. Sometimes it satisfies the community's reasonable expectations. Sometimes it does not.
Where it does not, State regulation and public provision may be needed to
correct the market failure.

This chapter is concerned with the mixed health economy. It examines the ways in which the State can maximise the gains from health
trade while keeping the potential downside at bay. It does so in six sections headed, respectively, 'Taxes and subsidies', 'Laws and regulations',
'Infrastructure', 'Marketing', 'Global public spillovers' and 'The right to
care'. The public interest in growth, employment, competition and justice
is not always served by the freedom of trade. This chapter examines the
policy tools that a pragmatic State can use to shunt the carriage on to a
more promising track.

It is never good to exaggerate the contribution that the State can make.
Governments do not have perfect knowledge. There may be issues of
bribery, corruption or electoral advantage. There may be pressure from
landed grandees or industrial barons who demand special privileges for
their own specific sector. There may be an ill-defined apprehension that
goods are tangible while services are evanescent. It would clearly be wrong
to expect too much from the State. It would, however, be just as wrong to
underestimate the contribution that public policy can make.

8.1 TAXES AND SUBSIDIES

Tax allowances reduce the cost of doing business. A Government which
wants to encourage domestic or transnational investment will provide
exemptions for the capital and construction costs of pioneer firms in priority areas such as health. It will allow tariff-free importation of equipment
and drugs where a treatment-centre can argue that the inputs are needed
to compete in the global market. It will offer accelerated depreciation
and tax-holidays in the expectation that infant entrants will in the long
run make up the revenue shortfall. It will fine-tune its exemptions by
concentrating export patients in dedicated hospitals and targeted wings.
Concessions such as these have long been granted to manufacturing

industry. Extended to services, they would share the risks with the tax-payers. There is no expectation that the profits will be shared as well. The social spillovers will come later. They will take the form of trade creation, reduced unemployment and the dynamic of growth.

Thus, in the Philippines, the 600-bed St Luke's Medical Center at the Bonifacio Global City (its aim is to be better equipped than 95 per cent of hospitals in the United States) pays tax at a concessionary rate of 5 per cent in lieu of all national and local taxes. It is able to do this since it is registered with the Philippine Economic Zone Authority as a 'medical tourism park'. Profits from services delivered exclusively to foreigners were tax-free for the start-up four years. Fixed capital enters the country duty-free. Very similar is the position in Malaysia, where the Industrial Development Authority has established a 61-kilometre 'wellness zone' at Port Dickson. Investors wishing to open medical facilities in the zone are welcomed in with a battery of fiscal incentives. One of these is the 70 per cent tax exemption (valid for 10 years) on corporate income generated from foreign citizens.

As well as exemptions for the hospitals, there can be rebates for the tourists. Indirect taxes such as the value added tax and the goods and services tax are often refunded at the airport to non-residents who have spent money on commodity exports. Foreigners who buy a computer get their purchase tax back. Not so if they buy a hernia repair: then they have to bear the whole burden themselves. Since indirect tax in some countries can be as much as 25 per cent, a waiver could make a difference to an uprooted customer torn between a rebating and a non-rebating State.

Local people going abroad could themselves be offered a fiscal offset. Patients who relieve pressure on overloaded facilities could at the very least be allowed to deduct the cost of overseas treatment from their taxable income. Especially will this be so if they are the clients of a National Health Service. Having prepaid at home, they may find it inequitable that they should have to pay twice.

It is here that the distinction between health tourism and recreational tourism becomes important. The tax allowance will be for medical treatment in a recognised institution. It will not be for a restorative holiday on a yacht. The rule is a straightforward either/or. Reality, in contrast, is a kaleidoscope of differentiation. The National Health Service does not provide cosmetic surgery or assisted suicide on demand. Should the strict Inland Revenue adopt the same distinction between needs and wants when it separates the legitimate from the liable? Doing so, it would authorise an allowance for an as-of-right necessity consumed abroad but would at the same time refuse an exemption to a marginal luxury which the Ministry of Health had defined to lie below the line. The line is not easy to identify.

One person's luxury is another person's necessity. The alternative to paternalistic judgmentalism is, however, unlimited tax relief which makes it impossible to raise adequate revenue for the State.

As with the tax relief, so with the concession and the grant. Where the Government is a major landowner it may release State land on favourable terms. It may provide seed-corn cash to new hospitals which have committed themselves to the export drive. It may even lend to foreign patients who would otherwise have gone elsewhere for care. Subsidies for outsiders in preference to locals are always an embarrassment. If jobs are created and a multiplier turned loose, the Government might nonetheless decide that the long-run gains outweigh any short-run antipathy. This is particularly so when bank credit is not available, self-funding is not enough and the would-be lack the track-record, detailed accounts, political contacts or scale economies they would need to attract venture capital.

Entrants and entrepreneurs in all industries find start-up resourcing a significant barrier. Apollo in India is big enough and successful enough to negotiate a loan or launch a new issue. It will be cited with approbation at events such as HealthInvestor's Investing in Medical Tourism conference. Smaller, newer clinics will find it more difficult to get a foothold in the trade. It is they who will treat the State as their lender of last resort. The same may be true of search engines that have disproportionate local content or where users ride free on open access. RevaHealth.com, which receives funding from Mianach Venture Capital, lists clinics worldwide, including 60 in Singapore. Importantly, it lists so many Irish clinics that it qualifies for a grant from Enterprise Ireland. The argument may be made that without the support it receives from the non-commercial State it would not be able to recoup the costs of its list.

Taxes and subsidies, as with all public policies, must be even-handed and transparent. State-owned hospitals must not enjoy additional priority over and above their preannounced allocation. Independent budgeting might be required in order to force State-owned competitors to be efficient. There must be no suspicion that favouritism is being shown to a close relative of a Cabinet Minister or to the business partner of a senior civil servant. More difficult to police is the entrepreneurial opportunist who pleads for an incentive when in fact he would be making the same investment even without the concession.

There is no point in paying people to do something that they would be doing anyway. It is never easy to know which businessman is exaggerating for effect and which one is genuinely stranded at the margin of indifference. Errors of omission are, however, at least as serious as the over-funding of the venal. If the market cannot redress the shortfall, then the State must do what the social interest demands.

8.2   LAWS AND REGULATIONS

Property rights must be well defined if investors are to chance their capital. The law of contract must be enforced impartially. There must be a recognised hierarchy of appeals. Patents must be protected. If a new endoscope or a wonder drug is easily pirated, the danger is real that First World innovations will not be taken abroad nor intellectual property developed.

8.2.1   Intellectual Property Rights

On the one hand there is the pecuniary incentive to do marketable research. On the other hand there is the deadweight loss of monopolistic inefficiency. Since the marginal cost of replicating existing technology is extremely low, there is an allocative argument against exclusionary appropriation. Growth economists since Adam Smith have, however, come down strongly in favour of a short-run surplus that makes the risks and the costs worthwhile. New discoveries break the mould: 'The public is afterwards to reap the benefits' (Smith, 1961 [1776]: I, 278). The public which is to reap the benefits should not, Smith is saying, expect the new ideas to be a free gift.

Some economists are satisfied with restriction and protection in forms such as the WTO's Agreement on Trade-Related Aspects of Intellectual Property Rights (TRIPS). Others are less convinced. The WTO itself affirmed in its Doha Declaration that good health had to come first: 'We agree that the TRIPS Agreement does not and should not prevent members from taking measures to protect public health. . . . and, in particular, to promote access to medicines for all' (World Trade Organization, 2001).

Stiglitz, writing specifically about drugs, is one of those who has expressed serious doubts about ownership locking-in: 'The most adverse consequences for health arise from provisions in trade agreements that are designed to restrict access to generic medicines' (Stiglitz: 2009: 364). The victims, as in the case of the new breast cancer BRCA test, might not be able to pay: 'In the USA, the high price that Myriad Genetics, the holder of the BRCA patents, will charge for genetic tests – over $2500 – means that many women, who could otherwise have been tested, discovered that they were at risk, and taken appropriate remediation, might die instead' (Stiglitz, 2009: 364). Branded drugs can cost eight to ten times as much as a local generic. It is a major obstacle to out-of-pocket payment, especially in countries where great numbers are trapped below the poverty line or where a balance of payments deficit rules out significant importation. High costs cost lives. Patent protection does not protect the patients whose lives

are lost for want of an affordable generic. It does protect the pharmaceutical lobby which puts its wealth and influence behind a brand-name
monopoly position.

Oxfam is alarmed by the juxtaposition of high profits in the US, tuberculosis and AIDS abroad: 'The ten largest U.S. drug companies made
$35.9 billion in profit in 2002, with a rate of return for shareholders of
27.6 per cent, more than two and a half times the Fortune 500 average
of 10.2 per cent' (Oxfam, 2003: 2). Stiglitz sees little relation between
private rewards and social returns. The windfall, he says, is clearly being
squandered: 'Drug companies spend far more money on advertising and
marketing than on research, far more on research for lifestyle drugs than
on life-saving drugs' (Stiglitz, 2009: 364).

The poorer countries enjoy less protection because of the world skew-
ness in R&D. The richer countries enjoy more protection for the well-
known reason that money talks. One consequence of the imbalance
is that countries with a fat book of patents can demand super-normal
prices even from backward countries that have no surplus to spare. Data-
exclusivity need not be in the global public interest. The least-developed
countries have accordingly been exempted from the TRIPS commitments
at least until 2016. The richer countries in the WTO signed up to patent
protection from 2005. Free trade agreements made bilaterally between
member-States often reinforce that protection.

Intellectual property rights are not, of course, ever 100 per cent secure.
Producers must apply for a patent in each country where they trade.
Improvements in some jurisdictions belong to the facility that has added
the value. Small changes make possible the evergreening of the monopoly:
it is done through a sequence of TRIPS-compliant 20-year renewals.
Legislation varies: the same procedure will be registered in one territory
but open-access in another. Mimicking is sometimes allowed. The proviso
is that a part of the formula, often relatively small, must be different from
that of the proprietorial original.

Sometimes even a registered patent can legally be broken. It has hap-
pened in countries such as Brazil and Thailand. Where the World Trade
Organization deems that the alternative would be a 'national emergency. . . . of extreme urgency' (World Trade Organization, 2001), copies
of drugs such as the HIV-antivirals Kaletra and Plavix can legitimately
be mass-produced without the consent of the patent-holder. Over 580,000
people in Thailand are known to be living with AIDS. Worldwide, the
figure is 42 million. Copying ('compulsory licensing') would save lives.

Generic versions of first-line AIDS drugs have reduced the cost of the
cocktail from US$10,000 in 2000 to US$130 in 2009. While even US$130
will be an insuperable hurdle for an uninsured slum-dweller on US$1 a

day, it is considerably less than US$10,000 which prices out even the lower middle class. There is also a cross-border benefit. Some sufferers travel to foreign countries to purchase the supplies that at last they can afford. The pharmaceutical tourist will often be able to buy virtually the same thing but at a lower price if he leaves his comfort-zone and goes abroad.

8.2.2 Quality and Safety

The Ministry of Health must track medical outcomes to ensure that survivals and recoveries are in line with world good-practice. It must enforce the professionally-sanctioned conventions that are conducive to good health. The kitchens must be hygienic. There must be a fire escape. There must be an emergency generator. Blood banks should be licensed. Records should be kept. Accounts should be audited. Reserves, bonds and insurance should be adequate. Medical staff should have proper credentials. Guidelines and inspections in areas such as these offer valuable protection to the health-worker and to the patient.

Inevitably, however, there will slippage. In terms of variety, price and convenience, State guidelines impose costs of their own. Electronic services are expensive or impossible to police. As for the treatments, some residents escape the restrictions by paying for their first choice abroad. A liver transplant discouraged at home is transplant capacity expanded overseas. Some residents, remaining at home, have to live within the law. Prohibitions and licences will often mean economic welfare clumsily blocked off. They will deprive locals of jobs and incomes. Jobs and incomes make a difference to deprived people struggling with malnutrition and poverty.

If liberalisation is conducive to growth, and if growth is conducive to health, then that in itself would be a humanitarian argument in favour of a free world market. Yet the position is not clear-cut. Pro-poor, pro-health legislation might do more for the absolutely deprived than would the lifting of restrictions. Also, the elimination of Pigovian taxes and protective tariffs might reduce the reserve of public finance that had been available to fund housing and hospitals for the underprovided. Laissez-faire is not necessarily preferable to a State that is up and doing. Sometimes sensible paternalism will do more for the standard of health.

8.2.3 Price Guidelines and Controls

The State can restrict quantity. It can limit entry into the medical schools and the profession. It can insist upon demonstrated proof of need before a new hospital is allowed. The State can also take a lead on price. A published table lacks the haggling and bargaining of the Adam Smithian market-clearing mechanism. Perhaps, however, fixed or suggested norms are the superior alternative if costs are to be contained and patients' ignorance not be exploited for a windfall gain.

Supply and demand might be reliable enough in the marketplace for apples. Medical care, however, might be different. Information asymmetry, radical uncertainty, supplier-induced demand and the profit motive can be a serious threat to the Hippocratic ethic. They can mean that the supply side will have things all its own way. One inference is that second opinions should be encouraged and comparisons made to pick up unnecessary surgery. Another inference is that responsible fee-setting might have to be removed altogether from supply and demand. Fees might have to be recommended by boards, ministries or associations because the mutually-acceptable price is at once inequitable and inefficient.

In Singapore the fees of doctors in the public sector are determined by the Ministry of Health. The fees in the private sector are not. They are set by whatever the traffic will bear. Prior to 2006 the Singapore Medical Association (SMA) issued Guidelines on Fees (GOF). These benchmarks restricted the power of private sector doctors to squeeze windfall rewards out of pain and anxiety. While individual professionals could deviate from the recommended charge, they had to inform their patients in advance. If they failed to do so, they were required to refund the difference.

In 2006 the Competition Act put paid to the GOF and professional fees went up. Medical tourists were especially exposed. In the country for only a short visit and without the back-up of a local general practitioner, they had no standard of comparison. They did not know if the fee they were quoted was reasonable. Private practitioners were known to charge S$32,000 for a knee reconstruction that the GOF had previously priced at S$2700 to S$4400. They were asking S$100,000 for cholecystectomy when the GOF had suggested only S$3500 to S$5500. Lee was in no doubt that a mistake had been made and that the answer would have to be controls: 'Medical care is not a commodity. . . . Reviving the GOF would provide one solution to the problem of overcharging' (Lee, 2008: A23).

In South Korea the Ministry has a GOF of its own: 'Medical fees have been strictly controlled by the government and remain at a fraction of the prices in the United States and even cheaper than those in China and Singapore' (Lee, 2009). The cost of medical attention in Korea is between one-fifth and one-third of that in the United States. The primary reason is that prices are not left to the invisible hand. Only the locals, however, qualify for the controlled rates: 'Many foreigners are paying two to three times more. . . . Tourists coming to Korea in the hopes of cheap medical care may feel cheated' (Lee, 2009). Taxis and hotels do not shade their charges. Hospitals do so, claiming that it costs them more to treat a foreigner. Dual pricing protects the Koreans. It does little to win the confidence of medical tourists. They do not want to pay over the odds.

Singapore and Korea have shown that the State, either directly or through self-regulating professional bodies, is in a position to influence or fix the fees. Yet it might be premature to conclude that the free market is intrinsically incapable of pricing the product. Often it happens that market failure is proclaimed when the truth is that the free market has not been given the chance to succeed.

As earlier chapters have shown, the individual will not necessarily be negotiating and navigating in a void. Family doctors, medical facilitators, outside advisers, insurance companies are only some of the agents whom the principal will consult when an informed decision has to be made. The purchase of a house presupposes the involvement of an estate agent to shortlist the property, a lawyer to confirm good title and a surveyor to check for subsidence. The purchase of a house is more complicated than the purchase of an apple. Yet people somehow manage to find their way through the maze without the need for a GOF.

If supported choice can succeed where unaided choice cannot, then there is much the State can do to unfreeze the conditions of supply. One of its most pressing duties is to ensure that adequate information is available in the public domain. The State can insist that medical charges be posted on the Internet and published in the press. The State can encourage medical advertising in order that consumers become aware of the alternatives. An important function of the State might be to facilitate access to data and statistics. Complementing the market, the State would in that way be making devolved choice more rational and more focused.

The State could at the same time use economic policy to bring about a level playing field. It could insist that health insurance guarantee global coverage in order that consumers have the freedom to shop worldwide. It could make labour and capital fully mobile in order to promote an international input market. It could ensure that occupational licensing is not so restrictive as to inhibit new demarcations. It could demand that professional standards not be so convention-driven as to seal in windfall rents.

The State could phase out tariffs, quotas, priority procurement and exchange controls even if the consequence is that uneconomic local business is competed away by unembedded multinational enterprise. The State could withdraw the monopoly mandate from a National Health or a national insurance system even if the national ideology of a common entitlement has to move with the times. The State may even have to explore the case for privatisation. Entrepreneurial entry and active rivalry might be able to keep the cost down. A centrally planned system may lack the incentive to satisfy consumers who have no other choice.

Market liberals say that near-substitutes make suppliers responsive, flexible and eager to please. They look to rivalry among service providers for the rise in quality and the fall in price that have been observed in the manufacturing sector whenever refrigerators, computers and children's toys have been exposed to the cold shower of global undercutting. Yet pragmatism is essential. Economies of scale may mean that the health system is a natural monopoly. Orderly markets may be a reason for collusion and cartel. Market freedom is a means. It is not an end. Sometimes the public interest will be better served by large organisations and cooperative networks than it will by price wars and corner-cutting.

8.3   INFRASTRUCTURE

Adam Smith assigned to the State 'the duty of erecting and maintaining certain public works and certain public institutions, which it can never be for the interest of any individual, or small number of individuals, to erect and maintain' (Smith, 1961[1776]: II, 209). Profit-seeking business, he said, has no economic incentive to supply roads, canals and harbours. If the State does not supply these foundation prerequisites and pay for them out of tax, then the danger is real that they will not be provided at all.

Health tourism, like all tourism, presupposes a reliable infrastructure of essential services. In debt to Adam Smith, it looks to the State to ensure that the facilities will be available even if the commercial sector is deterred by the multiple externalities that ride free whenever ticketing does not repay the cost.

8.3.1   The Core Package

First and foremost there must be law and order. Tourists and health tourists do not warm to wars, coups, currency crises, violent demonstrations, terrorist anarchy, ethnic conflict and political instability. There must be safety and security. No one will want treatment in a country where travellers are being mugged, aggressive beggars make the pavement an obstacle course, bombs go off in the streets and corrupt policemen ask for a bribe. The judiciary must be impartial. Patients will be reluctant to seek care in a country where contracts are not enforced.

The banking system must be trustworthy and efficient. Patients who need to convert currency or transfer funds will shy away from a financial sector that breaches confidentiality and is on the point of collapse. They will be discouraged by unpredictable exchange rates and complicated regulations. They will, on the other hand, be receptive to a common currency such as the euro which makes transactions straightforward. Prior to check-out they will want an itemised bill. That in turn presupposes a sophisticated computer network that can track all the components in the medical episode.

Individuals must be free to come and go. Permission to leave one's country plus the high cost of obtaining a passport can be a deterrent to going abroad. Health tourism, like all tourism, will flourish best where the legal formalities are kept to the minimum. While the importing countries must make the arrangements that suit themselves, an exporting country must regard easy entry as a part of the infrastructure that attracts the clients in.

Visa-free entry is a case in point. Puerto Rico is treated as a part of the United States for purposes of entry and exit. Thailand and Singapore stamp EU and US passports based on the information in the landing card alone. The North American Free Trade Agreement (NAFTA) allows Americans to travel freely to Latin America. Malaysia permits short stays without a visa for nationals from most developed and regional countries. Patients wishing to stay longer in Malaysia can (supporting their case with proper financial and medical documentation) apply for a special medical visa. It is valid for six months. It used to be valid for 30 days. There is no requirement that the individual should enter the country on a group tour. Extensions are not difficult to obtain where there are complications or where the patient requires post-surgical care. In Korea the medical visa for long-term care is for one year. Some nationalities such as Kuwaitis do not require any visa at all for short stays.

In India the equivalent visa is valid for 36 months. The M-visa in India is a multiple-entry permit issued to the patient and up to two family members. The M-visa is normally approved within 48 hours. Patients who do not want to wait can enter as ordinary tourists and ask the hospital to help them to convert. There will possibly be a visa on arrival for medical emergencies. Quick turnaround is important. Simplified procedures and an early decision will frequently make a difference to a patient who cannot wait ten days or more to see a doctor.

Infrastructure is law and order. It is also roads. Medical tourists do not want to bounce through muddy potholes on a feeder sliproad or be caught in motorway gridlock where they have to breathe in noxious fumes. Governments must ensure that motorways exist which get sick people where they want to go. It may, however, be a mixed blessing. Public money might be used for new roads that go to five-star resorts and glamorous treatment centres. Those roads, however desirable in themselves, might bypass the silent villages that have an equal claim on market access for their green revolution. Trickle down might give way to privilege.

Where the journey is cross-border, overland investment will have to be made on a multinational basis. A geographical region often spans more than a single State. Bahrain needs good road links with Saudi Arabia and Qatar. Laos needs quick access to Thailand.

Many tourists will go by plane and not by road. A user-friendly international airport is a further element in the health care infrastructure. The Hadassah University Medical Center in Israel is less than an hour from the Ben Gurion International Airport. There are direct flights to Eilat from Moscow and St Petersburg where Israel is sourcing patients. Panama City benefits from direct flights to Los Angeles, New York, Houston, Miami and other destinations. Patients prefer not to change planes. Chiang Mai has a runway suitable for jumbo jets. Iloilo does not.

Airports must have facilities for the disabled and the seriously ill. Oxygen, beds, wheelchairs and stretcher services must be available. Ambulances must be allowed on to the tarmac to take a suspected heart case off the plane. Air ambulances must have a place to land. Helicopters and helipads will be essential where access roads are bumpy, congested and impassable in the monsoon. More generally, the health traveller arriving at an international airport does not want to be met with long queues, overhead fans and surly customs officers. First impressions count. Sick people, like healthy people, prefer a well-presented concourse, comfortable seating and easy access in to town.

As well as transportation, there must be public investment in basic utilities where these cannot be released for commercial development. Electricity and water supply are the *sine qua non*: blackouts and burst mains can cost patients' lives. Telephones and postal services ensure core connectivity: good communications make possible a seamless healing web. Clearly, not all of the utilities have to be public. Drinking water can be bought and sold. Mobile handphones are as good as a fixed land line. Hospitals have their own generators and water-purifiers. Commercial television, the Internet link and the satellite dish all reduce social dependence on the State-run monopoly. There is much that commerce can do. Where the profit-seeking, however, falls short of the need, then the sewers, the traffic lights and the dykes will have to become a charge on the State.

The State will also have to become the trainer of last resort. Without public investment in education and skill, there is likely to be a severe shortage of medical personnel. India, in its eleventh Five-Year Plan for 2007–2012, estimates that the manpower deficit will reach 200,000 dentists, 600,000 doctors and 1 million nurses. Rising pay will increase the intake and stem the outflow. Even so, the upfront cost is an entry barrier and medical schools will never be able to charge economic fees that price in the third-party benefit. There is no alternative but to rely on scholarships, subsidies and public provision.

8.3.2 The Economics of Critical Mass

The steel industry was concentrated in Solingen and Sheffield. Printing was situated in Fleet Street and Paternoster Square. Alfred Marshall was in no doubt that industrial districts are a high-return network of interdependencies: 'Each man profits by the ideas of his neighbours: he is stimulated by contact with those who are interested in his own pursuit to make new experiments' (Marshall and Marshall, 1881 [1879]: 53). Silicon Valley is a twenty-first century illustration of geographical synergy. So are the numerous ventures into critical mass that are taking place in the broad field of health.

In Maharashtra the Lavasa Medicity will accommodate not just hospitals, five-star hotels, a convention centre and a golf course but a business research centre operated by Oxford University. In the UK the Manchester HealthCity is going up next to the Piccadilly railway hub: it is hoping to attract anchor health providers from Britain, continental Europe and the USA. In Korea there is a plan for an all-embracing Healthcare Town at Jeju. Apart from an integrated resort, the complex will boast a comprehensive range of hospitals, therapies and medical facilities. As with Harley Street in London, health care at Jeju will be a one-stop shop. Services will be convenient and on site.

What is striking about medicities such as these is that no single investor is large enough to bring the entire project to fruition. Oxford is involved at Lavasa. Johns Hopkins has made a commitment to Nagpur. The Berjaya Corporation, based in Malaysia, is in partnership at Jeju. KPC Healthcare Services, based in California, is involved in the integrated, holistic health care city being planned in West Bengal. A medical complex is a major undertaking. Many parties will contribute. They will share the work, the cost and the responsibility.

Consider the case of Cebu. In the Philippines the Cebu Health and Wellness Council (CHWC) is seeking to position the island as a leading treatment centre. The CHWC is a consortium of hospitals, dentists, hotels, resorts, property developers, tour operators, travel agents. The Philippine Dental Association and the Spa and Wellness Association of Cebu are members. So is Metro Pacific. A Hong Kong-based industrial group, it is intending to make a considerable investment in an established recreational vortex already accounting for half of the country's tourist arrivals. The Departments of Tourism and of Trade and Industry are in the consortium as well. Their involvement ensures that the public interest will be given a proper hearing.

Also in Cebu is the Dental Implant and Multidisciplinary Oral Care Center. A total of 23 dentists, with venture capital from business but not

from the State, have banded together to establish a single facility group-
ing a variety of dental practitioners. The dentists are at once collabora-
tors (in that they promote the centre and the island) and competitors (in
that they seek to expand their personal market share). Their joint venture
recalls the 130,000-square-foot Ivy Health Mall in the Punjab. The mall
brings together a range of health-related services in a single health-specific
forum. Foreigners and locals alike derive the benefits from self-interest
and commercial collaboration.

In Thailand there is the four-floor Bangkok Medical Complex.
Developed in alliance with Singapore-based Pacific Healthcare, it accom-
modates medical and dental clinics, a spa, an organic supermarket, a slim-
ming centre and a range of lifestyle-related facilities. Its business model,
built around locational cross-selling in a building which also devotes
floor space to boutiques, condominiums and restaurants, is commercially
viable. The market succeeds. It does not fail.

Tie-ins between complementary stakeholders help to make up an attractive product. Airlines and hospitals are an obvious mix. In Hong Kong the
Union Hospital (Trent-accredited) and Dragonair Holidays (a subsidiary
of Cathay Pacific) are working together to bring in middle-class mainland-
ers. Visitors are being offered flights, frequent-flyer miles, accommodation, sightseeing, shopping bundled together with a full medical check-up.
Further south, Malaysian Airlines is marketing a similar stop-over in
Kuala Lumpur. Not only does the deal cover a good-class hotel (with
buffet breakfast), it also guarantees a choice of five diagnostic procedures
at the HSC Medical Center. Blood and urine tests, ECG, X-ray, abdominal
ultrasound, bone scans, 64-slice MSCT are among the options. Passengers
can also ask to consult a TCM practitioner.

Airlines can complement hospitals. So can airports. An illustration
would be the plan to create a world-class medical centre next to the
Incheon International Airport in Korea. Hanjin Corporation, Korean
Air and the Inha University Hospital, all three members of the same conglomerate or *chaebol*, are behind the project. The group has a foothold in
construction and travel as well as medicine. The centre would service the
needs not just of local residents but of airline passengers and airport staff.
It would in particular be able to attract health care tourists who wanted
to take advantage of the hub location for check-ups, cosmetic surgery or
more elaborate procedures.

The airport itself would become a health care destination. It is already
happening in Munich. There the Munich International Airport (a privatised corporation) runs a clinic with two operating theatres and 13
beds. Plastic surgery, gynaecology, orthopaedic treatments and other
specialities can be pre-booked. The clinic is prepared to collect patients at

the aircraft and take them through immigration. After the visit it ensures that they continue seamlessly on their way. The tie-in is a logical one. An airport is a convenient place for a check-up or even for a day-case procedure en route from London to Istanbul.

There can be a tie-in with airlines and airports. There can also be a tie-in with accommodation. Ascott International in Vietnam puts the residents of its Somerset serviced apartments in touch with medical facilities such as the BNH Hospital. A free scheduled shuttle is provided. Transfers are important for a patient who is going back each day to the doctor's office. Short-stay units too can contribute to health tourism through a safe and comfortable environment. Hotels near an intensive care unit should be briefed to keep oxygen onsite. They should train first-aiders in resuscitation and teach them to respond to cardiac arrest. Guests will want stress-free conditions, English-speaking staff and room service. They may need a special diet, often low-fat or gluten-free. They may need special fittings in the bath. All of this can be provided by a familiar name such as Marriott, Ramada or InterContinental. In that sense the hotel chain and the treatment centre have real opportunities to partner one another in the delivery of a single product.

Whether a consortium, a joint venture or a tie-in, what is clear is that the contribution of private initiative must not be underestimated. Critical mass was possible in Solingen or Paternoster Square even under the hands-off regime of Victorian laissez-faire. It is conceivable that critical mass will evolve just as spontaneously in Dublin's Beacon Court or the Dubai Healthcare City. Adam Smith's criterion of 'never for the interest of any individual, or small number of individuals' may have been left behind by Adam Smith's well-publicised commitment to mutual benefit through self-seeking exchange.

Yet there is a case nonetheless for public–private partnership. Where the end is to group institutions on a single site, the medical complex can be significantly advanced if the umbrella body includes the State.

The State has overview. Active as it is in urban planning, it is able to see the links between the police, the fire services, an airport, a development bank and a special economic zone. The whole is more than the sum of its parts:

> No single advantage is necessary or sufficient for medical tourism to take off; but some combination of them is. . . It is not enough to have a cheap labor force – it also has to be educated; it is not enough to have hospitals – they also have to be hooked up to electricity and water (Bookman and Bookman, 2008: 95).

Coordination is the input–output table that makes the trains run on time. Aid must mesh with investment. Health must be linked to law. Law must be linked to transport. Where one building-block is missing, the State can fill the gap without challenging the private property developers or the private cosmetic surgeons who are successful in making their own small contribution to the whole.

The State can fill in the blanks. It can also initiate the contacts. Where there are numerous players and a need to move fast, the State is in a position to unify the disparate without a ruinous overhead in side payments and transaction costs. In Malta it was not gain-seeking capitalism but two public-sector bodies, the Malta Tourism Authority and the Healthcare Authority of Malta, that brought together the doctors, dentists, hospitals, spas, travel agencies and public bodies. It did so under the aegis of a single parastatal organisation called Malta Healthcare.

The State, moreover, is a fixed point. Businesses come and go. The State goes on and on. The fact that debts are normally honoured and institutions seldom revolutionised is not lost on risk-takers, local and foreign. InterHealth Canada specialises in developing and managing hospitals: the State is in a position to offer it a 25-year franchise while retaining the equity for itself. Two British financial institutions issue a Malta Healthcare credit card with which UK residents can pay for surgery, travel and accommodation: they would not do this if they thought that Malta Healthcare was teetering on the edge. Battelle and other research majors are attracted to high-tech parks in Korea: they are gambling that the State will also be attracting the complementary businesses that they require. This is not to say that management, credit and networks would be inconceivable in the absence of the nanny who knows best. What may be suggested, however, is that automaticity takes time while centralisation can be the political economy of speed.

8.4   MARKETING

Health tourism, like all tourism, has to cry its wares. Price and quality are not enough if potential customers are not aware that the selling points exist. In some cases it will be the clients who visit the websites and consult the travel agents. In other cases, however, it will have to be the supply side that takes the initiative. The doctors will have to reach out to potential customers. The hospitals will have to draw paying business in to the shop.

Individual providers are already active in salesmanship. They publicise their services and network their coalitions. They nurture continuing links with tour operators, insurers and self-funding company plans. They establish new alliances with resorts, hotels and referring practitioners. They contact immigrant minorities to inform them of medical resources in their country of origin. They leaflet self-help groups to mark the opening of a retirement community abroad. They work with medical facilitators such as Serokolo in South Africa. In doing this, the doctors and the hospitals are recognising that cross-border entrepreneurship is a fact of life. It is not enough for them to wait passively for sick people to come through their door.

In some cases, rather than acting on their own, the private providers will band together. An example would be the Indian Healthcare Federation: open to all private hospitals, it enables them to publicise their product as a club. The Association for the Promotion of Costa Rican Medicine (PROMED), made up of six health consortiums, three private hospitals, several universities, a cross-section of hotels exists to promote Costa Rica as a medical hub. The Medical Tourism Chamber of Commerce in Poland brings together the private stakeholders to promote Polish health care. Cross-national bodies such as the Medical Travel Association lobby Governments and publicise initiatives. London Medicine in the UK represents the private institutions. The National Health System Overseas Enterprise (NHSOE) markets the public providers. Joint marketing spreads the overheads of scale. Only one brochure has to be printed, only one roadshow sent out, only one stall staffed at an international conference. It is also an acknowledgement that critical mass is a public good. To make the market aware that Singapore General can straighten the nose is to make the market aware that Singapore itself is a medical nucleus. Singapore General gains. Raffles and Gleneagles gain as well.

That, however, is precisely the reason why a private consortium might not be able to market effectively. Since membership is not compulsory, opt-outs can play the free rider on the spillover awareness that is paid for by others. In an attempt to bring in the marginal, the collective may offer 'selective incentives' (Olsen, 1965: 51) such as bulk-buy discounts from hotels, airlines and pharmaceutical companies. Members-only concessions would make participation more comprehensive. Industry-wide inclusion would spread the costs of marketing. Banding together would make it easier for the de facto cartel to raise prices and discourage new entry at the cost of the wider public interest. Collusion is attractive. Even so, the temptation to abstain can be at least as great.

The answer might have to be the State. In country after country the State has been drawn in to the international marketing of health. In accepting this responsibility the State has acknowledged that whole nations as well as isolated providers are in competition for the inbound tourist trade.

In most countries the national tourist board publicises health care even as it publicises the country's other attractions. In Turkey the Culture and Tourism Ministry promotes the hospitals as well as the Topkapi museum and the Cappadocia Cave Hotel. It holds exhibitions in London, Antalya and elsewhere to make agents and other foreigners aware of what Turkey has to offer. In India, with aid from the Marketing Development Assistance (MDA) scheme administered by the Ministry of Tourism, the Tamil Nadu Tourist Development Corporation supports not-for-profit Meditour India in a bid to attract health care tourists to Chennai. It is represented at India Tourism's Medical Tourism Expo in London. Only accredited hospitals, preferably JCI, are included in its package.

In Thailand the Tourism Authority of Thailand (TAT) makes information available through Thailand's embassies, through its website and through its own well-situated missions abroad. Believing the Asian emerging economies to have exceptional potential, TAT has concentrated in the East on markets such as India and Vietnam. In Indonesia it has filmed health-related commercials featuring famous local actresses.

Thailand has the TAT but no dedicated medical agency. Other countries have opted for a more focused, more targeted approach. In Cyprus there is the Cyprus Health Service Promotion Board. In Korea there is the Council for Korea Medicine Overseas Promotion (KCMP). Jointly sponsored by the Korea Tourism Organization and 35 private providers (few of them with experience in advertising and salesmanship), it uses publicity and proactive marketing to link up domestic clinics with medical travellers. It has a website, publishes a booklet and represents its members at international conferences. In selling Korea it works with travel agencies and tour operators as well as with the Korean Ministry of Health. The Ministry funds half the Council's budget.

The public sector also operates the Korea Health Industry Development Institute. The Institute has satellite offices in Washington DC, Beijing, Shanghai and, dealing with the whole of the EU, Glasgow. Americans make up 34 per cent of all foreign patients seen in Korea. Many of them are Korean-Americans. There are almost 2 million ethnic Koreans in America. A large number of them are self-employed and without health insurance.

The Seoul Municipal Government through the Seoul Global Healthcare Business Center has formed a network of hospitals and travel agents active in recruiting international patients. It has a list of hospitals with an international department where doctors speak foreign languages such as English, Chinese and Japanese. Communication is a major problem, especially as Korea is seeking to tap into new markets such as Kuwait, Mongolia and Russia. Most South Koreans are not fluent in other languages.

In 2005 Korea attracted 760 foreign patients. In 2008 the number was

27,800. By 2013 the country is hoping for 100,000. The influx will be worth US$199 million. The spillover impact on growth, employment and invisible exports will be considerable. Recognising that there is a national as well as a private stake, the Government has used a quota to ensure that sufficient beds will be available. The 44 largest hospitals (including the 'Big Four': Seoul National University Hospital, Samsung Medical Center, Asan Medical Center and Yonsei Severance Hospital) have from 2009 been required to reserve 5 per cent of their beds for overseas-based patients. An alternative would have been to reserve an equivalent number of beds in foreigner-only hospitals. The emphasis on beds may be exaggerated. Not all health tourists require hospital beds.

In Malaysia there is the Corporate Policy and Health Industry Division of the Ministry of Health. It collaborates in an umbrella body called the Malaysian Healthcare Travel Council with the Malaysian External Trade Development Corporation, Tourism Malaysia, the Malaysian Association of Tours and Travel Agencies, Malaysian Airlines and the Association of Private Hospitals of Malaysia. The contribution of Malaysian Airlines is similar to that of the airlines in India. There the Ministry of Tourism has negotiated free air passage for the companion of a health tourist travelling on Jet Airways, Kingfisher or Air India.

In the Philippines the Department of Health participates in a multi-party initiative called the Philippine Medical Tourism Program. In Turkey the Ministry of Health and the Ministry of Culture and Tourism are sponsoring the Association of Improving Health Tourism. In Taiwan the Department of Health contributes to the Office of Task Force on Medical Tourism. Supported by the State in all three cases, the objective is to publicise what the country has to offer. The underlying premise is market shortfall. The private sector by itself would do what it could but it would not maximise the incomer potential.

In Israel the parastatal International Medical Services operates 12 offices in foreign countries. Situated mainly in territories such as Mongolia, Nigeria, Ukraine, Kazakhstan and Russia which have only limited top-notch facilities, these offices funnel patients to treatment centres in Israel which the IMS is convinced will enhance the national brand name and prime the pump through word-of-mouth. In Cuba there are Cubano Turismo y Salud and SERVIMED. In Australia there is AusHealth. In Singapore there is SingaporeMedicine.

Launched in 2003, SingaporeMedicine is a multi-agency consortium. It receives funding from the Ministry of Health, the Economic Development Board (which spotlights sunrise industries and pioneers), International Enterprise Singapore (which spearheads business expansion into the region) and the Singapore Tourism Board (which seeks to grow the recreational market in the interest of income and jobs). It suggests joint ventures and new sources of finance. It communicates information about overseas business practices. It provides connections to existing business networks. It collaborates in online initiatives such as Singapore Destination Medicine in order to market Singapore facilities and streamline the search. SingaporeMedicine refuses to represent local practitioners or institutions that go in for sharp practices, kickbacks, fraud, price-gouging or misleading advertising. The consumer can assume that the notoriously unprofessional will have been impartially weeded out: 'This type of national endorsement from a government agency could increase the confidence of patients preparing to travel to the country for treatment' (Deloitte Center for Health Solutions, 2009: 5).

SingaporeMedicine serves as a 'one-stop-shop' for the incoming traveller. Acting as a consortium, it ensures that the ministries and Government bodies will work together rather than duplicating each other's campaigns. SingaporeMedicine collaborates with the care providers, mainly private but occasionally public, to prepare health tourism packages. It assists the incomer to obtain a visa, to find a doctor, to arrange accommodation. It publicises Singapore through its advisory centres abroad. It showcases Singapore options at international business forums such as the Medical Travel Consumer Fair, the Health Tourism Show, the International Health Tourism Exhibition, the International Medical Travel Conference, the Medical Travel World Congress, the National Conference on Healthcare Consumerism, the International Congress on Medical Tourism and a number of other health-related trade fairs. It represents local suppliers at general trade travel fairs such as the World Travel Market. It has been known to have a stall at international medical conferences and seminars.

SingaporeMedicine has been proactive in targeting promising markets. One of these has been the Middle East. SingaporeMedicine represents Singapore hospitals at high-profile events such as Arab Health in Dubai. It has collaborated in the launch of an Arabic translation (also available online) of *Patients Beyond Borders: Singapore Edition*. It has assisted the Singapore Government to conclude Memoranda of Understanding with foreign Governments such as the United Arab Emirates. Bumrungrad has a contract with Dubai and Saudi Arabia that allows for treatment in Thailand at the home country's expense. SingaporeMedicine is taking the initiative in order to secure similar arrangements for Singapore.

Individual doctors can market themselves and private hospitals can band together. Yet scale economies cost money. When all is said and done, experience suggests that there will be a perceived void that can most economically be filled by the State.

8.5   GLOBAL PUBLIC SPILLOVERS

The provision of public goods, the prevention of public bads, have long been regarded as a core duty of the State. Adam Smith himself defended 'the obligation of building party walls, in order to prevent the communication of fire' in the added-up language of 'the greatest good of the greatest number': 'Those exertions of the natural liberty of a few individuals, which might endanger the security of the whole society, are, and ought to be, restrained by the laws of all governments' (Smith, 1961 [1776]: 344–5).

Pigou, like Smith, looked to the State to correct the unintended externalities of 'uncompensated services and uncharged disservices' (Pigou, 1932 [1920]: 191) that were making free market capitalism another name for economic anarchy and mutual frustration. Pigou encouraged an omniscient and beneficent Government to use taxes and subsidies, patent laws and command-and-control, to bring private incentives into line with the marginal *social* cost and *social* benefit of the wider neighbourhood that surrounded the swap.

Where free riders cannot be excluded, where the spillovers are non-rival in consumption, where private property rights cannot be assigned, it is the conviction of political economists like Smith and Pigou that the State must take responsibility for the bent rod that commerce by itself will not bend back. A law prohibits the contamination of children's milk with melamine and dyes. A tax makes it expensive to release carcinogens into the air. A grant internalises the externality of life-saving basic science. The underprovision of spillover goods and the overprovision of bystander bads are the ugly face of the unmanaged market. The State is the elected representative that puts the matter right.

Globalisation, however, alters the nature of the debate. Smith's bank failures, Pigou's forest fires, were major spillovers that stopped dead where the passports where checked. A more international economy that phases out the tariff barriers, universalises the Internet and encourages tourist traffic will be more exposed to the generosity and the carelessness of strangers. SARS, AIDS, TB, H1N1, H5N1, Ebola, the Nipah virus are global bads that, like the fish in the ocean, cross the borders without a permit. Laboratory research, medical education, the Salk-Sabin vaccine are global goods that, like the eradication of smallpox or the containment of a pandemic, gift good health even on countries that have not made the investment. Effluent in the river deprives *foreign* fishermen of their livelihood. Slash-and-burn dumps the haze and the smoke in downwind nations *abroad*. Globalisation is in the water and in the air. It is not just the health tourists who are crossing the borders. It is public health and public illness as well.

Where the spillover is accessible to all if it is accessible to any, Smith and Pigou had no doubt that the answer would have to be the State. That, however, is just the problem. There is no supra-national sovereignty. There is no international regulator. There is no effective courtroom. There is no cosmopolitan police force. There is no world authority with the power to tax, to compel or to quarantine. There is no border-free Ministry of Finance that can compensate the victims of Smithian, Pigovian legislation for the loss of jobs and exports, potential savings and multiplier consumption. There is no border-free Ministry of Health that can guarantee the neighbourhood clinics that can deliver the incremental injections that can eradicate polio worldwide.

Politics has lagged behind economics. Communicable diseases, environmental pollution, systemic inequities are no one's business precisely because they are everyone's business. It is a serious shortcoming. Medicines are being sold online. Telediagnosis is being bought across the exchanges. No dedicated authority is, however, taking responsibility for the quality of the product or the credentials of the supplier. Emissions and inoculations are monitored at home. Globally, however, the good Samaritans and the bad Samaritans are less likely to be politically shepherded into a course of action that they would not have selected on their own. There is a political void. It will have to be filled: 'Open borders and the free flow of private economic activity are one side of globalization. Concerted cross-border public policy action must be the other side if globalization is to serve as a means of improving people's lives rather than wreaking havoc on them' (Kaul et al., 2003: 2–3).

Global public policy is required if international collaboration is to contain the spillovers of homeless economics. There must be a general acceptance 'not just that global problems need local action, but also that local problems need global action' (Smith and Woodward, 2003: 260). A world Government or even a regional authority would be an acknowledgement of the interconnected destinies and the transnational risks that are the price of higher living standards and Ricardian prosperity. While relying principally on the nation-State for leadership, there are nonetheless a number of initiatives that can raise world citizens' felt well-being, self-perceived.

One initiative is cross-national regulation. Bilateral free trade treaties (FTAs), common markets such as the European Union (EU) and the North American Free Trade Agreement (NAFTA), regional customs unions such as the Caribbean Community (CARICOM) and the Central American Common Market (CACM), all contain clauses that promote the goods and restrict the bads. The Agreement on Trade-Related Aspects of Intellectual Property Rights (TRIPS) ensures cross-border protection for patents, copyrights, trademarks and designs. The European Court of Justice (ECJ) protects the e-consumer by insisting upon full disclosure of e-commerce contact details.

The World Health Organization (WHO) issues International Health Regulations, not always binding, to make medical standards consistent and stop epidemics in their tracks. The World Trade Organization (WTO) has the power to ban trade in products deemed detrimental to public health. The only restriction is that the prohibition should not discriminate by country of origin or introduce a wedge between home and foreign producers. The United Nations uses its authority for moral suasion: the UN Declaration on Human Cloning is a recommendation but not a prohibition. Only the United Nations Security Council can promulgate an edict which has the force of law. Sanctions for non-compliance are, however, not easy to enforce.

As well as cross-national regulation, there can also be cross-national support. The European Science Foundation sponsors high-quality basic research at the supra-State level of 30 European nations: otherwise the research agenda would be 'set by private industry, which is influenced by interests of commercial profitability rather than social need' (Ghosh, 2003: 122). Multi-government bodies like the United Nations Children's Fund (UNICEF) and single-Government agencies like the US Agency for International Development (USAID) do what they can for the health have-nots in poor countries where the State lacks the fiscal means. Areas such as childhood immunisation and the eradication of malaria are at once humanitarian and cost-effective.

At the non-State level, private philanthropists and cross-national charities are active in the promotion of good health. An example would be the Bill and Melinda Gates Foundation which pledged US$6 billion – equivalent to the budget of the World Health Organization for the whole of the seven years from 1999 to 2006 – to battle underfunded diseases like AIDS/HIV and tuberculosis (Cohen, 2006: 162). It is not only the State that can correct a market failure.

The money is considerable. Even so, about 2 million children still die every year from vaccine-preventable diseases. Democratic compulsion and higher taxes may be needed if the global public good is to be properly resourced. Yet mandatory transfers at the international level are few and far between. Compliance is the ultimate yes-but:

> Smallpox eradication may have been the best social investment the world ever made. It also saved millions of lives. And yet, despite repeated requests by the WHO for financial assistance, between 1959 and 1966 only eight countries donated cash to the effort. The total contribution: just $27,345. This is an astonishing demonstration of free riding behavior. If a global public good of

this extraordinary nature cannot be financed voluntarily, you have to wonder if any can be (Barrett, 2007: 124).

All the countries were in favour of eradication. Only eight were actually prepared to pay for it.

Cross-border regulation is needed. Cross-border support is needed. Needed too is cross-border provision. An integrated response is essential if non-territorial diswelfares are to be eradicated. Cooperation alone can produce a plus-sum outcome. A single nation cannot install tsunami early warning sensors for the whole of the Indian Ocean. A single nation cannot prevent weapons of nuclear destruction from falling into the hands of madmen who will globalise the fallout. What is needed is for the effort to be a joint public venture. There is no other way: 'If the Earth is "saved" for one country, it is saved for every country, including those countries that may not have contributed to the effort' (Barrett, 2007: 3).

Cross-border provision can be a regional concern. An illustration would be the eradication of schistosomiasis in West Africa. The black flies that cause river blindness can travel up to 500 kilometres in a favourable wind. This means that the elimination of the vector will only be successful if all eleven countries in the region become actively involved:

> In human terms, the program has prevented 600,000 cases of blindness. In development terms, it has opened up 25 million hectares of arable land to agricultural development – land that was abandoned to the black fly. In economic terms, it has earned a 20 per cent return on the money invested. All of this would not have been possible were only some states to control this disease. An international effort was required (Barrett, 2007: 172).

What all can do one cannot. It focuses the mind.

Cross-border provision may also presuppose an international effort. It is not just the doctors and the patients that cross the borders but the germs and the innovations as well. AIDS has killed over 25 million people since it was first diagnosed in 1981: contact tracing in an age of mass tourism requires a concerted response. A credit crisis in one country becomes a major recession worldwide: central banks must collaborate and beggar-my-neighbour protectionism must be avoided. Tuberculosis in the United States is seven times more common among the foreign-born: foreign countries could contribute to world good health through comprehensive screening and early treatment. Skin cancer and cararacts can be caused by ultraviolet radiation: the ozone layer, serving as the buffer, will continue to be thinned by chlorofluorocarbons unless the world as a whole redesigns its household appliances. One country can regulate its own CFCs. It will not be enough. The protection of the ozone layer is a *global* public good. *Global* public policy is inevitable if good health for all is to be ensured.

As politics becomes ever more transnational, however, so the nature of governance itself will have to be reappraised. Different stakeholders want different things. The intensity of desire is not always and everywhere the same. Non-governmental organisations must not become an extra-parliamentary opposition that shouts down the representatives of the people. Democracy will have to be deepened even as it is widened. The need, in sum, will be for what Held and McGrew have described as 'a process of double democratization': 'A double-sided process. . . . means deepening democracy within national communities, as well as extending democratic forms and processes across territorial borders. . . . This double-sided approach involves reconceiving legitimate political activity in a way that disconnects it from its traditional anchor in fixed borders and delimited territories' (Held and McGrew, 2003: 194). Cosmopolitanism will be the new citizenship. *Global* policy will be an ever more important part of the battery upon which the policy makers will draw in their attempt to curb market failure.

8.6 THE RIGHT TO CARE

It is often asserted that access to health and health care is an irrevocable entitlement: 'The enjoyment of the highest attainable standard of health is one of the fundamental rights of every human being without distinction of race, religion, political belief, economic or social condition. . . . Governments have a responsibility for the health of their peoples' (World Health Organization, 1962 [1946]: 1). Sometimes an acknowledgement of natural rights in the tradition of John Locke and sometimes the embodiment of citizenship consensus in the sense of T.H. Marshall (Reisman, 2007: 223–9), what is clear is that health care is generally perceived as a thing apart. Health care is absolute. Tourism is only relative: 'Tourism does not share the health sector's politically charged premise. No government claims that each citizen has the right to enjoy a beach vacation; no government subsidizes the rental car industry' (Bookman and Bookman, 2008: 69). Tourism is only economics. Health care is emotion and heart.

Health care is sometimes said to be a natural right. If it is, then health tourism ought to be welcomed precisely because it means that more people are being treated and getting well. Health care, however, is sometimes said to be a national and not an innate entitlement. It is often felt to be a bounded expression of a single community's uninterrupted nationhood.

If the right to health is indeed the commitment we make to our own, then health tourists must be seen as our rivals and not our brothers. A Them and not an Us, health tourists are outsiders who are leaving the local people to suffer and die.

The gap between the foreigners and the locals is a cause of particular concern in poor countries where doctors and supplies are genuinely thin on the ground. India is a case in point. India offers world-class medical facilities for the middle-class and upper-class families who can afford to pay. It offers far less in the villages and in the slums:

> Fewer than 50 per cent of India's primary health centres have a labour room or a laboratory, while fewer than one in five have a telephone connection. . . . Moreover, fewer than one in three primary health-care centres stocked essential drugs, in contrast to the situation in many new urban medical centres. . . . Health care in India's rural districts is poor, dogged by shortages of trained health workers, a lack of funds and corruption. Many patients resort to quacks or seek no medical care at all, since private practitioners are beyond the means of most (Chinai and Goswami, 2007).

In the United States there are 26 doctors per 1000 of population. In the United Kingdom there are 23. In India there are 6. In Zambia there is 1 (World Health Organization, 2009: 98, 102). The enclaves and the ghettoes are an inequality. Yet the inequality was there even before the health tourists arrived.

Many Indian doctors have taken advantage of globalisation to migrate not just to Apollo but to north London or San Francisco. Internal brain drain or external brain drain, the end result is the same. A doctor in Beverley Hills is not a doctor in impoverished Bihar. Meanwhile, prices in India go up as the foreign health tourists crowd in: 'By one estimate, an extra 100,000 patients seeking medical treatment in Thailand leads to an internal brain drain of between 240–700 medical doctors. This has exacerbated shortages of medical professionals in Thailand, especially in the public sector and in rural areas' (Arunanondchai and Fink, 2007: 20). Governments cannot be seen to be transferring facilities to foreigners that are needed for locals.

Telemedicine at least might narrow the gap. It might allow the diagnostic potential and even the treatment centres of a modern urban hospital to be put at the disposal of the isolated and the impoverished. Chanda, however, is not convinced. Chanda argues that telemedicine will be all but irrelevant in the absence of back-up local professionals and a reliable electricity grid. He also states that telemedicine concentrates scarce resources on high-cost cure when it is prevention and promotion that would contribute far more to the health status of the absolutely deprived:

Given the lack of telecommunications and power sector infrastructure in many developing countries, telemedicine may not be cost-effective. In such cases, public sector resources for telemedicine may be better invested in improving basic health care facilities for disease prevention and cure, and in areas where there is a direct impact on the poor. The risk is that telemedicine will channel revenues away from rural and primary health care and towards specialized centres, thus concentrating on technologies which cater to the affluent few in developing countries (Chanda, 2002: 38).

The objection is sometimes raised that the care may be domestic but that the beneficiaries are not. Organs are transplanted into foreigners because the residents cannot put in a realistic bid. Health tourism is the Raj all over again. More for Them means less for Us unless public policy does what the private sector never can.

One step is to insist that five-star hospitals should provide free or low-cost treatment for an agreed-upon number of needy locals. A hospital would in this scenario only be granted a licence or a tax exemption if it promised to set aside a *pro bono* floor. It would cross-subsidise the destitute through a mark-up on its full-fee business. Some of that business will be foreign. Hospitals which wish to treat foreign patients will be required to admit social insurance and hardship cases as well. Otherwise they might be asked to refund the social investment in medical education that its doctors take with them when they resettle in the private sector.

There is nothing in the GATS that prevents Governments from levying special taxes on top-end hospitals or imposing higher charges on non-resident patients in order that the residents and the poor might be the beneficiaries of an earmarked transfer. The locals themselves might be means-tested to generate additional resources for the genuinely deprived. The model for internal cross-subsidisation would be the American private sector which, albeit reluctantly, is often prepared to take in the uninsured. Some will be on low-reimbursement Medicaid. Some will have to be written off as bad debt. The hospitals which admit the charity cases will pass the mark-up on to the patients who can pay.

Downward redistribution is the intention. The outcome will often be something else. Where the contract does not clearly specify the throughput and the cost, a hospital will be able to exploit the ambiguity by means of lightning consultations, second-string equipment and poor-practice care. There is unpoliced default. There is also nepotism, favour-buying, *guanxi* cronyism and downright fraud. State sector or private sector, hospitals too can become emmeshed in the web: 'It is well known that the free patients on their list are relatives of hospital staff, bureaucrats and ministers' (Duggal, 2003). There may even be popular resistance to the notion that a foreign-owned hospital has bought its way into the country by promising to deliver a merit good that is not a business tradable but rather a sacred trust: 'The idea of foreign medical institutions providing essential services to the local population may be perceived as encroaching on national sovereignty' (Arunanondchai and Fink, 2007: 2).

Transferable payment is a possible solution. Tax-financed vouchers, means-tested grants, medical savings accounts and universal health insurance all have the advantage that they are patient-led: 'One way to remedy the problems linked to the dual structure is to facilitate the use of private hospitals by nationals by making the government's health care subsidy portable, to be used in the hospital of the patient's choice' (Blouin, 2006: 179). Where the money follows the patient, public and private hospitals will compete to attract customers from all income groups. Higher volume could reduce the average cost. The Government would provide some hospitals but would pay for others: 'Similar to the porosity for specialists, the porosity for patients would neutralize the perception of disparity in access to private facilities and expertise' (Ministry of Trade and Industry, 2003: Annex 2, 9). Even foreign hospitals can enter into the race. Often the appropriate treatment will not be offered locally. In this case, there is no reason why even poor people should not be allowed to spend their portable resources abroad.

Competition keeps the suppliers on their toes. There is also new entry. Foreign capital servicing tourists services locals as well: 'National policy-makers may have to consider that opening the system to foreigner providers may create an opportunity to rebalance the system' (Blouin, 2006: 183). So long as the entitlements are portable, there is a sense in which a new hospital attracted in from abroad may be said to confer a real benefit on local people as well. The supply of appointments goes up. Waiting times go down. Patients who would have made great sacrifices to travel abroad can gain the same standard of access at home. Foreign capital can be a complement to brotherly citizenship. It is a win–win game.

Governments can shape and influence the high-end private sector. Yet there is more to good health than the high-tech cutting edge. One of the most valuable contributions a health-promoting Government can make is to put money into preventive infrastructure. There is always and everywhere a need for safe drinking water, hygienic sanitation, adequate housing, health education, family planning, appropriate immunisation and particulate-free air. At the level of cure there should be provincial hospitals in less accessible areas that can deal quickly and affordably with the maladies of poverty such as diarrhoea caused by poor sanitation and respiratory disease brought on by biomass fuel even as they face up to the more universal conditions of hypertension, cancer, diabetes and AIDS. There is also the option of levelling down.

Beds, manpower and equipment are in short supply. It is easy to say that money plunged into the expensive technology that rich foreigners tend to demand would be better used for less-specialised, less capital-intensive procedures that would boost the health status of far greater numbers, most of them citizens. In a sense it is a tautology. Resources used at one end of the spectrum are not being used at the other. Prima facie there is a trade-off. It is the duty of the State to ensure that the *favelas* as well as the health tourists get a reasonable share.

Levelling down, the State could Robin Hood the outsiders by keeping down the foreign patients, keeping out the foreign hospitals, keeping in the domestic professionals who would otherwise have gone abroad. It is not a sensible strategy for a society that wants to use health tourism as an engine of economic growth. Levelling up would be a better way of making access more equal without having to compromise either on material advancement or on tolerant freedom of choice.

One way to improve access in pockets of neglect, geographical and social, would be to pay above the norm. Doctors willing to practise in remote areas might be offered differential capitations and hardship supplements. Infrastructure should be improved: there is no paediatrician in the northern two-thirds of Ghana, private housing is poor and the number of good schools for the doctors' own children is very limited. Returning expatriates might be promised relocation allowances, income tax rebates and updating sabbaticals in foreign countries. Undecided new graduates might be tempted with job security, retirement benefits, short courses, modern equipment and competitive salaries. They might be encouraged to practise in both sectors. Dual appointment would not only increase State-sector supply but attenuate the perception that subsidised patients cannot consult top specialists. Doctors might be given the opportunity to participate in research projects. Some of these projects will have the additional advantage that they adapt international results to conditions on the ground.

Self-interest is more than money alone. It would have to be: since private-sector doctors in Thailand earn from four to ten times as much as their public-sector counterparts, the State is unlikely to be able to match the remuneration package outside. Overwork, absenteeism and low morale sap the strength and thin the ranks. Lack of established posts, of a reasonable career structure and of opportunities for postgraduate training drive young people abroad. Clearly, attraction strategies and retention strategies alike are essential. They will ensure that the balance of skill and social background is not disrupted in the free clinics and the village infirmaries even if mobile manpower moves into the private hospitals, into the cities or goes abroad.

Another way of upgrading the underprovided would be to require all professionals trained in public universities or on public scholarships to do medical national service for a mandatory period of three to five years. They would serve out this bond among the under-doctored who most need their help. Medical education is heavily subsidised by the State. It is the fiscal balance and not just the domestic product that feels the strain. Each migrating African professional represents a loss of US$184,000 to Africa. The financial cost to South Africa, 600 of whose graduates are in New Zealand, is US$37 million (Eastwood et al., 2005: 1894). There is a solution. Recipient nations could be asked to reimburse developing countries for the tax-funded investment in training that is lost through the migration of health care professionals. There is little or no chance that this solution will be adopted.

What is feasible, however, is an expansion in the medical schools. If the foreigners are coming in and the locals are demanding more, there is no alternative to increased capacity in the nation's teaching hospitals. Buildings and seats are not enough. It will be necessary to recruit additional academics and in-service mentors to complement the new facilities. Not everyone will accept that this can be done quickly without some debasement in the quality of care.

It is, of course, not just in the poorer countries that medical schools should be producing more graduates. In Britain 28 per cent of the physician workforce is foreign-trained. In Norway it is 12.7 per cent. In France it is 3 per cent. In Japan it is 1 per cent (Mullan, 2005). If the richer countries were to augment their domestic supply, their need to bring in medical migrants from poorer countries would be that much less. Such a strategy would also be a bulwark against anticipated loss. New opportunities in India and other poorer countries are bound eventually to reduce the outflow of professional talent.

Bilateral agreements would be a third way of staunching the outflow. A receiving country would continue to make up its shortfall with non-resident professionals but it would do this on the basis of rolling recruitment. Fixed-term work permits would be an incentive for a foreigner to come in for a limited period and then to be replaced by another. The revolving door means that expensive training will be lent to the richer country but that the bulk of the investment will remain at home.

It will be easier to implement such a plan if local students do not have to go abroad for their basic training. Qualified locals should instead go abroad for top-up training later on. They will then acquire incremental specialisation which they will subsequently bring home. Short absences are more likely to become permanent if a young person aged 18 goes abroad for five or six years. There is much to be said for adequate places in the local medical and dental schools if only because they build up loyalties and contacts within the local system. In sub-Saharan Africa 24 out of 47 countries have only one medical school. As many as 11 have no medical school at all (Eastwood et al., 2005: 1893). Retention is especially difficult if local medical students are already living in the West.

The local medical schools should in addition align their training programmes with local patterns of disease and levels of technology. Students who are taught to 'think Western' are more likely to be discontented with the problems, equipment and challenges in their Third World home. An imaginative Government might even site a medical school in a deprived part of the country. Students from the region are more likely to remain there because they already have roots. As for the others, incomers who have lived for five or six years in northern Ghana or in Bihar might decide that it is not all that bad.

9.   The Singapore experience

Medical tourism in Asia generated revenues of US$3.4 billion in 2007. It accounted for 12.7 per cent of health-tourism exports worldwide. Already attracting 1.6 million health tourists a year, health tourism in Asia is growing annually at the rate of 20 to 30 per cent (Velasco, 2008: 13, 15). Revenues are likely to be in excess of US$4.4 billion by 2012 (*USA Today*, 2006).

The market leaders are Thailand, India and Singapore. Other countries active in the Asian market are Korea, Malaysia and the Philippines. This chapter takes the example of Singapore to show what being a health care hub can mean on the ground.

9.1   THE SERVICE SECTOR

Singapore is a small city-State situated about 85 miles north of the equator. Its population is only 4.99 million. Its land area is 692.1 square kilometres. Singapore is an open economy. The ratio of trade (exports plus imports) to GDP, at 360 per cent, is probably the highest in the world. Its balance of payments is almost always in surplus.

Yet Singapore is a high-wage economy. Hourly compensation for manufacturing labour in Singapore stood at US$8.35 in 2007. In the United States the equivalent average was US$24.59. In Japan it was US$19.75. In Denmark it was US$42.29. Production workers' pay in Singapore was only 34 per cent of the equivalent level in the United States. It is no cause for complacency. Production workers were paid only US$6.58 in Taiwan, US$5.78 in Hong Kong, US$1.10 in the Philippines, US$0.61 in Sri Lanka (Bureau of Labor Statistics, 2009: Table 8). Even after adjusting for higher productivity in Singapore, the risk is real that cheap foreigners will hollow out the manufacturing base.

Microelectronics, pharmaceuticals and petrochemicals are still competitive in the world market. The fact that Singapore is having to move up the value chain need not mean that it will have to abandon altogether the production of goods. Even so, industries like textiles and car assembly have already gone abroad. Other industries are considering relocation to China, Vietnam or Myanmar. Singapore is looking for new opportunities. It may fall to high-end services to make up the loss.

In some countries there has been a historical progression from the primary through the secondary to the tertiary sectors. In the United States about 84 per cent of the labour force in 1810 was in agriculture. By 2006 it was 2 per cent. In 1960 about 35 per cent of non-agricultural workers in the United States were making goods and 65 per cent were supplying services. By 2004 the figures had become 17 per cent and 83 per cent respectively (Blinder, 2006).

The United States is evolving into services. Singapore, on the other hand, has always been an emporium and an entrepôt. The services sector in 2007 was responsible for 66 per cent of the Singapore GDP. It accounted for 76.7 per cent of the jobs (Ministry of Trade and Industry, 2008: 151; Ministry of Manpower, 2008: 7). Manufacturing was 13.6 per cent of the GDP at independence in 1965. It peaked at 28 per cent in 2000. It fell to 25 per cent in 2007. It is likely to fall still further. There is almost no agriculture. What that leaves is services. Singapore has always lived through its intangibles.

Crucially, however, many of the services in the past have been labour-intensive. They have been low-value-added and non-tradable. Services like shoe-shining and window-cleaning created jobs when Singapore had surplus population. They made only a small contribution to growth and hardly any contribution at all to exports. While retaining the hairdressers, the dry cleaners and the taxi drivers, what Singapore will require in the future is not so much the chicken-rice hawkers who sell to locals as a skill-intensive cutting edge that can keep the nation prosperous in an increasingly competitive global environment.

Service exports are outpacing service imports. In 2007 Singapore had a surplus of S$8.6 billion on invisible account. In earlier years it had had a deficit. Total world trade is increasing more rapidly than world GDP. Service trade is increasing more rapidly than world trade as a whole. Ricardo's examples of wine and textiles seem strangely outdated now that services, growing fast, account for 20 per cent of all international trade (Smith, 2004: 2313). Singapore's total services trade (the sum of service exports plus service imports) was 62.2 per cent of its GDP in 2000. By 2007 it was 93.1 per cent. This highlights the increasing significance of international trade in services to the Singapore economy. Service exports in 2007 went mainly to Asia (50.2), Europe (20.3 per cent) and North America (15.3 per cent). The equivalent figures for service imports into Singapore were 31.8 per cent, 27.4 per cent and 27.6 per cent respectively (Department of Statistics, 2009: 2, 7).

The largest service tradable (accounting in 2007 for 35.2 per cent of service exports and 38.9 per cent of service imports) has always been transportation. Although in deficit by S$1.1 billion in 2007, at least the imbalance is becoming smaller over time. The Port of Singapore handles the second largest volume of shipping tonnage in the world. Changi, important both for freight and passengers, is the nineteenth busiest airport. Associated with such facilities are supporting or symbiotic activities such as warehousing, leasing, ship-chandlering and ship-repairing. Trade-related services generate a further 23.5 per cent of invisible exports, 7.8 per cent of invisible imports.

A second concentration is travel and tourism. Tourism accounts for more of world value-added than agriculture or defence. Growing at twice the rate of world GNP, it was 10 per cent of the total in 2005. In that year it represented 8 per cent of world exports (Bookman and Bookman, 2008: 21–2). The tourist sector employs 238 million workers throughout the world. This represents 8.4 of the world's workforce. Singapore in 2007 played host to 10.7 million tourists. They contributed 3 per cent to Singapore's GDP (www.stb.gov.sg). Travel receipts expanded by 15.3 per cent to S$13.8 billion in 2007. About 11.4 per cent of Singapore's service exports and 16.6 per cent of Singapore's service imports are generated by travel services. The net deficit is worth S$5 billion and is narrowing (Department of Statistics, 2009: 3). Rising incomes abroad are making it possible for foreigners to come to Singapore. An expected rise to 17 million arrivals would add up to a total spend in the hotels, restaurants and casinos of Singapore of at least S$30 billion. There are approximately 500 million tourists travelling for pleasure in the Asia-Pacific region. They generate revenues in excess of S$6.4 trillion. About 70 per cent of those tourists are Asians. China is poised to displace France (the front-runner in 2009), Spain and the United States as the single most important destination worldwide. The whole of South and East Asia is well-placed to share in the boom.

A third service area is business management. Singapore has expertise in consultancy, logistics, advertising, accounting, marketing and the law. Things can be sold from Singapore that do not originate there. Companies which trade in South-East Asia often locate their regional headquarters in Singapore. Business services make up 9.4 per cent of Singapore's service exports and 7.8 per cent of its service imports. Exports totalled S$11.5 billion, imports S$8.8 billion, in 2007. Higher growth in exports vis-à-vis imports resulted in a considerable surplus of S$2.7 billion (Department of Statistics, 2009: 5). Business services like engineering, communications and information technology complement the management component. They represent an additional 4.7 per cent of exports, 3.8 per cent of imports.

A further service area is banking, finance and insurance. About 10.2 per cent of service exports and 5.6 per cent of service imports arise from money-related activities such as deposit-taking, brokerage, underwriting, new issues, credit and foreign exchange. Singapore, with Hong Kong and Shanghai, has a major regional and international profile in these activities.

Finally, there are the human services. One of these is health. The World Health Organization estimates that international trade in health care represents less than 1 per cent of world expenditure on health. It is growing more slowly than international trade in other services. The picture is likely to change. The Economic Review Committee in 2003 identified medical attention supplied to foreigners as a sunrise source of jobs, value-added and exports in a post-industrial Singapore that would have to become a high-end services hub. It has some way to go. Earnings from health tourism were only 4 per cent of Singapore's total revenue from tourism in 2007.

9.2   HEALTH SERVICES AS A HUB

The potential is there. By 2050 there will be approximately 5.6 billion people in Asia. They will be 60 per cent of the world's population. Total consumer expenditure on health care services and goods in Asia will reach US$610 billion by 2013 (Ministry of Trade and Industry, 2003: Annex 1, 1). Consumer expenditure on health in Singapore will be US$3.9 billion. Consumer expenditure in China will be US$64.6 billion. Consumer expenditure in Japan will be US$421.9 billion.

There is no reliable estimate of the number of Asians who will be seeking health care abroad. A proxy, however, would be income. The Asian regional market, East, South, South-East, is already home to 4.8 million middle-class families with a household income of at least US$50,000 per annum. That figure of 4.8 million is growing at an annual rate of between 3 per cent and 5 per cent in the ASEAN region, between 5 per cent and 7 per cent in China and India. Some estimates suggest that over 50 per cent of households in China (and some 400 million households in India) will by 2020 have an annual income of at least US$8000. There will soon be 300 million people in Asia alone who are able and willing to pay for good quality medical care at an affordable price. Medical care in Asia costs from 6 per cent to 33 per cent of equivalent care in the United States (Grail Research, 2009: 5).

Incomes are rising. Numbers are going up. Nations, moreover, are growing old. The United Nations estimates that the over-60s worldwide will increase from 6 million in 2000 to 2 billion in 2050. In Asia the increase in 50 years will be from 3.1 million to approximately 1.2 billion. In South-East Asia alone it will be from 380,000 to 1.7 million (United Nations

Population Division, 2009). The rise in 40 years in South-East Asia will be of the order of 430 per cent (Credit Suisse, 2008: 15). Older people will be in a position to convert their demand into effective demand. By 2015 the over-65s in Singapore, Japan, South Korea, Taiwan, Hong Kong and Australia are expected to have assets in excess of US$1535.4 billion (Hedrick-Wong, 2007: 86).

It is a considerable market presence. As purchasing power increases and life expectancy becomes longer, Asian spending will go up. Private consumption will be augmented by public spending and non-Asian spending. Mitra is in no doubt that a great deal of money is at stake: 'The Medical Tourism market earned global revenues of USD 20 billion in 2005. . . . The Asian market comprising India, Singapore, Thailand and Malaysia stood at approximately USD 2.5 billion in 2006' (Mitra, 2007). The figures are likely to double or more than double within a decade. The figure of US$4 billion earned from 1.3 million travellers may be a conservative estimate (*Hotel Marketing Newsletter*, 2006).

The American market in particular has yet to be properly opened up: 'This has the potential of doing to the U.S. health care system what the Japanese auto industry did to American carmakers' (Uwe Reinhardt, quoted in Kher, 2006). Already 45 per cent of cross-border patients from North America are travelling to Asia for their medical needs: only 26 per cent are going to much-nearer Latin America and a negligible 2 per cent are going to the Middle East. Only 1 per cent of Latin Americans, interestingly, are choosing Asia: 87 per cent prefer medical care in the USA and 12 per cent select other Latin American destinations (Grail Research, 2009: 4). Despite the impressive figure of 45 per cent, Asian countries like Singapore are not dependent on America. Medical travellers in Singapore are likely to be drawn mainly from the region: Asia, the Middle East and the Pacific. Of all medical travel originating in Asia, fully 93 per cent remains in Asia. Singapore has state-of-the-art technology. Most of the region does not.

The potential is tremendous. Affluent foreigners, Asian and non-Asian alike, will be able to purchase health care in Singapore and not just at home. Foreigners spend over the odds: 'Hospital patients from abroad are prepared to pay high prices, illustrated by those in Singapore who spend S$2,680 (US$1,522) compared with an average of S$758 (US$431)' (Henderson, 2004: 177). Foreigners prefer the A-class wards. Foreigners have more complex procedures. Foreigners are loyal to their doctor: they undertake repeat visits for subsequent consultations even when recreational tourists are frightened away by a recession. Foreigners have hidden spillovers: usually accompanied by close relatives who patronise the hotels, restaurants and shops, each S$1 spent by a visitor generates S$0.63

of additional demand in the Singapore economy (Ministry of Trade and Industry, 2003: Annex 1, 5).

In 2000 about 150,000 foreign patients were being attracted to Singapore for care. Bringing in a total of S$354 million, foreign patients were contributing only 0.19 per cent in value-added to Singapore's GDP. The equivalent figure for the US at the same time was US$915 million. The Economic Review Committee was in no doubt that the potential was tremendous and that Singapore had to be on board:

> Singapore aims to increase the number of foreign patient visitors to 1 million per annum by year 2012. Of these, 100,000 are likely to be inpatient/day surgery cases while the bulk would be out-patient visits. This could generate some S$2.6 billion in value-added and add approximately 1 per cent to the then GDP. . . . The initiative has the potential to create 13,000 new jobs (Ministry of Trade and Industry, 2003: 1).

Foreign patients in 2000 represented only 4.3 per cent of all patients seen in Singapore. They accounted for only 0.25 per cent of the GDP. It was not the maximum that could be captured. Even if the target figure for 2012 proves unrealistic, the fundamentals are sound and the prospects good.

At the time of the Economic Review Committee Singapore was playing host to approximately 230,000 medical tourists. As Singapore landing cards do not ask about the purpose of the visit, and as the hospitals do not report the immigration status of patients (especially outpatients) to the Ministry of Health, it is impossible to be certain. Exit surveys extrapolating from 10,000 visitors sampled at Changi Airport by the Singapore Tourist Board suggest that there were about 646,000 medical incomers in 2008. There were 410,000 medical entrants in the good year of 2006. There were only 348,000 in 2007 when the sky darkened due to the economic slowdown and the fears engendered by the H1N1 epidemic (Velasco, 2008: 13). The apparent fall may have been the consequence of measurement error: 'This drop came as a surprise as all hospitals registered higher patient admissions and patient-days in 2007, as compared to the previous year. . . . Spending by these medical tourists increased by 30 per cent to S$1.7 billion during the same period' (Ministry of Health, 2009a).

An expenditure survey, also in 2007, found that 10 per cent of tourists' spending went on medical and health-related services. This was close to the 14 per cent for food and beverages with which the Singapore name is more commonly associated (Singapore Tourism Board, 2008: 8). Allowing for the accompanying relatives and the spillover shopping, the gain is likely to have been much more. Even in a bad year, health tourism is good business.

Despite the occasional fall in entries (which may be due to sampling error), it is relatively certain that the trend is up. Yet the numbers are not large. About 150,000 foreign patients were seen in India in 2003, 450,000 in 2007 (Velasco, 2008: 13). In Thailand in 2005 there were 730,000 foreign patients (Yoopetch, 2006: 307). In 2007 there were 1.54 million (Grail Research, 2009: 5). What this means is that Singapore in 2007 was playing host to less than a third of the health travellers who were flocking to Thailand.

Foreign patients in Singapore came mainly from Indonesia (51.7 per cent), Malaysia (11.4 per cent), United States and Canada (5.1 per cent), the United Kingdom (3.7 per cent) and Japan (2.9 per cent). The Indonesians alone are estimated to have spent S$358.6 million in 2005. Vietnam as it develops is becoming a major source of business. In 2008 about 30,000 Vietnamese nationals travelled abroad for care. Many of them chose Singapore for their health.

The bias towards the region – about 70 per cent of foreign patients in Singapore come from the ASEAN countries – is a reminder that medical travel need not have a worldwide catchment. Patients going to Cuba come mainly from Latin America and the Caribbean. Patients going to Jordan come mainly from the Arab Middle East. That said, Singapore is actively looking beyond the neighbourhood to refresh its patient pool. There is increasing demand from India, China, Bangladesh, Russia, the Ukraine and the United States.

About 30,000 of Singapore's medical tourists are coming for cancer treatments, open heart surgery and other major interventions. The majority are coming for routine check-ups and simple procedures such as hernia repair. Day-case surgery without an inpatient stay will often meet their requirements. In 1996 36 per cent of all surgery in Singapore was day-case. In 2006 it was 57 per cent.

Foreigners will be coming to Singapore. Singaporeans will be going abroad. Trade is a two-way street: 'We should allow it as consumers would benefit through such increased competition across the border' (Khaw, 2009). Historically, Singaporeans have had to pay out-of- pocket or through private insurance for elective medical care consumed overseas. Earmarked medical savings accounts ('Medisave') have been restricted to treatment in Singapore itself. The only exception has been cover for a medical emergency such as a heart attack abroad. From 2009 the system was made more liberal. A draw-down for medical care overseas was agreed in principle. Singapore, here as elsewhere, will proceed by small steps. Caution will remain the order of the day:

> Overseas Medisave use will only be limited to hospitalisations and day surger-
> ies. The overseas hospital should have an approved working arrangement with

a Medisave-accredited hospital in Singapore. Medisave claims can only be made through the Singapore hospitals, and subject to the following conditions: (i) Overseas use of Medisave should be limited to patients normally resident in Singapore; (ii) The local attending doctor should certify the patient's condition and necessity of medical treatment; and (iii) The referring local hospitals remain accountable for patient satisfaction and good clinical outcomes for patients referred overseas, at the same standard as if the patients were treated in Singapore (Ministry of Health, 2009c).

Patients are being allowed to stretch their Medisave dollar by seeking elective procedures from recognised medical providers overseas. Safeguards against extravagance, fraud and shoddy workmanship are nonetheless in place. The procedures will be no more than those allowed under the Medisave regulations at home. The providers will be the tried-and-tested contacts of a Singapore centre that knows them well. A more limited scenario would have been to outsource the tests but to retain the bodies. The compromise that has been adopted, while not fully demand-led, is not the least liberal that could have been proposed.

The criticism is sometimes made that restrictions on the international portability of Medisave are a non-tariff barrier. A full body check-up costs about S$750 in Singapore. It costs S$500 at Bumrungrad. Cataract removal costs about S$2500 in Singapore. It costs S$1800 in Malaysia. Since Medisave balances belong to the patient, it is sometimes said that demand-led shopping would allow the patient to secure the best-attainable value for money. The objection is the familiar one, that medical paternalism is essential because the ill-informed cannot make a fully rational choice. There is, however, another consideration as well. It does not do much for Singapore's image as a medical services hub if its own people are regularly travelling to other countries for care.

9.3   HOSPITALS AND PATIENTS

There are 14 public hospitals and speciality centres in Singapore in the public sector. They have 72 per cent of the bedstock. The public sector provides hospital care for 80 per cent of resident patients. There are also 16 private hospitals and a large number of walk-in clinics (Ministry of Health, 2009b). Hospitals in the State sector tend to be larger. Singapore General Hospital has 1516 beds. Tan Tock Seng has 1400. There are only 380 beds in Gleneagles and 505 in Mount Elizabeth. Every major hospital in Singapore is JCI-accredited.

The two main groups in the private sector are Parkway Holdings Limited and the Raffles Medical Group. Parkway is the market leader.

It accounts for 70 per cent of private hospital care in Singapore. It has four hospitals: Gleneagles, Mount Elizabeth, East Shore and a 350-bed hospital in the Novena area, constructed in the recession but bullish about growth. The Group practises centralised procurement in order to secure economies of scale. Parkway also operates the Parkway College of Nursing and Allied Health. The aim is to develop the talent pool and alleviate the nursing shortfall.

Parkway, with 16 hospitals and more than 3300 beds in the region, is the largest health care service provider in Asia. It treats nearly half of all medical incomers in Singapore. About 40 per cent of its patients in Singapore and of its local revenues are non-resident in origin. About 59 per cent of its foreign clients are from Indonesia (Credit Suisse, 2008: 11). Jakarta is only an hour away by plane. American agencies such as PlanetHospital and Companion Global Healthcare include Parkway in their global network of preferred providers. Fees (by diagnostic related group) are negotiated in advance.

Parkway encourages its doctors to give seminars in different countries. Some lecture abroad several times a month. In that way it builds up a network for referrals and follow-up, and also keeps the company's name in the public eye. Parkway markets and advertises abroad. It has patient assistance centres in 18 countries, including China, Ukraine, the United Arab Emirates, Saudi Arabia, Uzbekistan and Russia. Russia is a sunrise market since incomes there are growing more rapidly than the supply of reliable medical attention. While Russians in the western areas often prefer to go to Germany, Russians in Siberia and the Far East find Asia more convenient. Parkway in Singapore sees about 80 patients from Vladivostok and the Primorsky region a month.

The Raffles Medical Group has a network of 66 GP and specialist clinics in Singapore. The Group has centres which cater specifically to the Japanese community. Since visits to GPs recur at the rate of 4.5–5 times a year, satellite attention is a reliable source of earnings even in a downturn. Raffles has the largest network of family medicine and dental clinics in the Republic. As such it is well placed both to feed referrals to its hospital specialists and to deliver outpatient care. Some outpatient treatments (and most inpatient care) qualify for a Medisave reimbursement. The Group's flagship, Raffles Hospital, has 380 beds. Hospital doctors are paid a salary and receive performance bonuses. Fees paid by the patient go directly to the hospital. Labour accounts for about 70 per cent of the total operating costs of Raffles Hospital. Manpower is expensive.

About 35 per cent of the hospital's patients in 2008 were foreign. It had been 20 per cent in 2002. They come from 120 countries. Its largest markets are Indonesia and Malaysia, followed by new sources of business such as Japan, Russia, Bangladesh, Vietnam and Mongolia. Patients from underdoctored countries often have undetected conditions: admitted for one problem, they will subsequently be treated for others as well. To assist in its marketing Raffles has representatives abroad. It has entered into a transnational agreement with Kaiser Permanente, America's largest health maintenance organisation. The Raffles Group also caters to a number of resident expatriates, many of them corporate clients. Image matters. There is a grand piano in the lobby and framed pictures on the walls. The feel is luxury alongside the competence.

Raffles offers health care financing to businesses and individuals through its subsidiary, International Medical Insurers (IMI). It has funded a part of its expansion through the placement of new shares. They were taken up by Temasek Holdings, the high-profile Singaporean sovereign wealth fund, and by the Government of Qatar. While the stake of each party (at 4.9 per cent of total equity) is not large, it is a strategic move to have such powerful investors onside.

As well as the two giants there are a number of smaller hospitals in the private sector. These include the West Clinic, Mount Alvernia Hospital and the Thomson Medical Centre. There are also private clinics such as Pacific Healthcare and the Camden Medical Centre. Clinics like these specialise in ambulatory treatment. In an emergency the hospitals are not far away. An integrated multiplex, Connexion at Farrer Park, is offering a range of choices (189 private medical suites, a 220-bed tertiary hospital, a 230-room luxury hotel) in a single 19-storey mall. Rents are high for medical suites situated near the major hospitals. The Paragon Shopping Centre (located next to Mount Elizabeth Hospital) had eleven floors of medical suites in 2009. Medical suites are experiencing a new and largely unnoticed property boom in Singapore. All private medical facilities in Singapore must be licensed and inspected by the Ministry of Health under the Private Hospitals and Medical Clinics (Amendment) Act of 1999. The standards required are so high as to deter frivolous entry.

Four foreign patients in five are being treated in the private sector (Khoo, 2003: 3). The State sector is less active in the market. In contrast to the private hospitals, about 95 per cent of patients seen at public hospitals (and 98 per cent of inpatient admissions) are Singapore citizens or permanent residents. Since medical tourists do not qualify for subsidised beds, there is no financial incentive for them to opt for public-sector care.

As for the suppliers themselves, the public hospitals do not make a deliberate effort to target foreign business. Not least because of the shortage of trained professionals and State bedstock, local patients, as the Minister of Health has explained, will remain their priority catchment: 'For us in public hospitals, our mission is very clear. Our primary objective is to look after Singaporeans' health, particularly those in the bottom half of the population who have no choice. If you are in the upper half, you can consider going to private hospitals or even foreign hospitals. But for the bottom half, we are the only provider for them. . . . We will never neglect local patients and simply chase the foreign patient load' (Khaw, 2009).

Locals must be guaranteed the affordable health care to which they are entitled. This does not mean, however, that the public sector should be indifferent to international business or to the revenues which such business brings in. The Minister of Health has made the position clear. Foreigners attracted by Singapore's reputation and standards should be given a warm welcome as well: 'I see no reasons why we should reject them just because they are foreigners. We will treat them within our capabilities and capacity. When we do long-term planning – whether it is manpower or capabilities – we will have to factor in foreign patient load' (Khaw, 2009).

All of the State hospitals are JCI-accredited. They have an international reputation for excellence. The successful separation of Nepalese conjoined twins was performed at the Singapore General Hospital. Successful stem-cell cornea transplants have been performed at the Singapore National Eye Centre. Singapore performed South-East Asia's first adult living donor liver transplant. Singapore performed Asia's first kidney cum bone marrow transplant. Singapore performed the world's first cord blood transplant from an unrelated donor to a thalassaemia patient. The National Cancer Centre and the Integrated Neuroscience Centre, public-sector facilities both located at the Singapore General Hospital, are major referral centres in South-East Asia. Singapore General is the only place in the region capable of treating patients with major burns. Singapore General Hospital, in partnership with the Shanghai Hospital Development Centre, is also involved in the Bao Zhong Tang Traditional Chinese Medicine Clinic. The Clinic offers Chinese TCM such as herbal remedies brought in from Shanghai in a treatment centre that has access if needed to Western X-rays, blood tests and operating theatres. The joint product is attractive to local Chinese. It is attractive as well to new patients from the region who welcome a range of choices under one roof.

The SingHealth Group, one of Singapore's four public-sector clusters, arranges follow-up in Dhaka's Square Hospitals for Bangladeshis who have had treatment in its hospitals. The Bangkok Hospital Medical Center has a similar arrangement for patients in Bangladesh. The public sector in Singapore is represented at health care events organised in foreign countries by SingaporeMedicine. Along with the private sector, it seeks in that way to promote health care facilities and options.

The public sector has been known to conclude deals with unexpected trading partners. An example would be the American supermarket chain,

Hannaford Bros, which provides a company plan for its 27,000 employees. Hannaford has made an arrangement (reinsured through Aetna) with the National University Hospital whereby its members can receive a hip replacement at the NUH for US$8000. The entire bill, including travel for the patient and spouse, is covered by the employer. Other American companies such as Snow Summit Ski Resorts are exploring similar arrangements in Singapore. No one can predict whether such schemes will in the end succeed or fail. It has to be recorded, however, that by the end of 2008 not a single Hannaford employee had taken advantage of the opportunity to travel to Singapore for a hip.

9.4 STRENGTHS AND WEAKNESSES

Health care is an area in which Singapore ought to be able to excel. It is well situated on the air and sea routes. It is not far from the big markets of Indonesia, India, North Asia and the Middle East. It has the port. It has a world-class airport with an extensive network of non-stop flights. Singapore is a clean-and-green place with a low level of harassment and crime. Its facilities are not paralysed by social conflict or monsoon floods. It has the advantages of a warm climate, high-quality infrastructure, luxury hotels with in-house spas. It has visitor-friendly immigration procedures. It has many years of experience in the tourism industry. It offers good facilities for the meetings, incentive trips, conventions and exhibitions ('MICE') market. It has two world-class casinos. It is home to a critical mass of foreigners who bring their relatives to Singapore for care.

Singapore is a multicultural society. Well-educated professionals can be found who speak not only English but Malay, Tamil or Mandarin as well. Medical interpreters fluent in other languages are available if required. Foreign doctors are welcome: at the National University Hospital, for example, Austrians, Greeks, Russians, Indians and other nationalities are 21 per cent of all doctors. Singapore, which is 15 per cent Muslim, is able to offer halal food, female doctors, prayer-mats and correctly-orientated prayer rooms. Many locals have lived abroad. British patients have been offered muffins because that is what the British like. Hospitals know how to source newspapers in Arabic or Russian.

Regulation inspires confidence: the Health Sciences Authority (HSA) sets strict standards on drugs, blood and equipment. Hospitals are comfortable, modern and well equipped. Advanced technology and medical expertise ensure that a wide range of procedures can be delivered. Singapore can field not just local enterprise but international names like Johns Hopkins and the West Clinic. Marketing initiatives have meant that the world is aware of Singapore. Singapore in 2000 was ranked best in Asia by the World Health Organization, sixth best in the world. Singapore has a good brand name.

Singapore has a reputation for clinical excellence. The Singapore Tourist Promotion Board found that 72 per cent of the patients surveyed had chosen Singapore because they or their referring doctors believed that Singapore could be trusted and that quality there was state-of-the-art (Ministry of Trade and Industry, 2003: Annex 1, 4). Singapore is known for organ transplants, stem cell transplants and other high-end procedures (Grail Research, 2009: 5). Koncept Analytics, profiling the competitive advantage of selected Asian suppliers, ranked Singapore as the best in Asia and among the best in the world. It was less confident about Thailand: 'Thailand. . . . is faced with tough competition from both ends, low-cost treatments from India and Malaysia as well as high-end medical services from Singapore. The price difference between Singapore and Thailand is also reducing at a significant rate' (*International Medical Travel Journal*, 2008d).

Ten hospitals and three medical centres in Singapore have been accredited by the Joint Commission International. The equivalent figures are ten in India, four in Thailand, two in the Philippines and one in Malaysia. A disproportionate number of all JCI-accredited hospitals in Asia (including Turkey) are in Singapore (Woodman, 2007: 58). Singapore hospitals are aware that they need the JCI certificate to attract international business. Interestingly, the first to win accreditation was the not-for-profit National University Hospital, in 2004. About 85 per cent of patients from the United Arab Emirates receiving treatment for cancer overseas are seen at the Johns Hopkins Singapore International Medical Centre. Many are Government-sponsored. Singapore is respected but the market is still a niche. Singapore only receives about 1200 patients a year from the Gulf.

Doctors, at least in the private sector, are available. Waiting times for international and local private patients are short. The average wait for joint replacement surgery in Canada is 253 days. In Singapore it can be arranged within a week (Grail Research, 2009: 6). While bed occupancy in the public sector has been as high as 84 per cent at the National University Hospital, 89 per cent at Tan Tock Seng and even 99 per cent at Shanghai General, in the private sector there is a considerable amount of underutilised capacity. Bed occupancy in the Parkway Group is about 60 per cent. This reflects the growing preference for day-case treatments: these made up 42 per cent of its total admissions in 2008 (www.parkwayhealth.com). In the Raffles Group, only 55 per cent of hospital beds were occupied on any given day in 2009. It is hard to be precise. Of 380 beds in its wards only 250 were operational. Additional beds will be brought into operation when there is a demand for capacity.

The number of hospital beds in Singapore has actually declined since 1997. There were 11,885 hospital beds in 2003 (just after the opening in 2001 of the new Raffles Hospital). There were 11,457 beds in 2008. In that period total hospital admissions rose by 8 per cent. Private hospital admissions rose by 25 per cent (Credit Suisse, 2008: 27). The difference in admissions may have been a reflection of the difference in capacity. If so, then the constraints are in the process of being overcome. While the private sector is adding Novena, the public sector is adding 550 beds through the green-field Khoo Teck Puat Hospital. It is planning additional hospitals in Jurong and Woodlands.

Yet demand is going up, and so is price. Quality and name are Singapore's greatest strengths. High price and rising price are, however, the medical sector's Achilles heel.

Singapore is not cheap by regional standards. Blepharoplasty to remove excess fat from the eyes costs between S$2500 and S$5000 in Singapore. In the US it would cost at least S$5800. In Thailand it would cost only S$600. Cardiac bypass surgery costs US$18,500 in Singapore. In Thailand it would cost US$11,000. In Malaysia it would cost only US$9000. It is not much comfort to learn that an equivalent bypass would cost at least US$130,000 in the United States (Woodman, 2007: 8). The calculation is a simpler one. Total knee replacement costs S$16,000 at Gleneagles in Singapore. Total knee replacement costs S$10,000 at Gleneagles in Penang. Which Gleneagles in the circumstances is likely to be the better buy?

Estimates made by the Deloitte Center for Health Solutions suggest that the average cost of medical attention in India is 20 per cent of the average cost in the US. In Malaysia and the Philippines it is 25 per cent. In Thailand it is 30 per cent. In Singapore it is 35 per cent (Deloitte Center for Health Solutions, 2008: 6). Even North Asia can cost less. Hip replacement costs US$5900 in Taiwan but US$10,000 in Singapore.

The patients who come to Singapore are a self-selected subset. They want Singapore excellence and are willing to pay. Their confidence is a compliment but it is also a temptation. There is in theory no systematic price discrimination and no deliberate cross-subsidisation. Foreigners and unsubsidised locals are quoted the same medical fee: if interpreters and transfers are required, they are invoiced separately. Standard billing according to an internal schedule ensures that patients bring in the same revenue surplus irrespective of their origin. The practice in the private sector can be different. Doctors in the private sector, as the Director of the National Neuroscience Institute has warned, can and do charge whatever the traffic will bear:

I know first-hand of an Indonesian patient who was charged $100,000 for a simple laparoscopic removal of a gall bladder, a procedure that usually costs $10,000 in the private sector. There have been enough cases of shameless profiteering to earn some hospitals here a bad reputation. . . . The Government hopes to promote medical tourism. But news of overcharging spreads very quickly abroad. Unless action is taken soon, greed will kill the golden goose (Lee, 2008: A23).

While all patients can be manipulated through information asymmetry into wasteful over-consumption at supra-competitive prices, foreign patients are more vulnerable than their local counterparts since they do not have the time to shop around. Data on prices and outcomes posted by the Ministry of Health on its website will improve transparency and facilitate comparisons. Perhaps, however, information by itself will not be enough. Singapore's good name is a valuable business asset. Dr Lee is warning that Singapore's brand name should not be put at risk for short-term gain.

There is another threat. The general rate of inflation in 2008 was 6.5 per cent. The rate of care cost inflation was 7.5 per cent. The absolute numbers went down in 2009. The high numbers were, however, a warning. There is a strong likelihood that the cost of care will accelerate again.

Singapore is at risk from an ageing population. The over-65s were 8.5 per cent of the population in 2008. They will be 18.9 per cent of the population in 2030. Old people put more pressure on scarce health care resources (Reisman, 2009: 22–33). Sheer numbers mean more treatments. Life expectancy is going up. Immigrants are coming in. Citizens and residents are likely to number 6.5 million by 2050.

New technologies and costly pharmaceuticals are putting a strain on limited budgets. Rising incomes make it possible for ordinary people to spend more on health. Reimbursement from compulsory Medisave is becoming more liberal: additional conditions such as diabetes and stroke are being added to the list. The Government's MediShield now insures 80 per cent of the population: the co-payment rate was reduced de facto in 2008 from 60 per cent to 30 per cent of the largest hospital bills. Private insurance is extending the options: whereas public sector MediShield reimburses no more than S$50,000 per annum, S$200,000 in the course of the policy-holder's life, some private plans offer S$500,000 for one year, an unlimited amount for a lifetime. It all puts the prices up.

Differential pricing can itself have an inflationary bias. Non-residents do not qualify for a subsidised bed. Permanent residents are entitled to only 80 per cent of the citizens' subsidy. Means-testing makes the lower-cost wards more expensive for the haves. The net result of social facts such as these might be to skew demand into costly A-class beds and the private sector. Spending in the private sector grew more rapidly than the GDP in the decade between the Asian economic crisis in 1997 and the world recession in late 2008: 11 per cent annually, as opposed to 8 per cent (Credit Suisse, 2008: 7). Private hospitals are gaining share. Medical tourism is contributing new admissions to the private sector. The private sector costs more. The care-cost index goes up.

Due both to rising quantities and rising prices, the share of medical attention in the GDP is increasing. Slower growth in the denominator combined with faster growth in the numerator is bound to speed up the rise. Some estimates suggest that the share of medical attention will reach 7 or even 8 per cent by 2030. Yet countervailing forces are in play. Day-case surgery and reimbursement by diagnostic-related group tend to keep down the average bill. Faster throughput can mean forward-falling economies of scale. Greater volume makes possible the accelerated depreciation of high-cost capital before it becomes obsolete. Surplus beds and manpower in the private sector contain the fees in a way that ceiling operation would not. Finally, there is the impact of competition from other regional hubs. So long as well-informed customers have meaningful choices overseas, so long as prices abroad are rising at a slower rate than in Singapore, there must be a limit to what a treatment centre in Singapore can charge.

9.5   THE OVERSEAS WING

Just as the patients can come to Singapore, so Singapore can go to the patients. The penetration of the foreign market by Singapore-based capital can take two forms.

The first is portfolio investment. In this case the local investor buys a paper stake in a physical asset situated abroad. Thus Health Management International, listed in Singapore, is the majority shareholder in the Mahkota Medical Centre in Malaysia. Temasek has bought its way into Bumrungrad. The Texas Pacific Group, based in the US, dominates the equity in Parkway Holdings. Parkway Holdings owns 40 per cent of the shares in Malaysia's Pantai chain of nine premier hospitals. The Malaysian Government's investment agency, Khazanah Nasional, holds the remaining 60 per cent (Chee, 2008: 2150). Khazanah Nasional owns 23 per cent of the equity in Parkway Holdings. It does this through its subsidiary, Mount Kinabalu Investments.

Parkway retains operational control of the Pantai net. It has not, however, been allowed to go beyond the 40 per cent stake because Parkway is foreign and the industry is deemed to be of strategic interest. There may also have been a commercial dimension. Pantai supervises medical checks for all foreign workers and also provides support services to the public hospitals. These concessions are said to be extremely lucrative.

The Parkway–Pantai link is a reminder that ownership need not be straightforward. Life was much simpler in the nineteenth century when the Marxian wage-slave knew the nationality and even the name of the moneybags for whom he toiled. Nowadays, things are all jumbled up. An American travels by Egyptair to Dubai to have plastic surgery performed by a London-trained Thai in a hospital that is managed by a German and owned by a consortium. Equity is faceless and footloose. Ownership is all around.

The second way in which a Singaporean business can enter a foreign market is through direct investment. FDI allows a single-product firm to expand without having to go conglomerate. Often it is part of a corporate plan which builds in the funnels of a vertically-integrated network.

An example would be the Parkway Group. It has 13 hospitals situated outside Singapore. In Malaysia it owns and manages the Gleneagles Medical Centre in Penang and the Gleneagles Intan Medical Centre in Kuala Lumpur. At the same time it is a shareholder in the Pantai hospitals, to which it provides management and expertise. Singapore, Penang, Pantai – the Group is in competition with itself.

In Bandar Seri Begawan the Parkway Group operates the 20-bed Gleneagles JPMC Cardiac Centre. In Mumbai it holds a 50 per cent stake (its initial investment was US$83 million) in the 500-bed Khubchandani Hospital: its partner is the Mauritius-based private company Koncentric Investments. In Kolkata it is in a 50–50 joint venture with the Apollo Group to run the Apollo Gleneagles Hospital: the location is ideal for patients from Sikkim, Nepal and Bangladesh as well as north-eastern India. In Shanghai, it treats Chinese nationals and resident expatriates on an outpatient basis at Gleneagles Medical and Surgical Center. Its clinic is situated in the evocatively named Tomorrow Square. Teleconferencing and videoconferencing mean that specialists in Singapore can be consulted without an unnecessary trip abroad. In case of need, of course, the patients are channelled upwards to the primary Parkway hospitals in Singapore. It is the international division of labour. Routine procedures are performed abroad. High-end procedures are performed in Singapore.

Parkway has five further clinics in China. It advertises in the print media and operates an English-language website. In all it has 22 facilities in five Asian countries: China, India, Brunei, Malaysia and Singapore. It also operates 42 international patient assistance centres outside of Singapore in places such as Russia, Myanmar and Pakistan. The result is an integrated chain. Parkway is the largest listed hospital operator not just in Singapore but in South-East Asia as a whole (Chee, 2007: 21; Chee, 2008: 2151).

In spite of that regional footprint, most of its revenues are generated in Singapore itself. In 2008 it earned S$633 million (67 per cent of monies received) from patients seen in Singapore, S$312 million (33 per cent) from its international transactions (www.parkwayhealth.com). About 26 per cent of its international revenues came from its commitments in the ASEAN region, and especially in Malaysia.

Raffles too, if on a much smaller scale, is investing abroad. It has four clinics in Hong Kong. These tap into South China as well as the local market. Raffles is planning further clinics in Myanmar, Sri Lanka, Vietnam, India and other countries in the East. As with Parkway, the model is a pyramid. Routine procedures and preliminary tests are performed in the patient's home country. Not only does this economise on time and money, it also enlists the on-the-spot knowledge of partners who know about health in their area and can advise on what local people can afford. More difficult cases are referred on to the mother hospital in Singapore. Cross-national investment integrates the Singapore specialist into the regional wheel. Follow-up monitoring is devolved to a Parkway or a Raffles centre abroad. One way or another, the parties complement each other.

Health cross-nationals are in the air. Thomson International in Singapore manages (but does not own) the Hanh Phuc International Women and Children Hospital in Vietnam. The West Clinic in Singapore has opened, with a local partner, a cancer facility in Shanghai. Pacific Healthcare in Singapore, working with Priory International in the UK, is managing the ten-clinic Bangkok Mediplex. Pacific Healthcare at its current offices in Singapore offers oncology, cardiology, psychiatry, sports medicine and other specialised services. It is collaborating with First Reit, a property-based investment trust, to put S$42 million into a 24-hour cancer centre. It has entered into a joint venture with the Yash Birla Group to open five specialist cosmetic surgery centres in India.

Partnered by Bumrungrad, Singapore Medical Group operates Lasik Surgery Clinic Alabang in the Philippines. Partnered by the Angeles City Foundation, it also operates LSC Angeles City. The Philippines is an English-speaking country. It has a population of at least 85 million people. The Philippines can be a major growth-area for service providers in Singapore who are looking for new challenges abroad.

9.6   A PUBLIC–PRIVATE MIX

Chapter 8 has suggested that coordination and leadership as well as entrepreneurship and individualism can be productive inputs in the health industry production function. The articulation of the parts to form a whole requires overview and vision. The Government in Singapore has taken responsibility for ensuring that the separate roads mesh into a consistent plan.

Health care has synergies with education. The schools and the universities in their own right are a major source of invisible exports. They are also a source of trained manpower for the knowledge-based health care sector. Faculties of biology exist in two of Singapore's four State universities: the local talent pool must be created before research and manufacturing can take off. There are two medical schools, one undergraduate (at the National University of Singapore), one postgraduate (a joint venture between the National University of Singapore and the Duke University Medical School in the USA). A third medical school, at the Nanyang Technological University, is at the planning stage.

The Ministry of Education, in consultation with the Ministry of Health, regulates the intake into the local medical schools. It also controls the number of foreign medical schools (in 2009 there were 140, in 1993 only 20) that are accredited as equivalent. In this way the Ministries exercise a check on both quality and quantity of professional entrants. Too few doctors means unacceptable waits. Too many doctors means supplier-induced demand. Too many *Singaporean* doctors means that other professions and sectors are being deprived of top talent. The Ministries of Education and Health, short-cutting the hog-cycle of market action and reaction, plan ahead to get the quantities right. The Ministry of Manpower issues appropriate Employment Passes to foreign professionals in order to facilitate selective recruitment without having to train or wait.

Medical education and health care fit in with growth areas like biomedical research and pharmacology. Gross expenditure on research and development reached 2.6 per cent of Singapore's GDP in 2008: in Japan it was 3.39 per cent, in the US 2.68, in the UK 1.78 (Economic Development Board, 2009: 2). There are opportunities for collaboration between the university-based scientists, the medical schools, the research institutes and the private laboratories that multinationals such as Novartis, Bayer, Schering Plough, Lilly, Baxter and GlaxoSmithKline are siting in Singapore. Clinician-scientists are pioneering new treatments and new drugs which will position Singapore at the high end of medical expertise. The subsidised and the for-profit laboratories will come to complement one another. To encourage top-drawer corporations to relocate their cutting-edge science the Government has constructed the Biopolis and the Fusionopolis research estates. They are conveniently located near the National University and the National University Hospital. The area will become an industrial region, rather like Marshall's Paternoster Square in printing or America's 'Silicon Valley' in the field of microelectronics.

Production accompanies research. Global names are manufacturing drugs and equipment on the spot. International biomedical companies invested more than US$500 million in Singapore in 2008 (*Medical News Today*, 2009). Some develop or adapt their products in Singapore itself. Others bring in research under licence from abroad. Merck produces anti-cholesterol medicines. Ciba Vision makes contact lenses. GlaxoSmithKline is manufacturing vaccines. The biomedical sciences industry generated output worth S$19 billion in 2008. The sector accounted for 7.6 per cent of total manufacturing output. Biosciences manufacturing value-added was 4.1 per cent of the Singaporean GDP in 2008 (Economic Development Board, 2009: 4). The trend is upward. Both the volume and the percentage are poised to double within five years or less. This is especially likely if the sector continues to diversify beyond traditional pharmaceuticals into medical technology, healthcare informatics and healthcare innovations. Already 10 per cent of the world's contact lenses are made in Singapore by firms such as Ciba Vision, Essilor and Alcon. The Government has made clear that foreign patients are only one strand in a complex health-and-wellness project that extends into science and engineering as well: 'We are positioning Singapore as a future-oriented Living Lab, for the industry to work with the public sector in co-creating, conceptualising, test-bedding and adopting innovative solutions, which could subsequently be exported' (Khaw, 2009).

There are tax incentives and even start-up loans for companies wishing to relocate their regional operations to Singapore. Singapore's location in the fast-growing Asia Pacific is attractive for outreach and local knowledge. Patents, designs and know-how are protected: royalties for intellectual property rights are the service sector with the largest deficit. Money for basic research is available from the National Medical Research Council (25 per cent funded by the Singapore Totalisator Board) and the Biomedical Research Council (a subsidiary of the Agency for Science, Technology and Research, A*Star) that have been set up to prime the pump. Welcoming legislation on embryonic stem cell research attracts research and development to a jurisdiction where it has more freedom. Singaporean and global talent ensure that there is an adequate reserve of world-class scientists. Local doctors are prepared to facilitate clinical trials. There is a link with medical care. Patients in Singapore who give their informed consent gain access to coal-face innovation before it becomes generally available outside.

10.   Health hubs in Asia

In 2007 2.9 million health travellers visited South-East and South Asia for medical treatment (Velasco, 2008: 13). About three-quarters of them had come for cosmetic surgery. Beauty tourism attracts more business than the hip and knee replacements, the full-body check-ups, the angioplasty and the prostate conditions which too are well represented.

It is a competitive market. Singapore in colonial times acquired a head-start reputation for clinical excellence. Other countries in the region are coming up. When in 2010 the Medical Travel Quality Alliance made a list of the world's best destinations for medical tourists, it found that no less than six of the top ten hospitals were in Asia. Fortis Hospitals, Bangalore, headed the list followed by Gleneagles in Singapore and Prince Court in Kuala Lumpur. This chapter discusses the nature of medical tourism in four of the Asian countries: Dubai, India, Malaysia and Thailand.

Yet the world is flat. It is six hours in the air from Kennedy New York to Juarez Mexico City. It is 19 hours in the air from Kennedy New York to Suvarnabhumi Bangkok. Nineteen hours is more than six hours. It is not much more if the price, the quality and the service are right. The country gives way to the region. The region gives way to the world. Like it or not, interdependence is here to stay.

10.1   DUBAI

Dubai, situated on the Persian Gulf, is one of the seven jurisdictions that make up the United Arab Emirates. Its population is 1.4 million. Less than 20 per cent of its residents are UAE nationals. More than 70 per cent are young South Asian males. The median age in Dubai is 27 years.

The oil upon which the economy was once built now accounts for only 6 per cent of the national product. It will be exhausted within 20 years. The most active sectors of the economy are construction, trade and finance. Health care is a new area that might be able to help the small but well-situated enclave to pay its bills.

Historically, patients in the Middle East have gone overseas. The Arab world has not been able sufficiently to provide them with high-quality

medical care. The situation is changing rapidly. The Dubai Healthcare
City (DHCC), a free zone with backing from the State, will be fully opera-
tional by 2011. Its market will extend beyond the emirate alone. There are
1.8 billion potential patients within a four-hour flight of Dubai. A number
of airlines fly to Dubai, including the two local carriers, Emirates and
Etihad. The DHCC is only four kilometres from the Dubai International
Airport. It is on the main road from Abu Dhabi. It will be on the new
Dubai Metro.

The DHCC will be a supermarket and a conglomerate. On a single site it
will bring together over 100 specialist clinics and at least nine private hospitals, JCI-accredited. It will field teaching institutions, research centres,
sports medicine, cosmetic surgery, conference facilities, physical rehabilitation, therapeutic spas. Hotels, apartments, a lakeside setting and
a carbon-neutral eco-friendly environment will strengthen its niche as a
wellness resort and a place of rejuvenation even as it will also be known for
its excellence in diagnosis and surgery. For recreation there will be nearby
facilities such as the Tiger Woods Golf Course and the Universal City. For
serious study there will be the 32 foreign universities based in the Dubai
International Academic City. It is the world's only free zone dedicated to
higher education.

The DHCC imposes no restrictions on foreign ownership or repatriation of profits. There are no taxes or customs duties. There is fast-track
company registration. There is a one-stop-shop service for visas and
permits. There is an open-door policy for skilled labour from abroad.
The DHCC, aware that new destinations are at a disadvantage, has made
every effort to attract top-end names. The list includes the Mayo Clinic,
the Moorfields Eye Hospital, the German Medical Center, the Samsung
Medical Center (the first outside South Korea), the Boston University
Dental Health Center and the Harvard Medical School Dubai Center
(supported by the Dubai Harvard Foundation for Medical Research).
Bumrungrad (partnered by Dubai World, a public-sector holding
company) wants to invest up to US$10 million in a 250-bed facility. It is
expected that famous institutions like these will be able to pull in long-haul
and regional patients with the promise of a Boston, a British or a Bangkok
standard of medical treatment in the Persian Gulf. Their presence gives
local people on-the-spot access to the best.

Some of the hospitals will be foreign-owned: an example is the American
Academy of Cosmetic Surgery Hospital. Others will be locally- owned but
managed by incomers: Johns Hopkins International will be in charge of
the Al-Rahbah complex. Regardless of ownership it will be common for
the hospitals to employ or invite foreign staff. Some will be resident in
Dubai. Others will fly in for one-off assignments. Some will not have a staff

appointment. Dubai Medical Suites offers short-term facilities (including surgical facilities) to visiting specialists without a hospital affiliation.

Care in Dubai will be cheaper than in the US or the UK. It will, however, be more expensive than in India or Thailand. Medical education in the Gulf is underdeveloped. Foreign professionals are the short-cut. Prices will rise as Dubai struggles to recruit top-class surgeons on the world market. It will be expensive to attract foreign-based Arabic-speakers back to the Gulf. The high cost of living will be a major concern. As for capital, investors will expect a competitive rate of profit. International hospitals must be paid for their name and participation. A precautionary mark-up must be added to compensate for cyclical shortfalls in a region that is overdependent on the fluctuating price of oil. At the end of the day, it is the patient who pays.

A cardiac bypass costs US$44,000 in Dubai. It costs US$18,500 in Singapore and US$11,000 in Thailand. Prices that are so far out of line will be a deterrent to the medical tourists that Dubai is trying to attract. Even Emiratis might continue to go to Germany, Thailand or the United Kingdom: 'In the UAE most medical tourism is outbound. . . . It will be an uphill struggle to even turn the flow around' (*International Medical Travel Journal*, 2008a). The UAE spent US$2 billion in 2007 to send its nationals abroad. The ministries of health in the Arab countries are the biggest spenders on cross-border health care in the world. As many as 70,000 UAE nationals sought medical treatment in Thailand in 2006 alone. The revenues were lost to local hospitals. It will be difficult to change the mentality that UAE health care is not value for money.

Aware that it cannot compete on cost with the East, the Ministry of Health is using the lure of world-class foreign consultants to attract high-net-worth clients who put quality and opulence above price. It is also introducing performance rankings and service ratings. These will spotlight five-star hospitals and professionals while weeding out the low-standard suppliers who could damage the image of the DHCC. It is taking advantage of the concentration of hospitals in a designated district to police outturns and de-register substandard clinics. It is vetting advertisements to ensure that publicity is dignified and truthful.

More expensive or less expensive, there are a number of non-price factors which are conducive to medical care in the DHCC. There is a high incidence of diabetes, hypertension, high cholesterol and smoking-related illness in the Middle East. There is a backlog of need in areas such as weight management, lifestyle counselling and preventive medicine. There is a shortage of professionals and treatment centres in the region. Visas to Western countries are not easy to obtain. Many Arabs (allowing for the fact that nurses and auxiliaries will often be foreigners on contract)

prefer to be treated in a cultural environment with which they are familiar. Incomes are rising: citizens are better able to pay for health. It should
also be remembered that 80 per cent of UAE residents are not citizens.
They are not covered by the State insurance scheme. Legislation making it
compulsory for employers to provide private insurance would at a stroke
create a huge domestic market.

Dubai has thought big. The problem is that a number of other centres
in the Arab world have thought big as well. Irrespective of the threat from
Bangkok and Chennai, they are chasing the same business with the same
business model. They are eating away at each other's market share.

An example would be the US$1.6 billion Dilmunia Health Island in
Bahrain. Health Island is an attractive resort on reclaimed land off the
coast at Muharraq. As with the DHCC, it will offer a range of clinics,
luxury hotels, diagnostic centres, cosmetic surgeons, alternative treatments, diabetes specialists. There will be supermarkets, cinemas, restaurants. There will be spas such as the US$1500-a-night Banyan Tree Al
Areen. Dilmu is the archaic name for the Garden of Eden. Paradise does
not come cheap.

Qatar is in the same market. The Hamad Medical City in Doha is
the second-largest hospital development project in the Middle East.
Oman is competing as well. There the Bavaria Medical Group has established a medical centre. In alliance with Qatar Airways and the Omani
Government, its strategy is to fly out its own doctors and to refer complicated cases back to Germany. The airlines in the region stand to gain if
two-way medical tourism reaches its projected targets.

There are already 38 JCI-accredited hospitals in the Gulf. Of those hospitals, 19, including the King Saud University Medical City in Riyadh, the
Sultan Bin Abdulaziz Humanitarian City in Riyadh and the Dr Soliman
Fakeeh Hospital in Jeddah (considered one of the top in-vitro centres in
the world) are in Saudi Arabia. Five are in Abu Dhabi. The Cleveland
Clinic will open a multispeciality facility. Parkway will manage the Danat
Al Emarat Women and Children's Hospital. Johns Hopkins has a ten-year
contract to operate Tawam Hospital. The Dubai Government, through
its business arm, Dubai Holding, has invested heavily in the planning and
infrastructure of the DHCC. It could usefully have coordinated its expansion with Saudi Arabia and Abu Dhabi which are already such prominent
players in the region.

Jordan, also competing in the Middle East, is the outlier. Despite its low
profile, it is nonetheless the only country in the Arab world to generate
more money from inbound patients than its own health care tourists spend
abroad. The Jordan Enterprise Development Corporation estimates that
revenue from medical tourism reached US$1.4 billion in 2009. Numbers

are growing by 10 per cent a year. Most of its 220,000 clients came from Iraq, Sudan, Yemen (where it has a health attaché), plus a small number from the US and the UK. Subtracting resident expatriates, the adjusted figure would be 120,000. The great majority were treated in (48 out of 60) private hospitals. Four of them have JCI status. The average occupancy rate in private hospitals in Jordan is only 64 per cent. There is enough room to accommodate new patients. Arabs who want to remain in the Arab world can go to Jordan. The DHCC will have an uphill struggle to convince them to try something new.

10.2   INDIA

Dr Prathap Reddy, Boston-trained, founder in 1983 of the first Apollo hospital, describes his vision in the following words:

> It is a dream to see healthcare as the catalyst to propel India to its rightful position in the world as a developed country, as a knowledge & economic powerhouse. . . . The total healthcare market in India is growing significantly and its contribution to the country's GDP will increase from the present 6 per cent to 8.5 per cent over the next ten years. Today, Indian healthcare is in a position to become the largest employer in the foreseeable future. With every hospital bed added, direct employment for five people and indirect employment for twenty-five is created. The generation of employment would help the nation grow in a way that would be the envy of every nation around the world (Apollo Hospitals Group, 2008: 12).

Dr Reddy sees health care as a major contributor to affluence and employment. Independent predictions confirm that the market is on course to reach the target. According to the Federation of Indian Chambers of Commerce and Industry, the health care sector (the figure includes health insurance) is likely to expand from US$22.1 billion (5.2 per cent of GDP) in 2007 to between US$50 and US$69 billion (6.2 to 8.5 per cent of GDP) by 2012 (Chinai and Goswami, 2007). Revenue from medical tourism will play its part. It was between US$656 and US$819 million in 2008. Growing at the rate of 30 per cent per annum, it will probably bring in US$1 billion in 2010, between US$1.87 and US$2.2 billion by 2012 (Velasco, 2008: 14). If so, India will be treating half the medical tourists visiting Asia in that year. Between 272,000 and 450,000 international patients sought treatment in India in 2008. By 2012 the figure might be 700,000. After that it might be much more.

The bulk of the international patients in India are treated in 45 hospitals. Eleven of them have received JCI accreditation. While medical excellence is undoubtedly a driver, the principal draw for Western travellers is likely to be the price. Heart valve replacement costs US$10,000 in India. It costs US$200,000 in the US. A metal-free dental bridge costs US$500 in India, US$5500 in the US. India is the lowest-price option. Some regions are especially cost-effective. Prices in Kerala are half what they are in Delhi or Mumbai, three-quarters what they are in Chennai. Demographics will keep the cost of labour down: half of India's 1.1 billion people are under 25. So will training. The large number of doctors and nurses in India is a guarantor of availability as well as price. An operation in Delhi or Bangalore can be scheduled within 24 hours. This is a considerable plus. As Dr Reddy observes: 'If you wait six months for a heart bypass, you may not need it anymore' (Reddy, quoted in Demicco and Cetron, 2006: 527).

There are some smaller competitors. The list includes the Artemis Health Institute, Max Healthcare and the Delhi Heart and Lung Institute. Wockhardt has six hospitals, two of them with JCI accreditation. Fortis has 13 hospitals. It also owns the Escorts Hospitals chain. The market leader is, however, Apollo.

The Apollo Group has 7500 beds in 43 hospitals (6 of them JCI-accredited). Some of its hospitals are in big cities like Chennai, Bangalore and Hyderabad but others are in smaller places like Pune, Ranchi and Mysore. It has over 1000 pharmacies. Pharmacies are a major growth area in a country where 98 per cent of medicines are purchased informally. Apollo has a nursing school and a network of clinics. It operates an air ambulance service. It has over 100 telemedicine centres. It is active (in partnership with Munich RE) in health insurance. It has good access to capital from banks and from the Reddy family which retains a controlling stake. Patients can be admitted quickly. The bed-occupancy rate is under 80 per cent. The bed stock is rising. The length of stay is coming down. The average currently stands at 5.9 days.

The Apollo Group is the largest private health care provider in India. It is based in Chennai. The health-travel capital of India, Chennai attracts 45 per cent of all health tourists from abroad and 40 per cent of domestic health tourists. Apollo's leading centre is probably its Indraprastha Hospital in Delhi. About 30 per cent of Group revenues come from medical tourism. It has treated over 2 million foreign patients. While a growing number are from the United States and Western Europe, the bulk of them have come from Bangladesh, Bhutan, Nepal, Sri Lanka, Pakistan and elsewhere in the South Asian region. Afghanistan, the Middle East and Africa are all part of its catchment. Its kitchen is able to prepare steaks, pizzas, Iraqi dishes and kosher food. It also sees a number of ethnic Indians from countries like Mauritius and the Seychelles. About 70 per cent of its doctors were either trained outside India (mainly in the US, the UK or Australia) or have practised there.

Apollo has links with hospitals in Bangladesh, Sri Lanka, Dubai, Mauritius, Fiji, Yemen and Tanzania. At some stage it may expand into Nigeria, Ghana, Lebanon and Kuwait. Not only will these initiatives provide locals with an alternative to treatment abroad, they will also offer competitive medical care to health travellers from third countries.

Apollo is not the only Indian chain to have a presence abroad. The Kerala Institute of Medical Science is operating the KIMS Bahrain Medical Center in the Gulf. Narayan Hrudayalaya is interested in Mexico. It also wants a presence in the Cayman Islands (only 52 minutes from Florida), where it is planning a 2000-bed hospital and a medical university. Singapore has an external wing. India is developing an external wing as well.

10.3 MALAYSIA

Malaysia too is establishing a presence in medical tourism. The Ministry of Health has identified 35 of the nation's 224 private hospitals as especially well placed to compete for an international clientele. The list includes such well-respected names as the Mahkota Medical Centre in Malacca and the Sunway Medical Centre in Petaling Jaya. In Penang there is the Gleneagles Intan Medical Centre and the Penang Adventist Hospital. In Kuala Lumpur there is the Subang Jaya Medical Centre and the Prince Court Medical Centre. Prince Court is fully owned by the Government's oil and gas corporation, Petronas. It is managed by the Medical University of Vienna in collaboration with the Austrian-based Vamed engineering group.

Medical care in Malaysia ranges from the curative to the aesthetic. In the curative field some of the leading research and treatment centres are the Tun Hussein Onn National Eye Hospital, Selayang Hospital, the NCI Cancer Hospital and the National Heart Institute. As for aesthetic procedures hospitals throughout the country have built up a considerable presence in plastic surgery. About 23 per cent of interventions supplied to foreign patients in Penang fall into this category.

The hospitals, with support from the airlines and the public sector, have formed the Malaysian Healthcare Travel Council (MHTC) to promote inbound travel. There are portals such as www.hospitals-malaysia.org and www.malaysiahealthcare.com which provide full information on the various centres. Despite the fact that only three hospitals in Malaysia are JCI-accredited, about half are ISO-certified, 83 are certified locally by the MSQH, and all have been inspected and licensed by the Ministry of Health. The Ministry of Health is one of the three partners in the

MSQH. The other two partners are the Association of Private Hospitals of Malaysia (APHM) and the Malaysian Medical Association (MMA).

In 2001 only 75,210 foreign patients came to Malaysia for care. By 2008 the figure had become approximately 370,000. They generated revenues of about US$76.6 million. The numbers are growing by 25 per cent to 30 per cent a year. Approximately 70 per cent of the foreign patients are from Indonesia (especially neighbouring Sumatra, the Riau Islands and Java: a day trip for a consultation, even combined with an afternoon's business, can easily be scheduled). A further 10 per cent are drawn from Singapore and 5 per cent from Japan. Patients from the UK, the US, Australia and the Middle East are an increasing proportion of the throughput. Eager to attract patients from old sources and new, Malaysia has liberalised its entry procedures. New arrivals who have been accepted by a hospital are permitted a six-month stay.

Singapore and Malaysia are in competition for the Indonesian market. Since between 200,000 and 1 million Indonesians are believed to go abroad each year for medical care (it is estimated that they spend in excess of US$1 billion), there is room for both players in the market. Malaysia has a head start in terms of linguistic and cultural affinity. Apart from that, serviced accommodation and leisure-time activities in the convalescent phase are considerably less expensive. Medical care itself costs less in Malaysia than in Singapore. Both countries have staff who can communicate in Arabic, Mandarin and Japanese as well as English and Malay. Both countries have spare capacity. The bed-occupancy rate (citizens plus foreigners) in the Malaysian private sector is about 80 per cent. Foreign patients are clearly not pushing the locals out. Waiting times are clearly not a deterrent.

10.4   THAILAND

Singapore was the regional leader in the colonial period. It was overtaken by Thailand in 2001. In 2008 about 1.5 million foreigners entered Thailand for medical treatment: 300,000 from Asia, 257,000 from Europe, 152,000 from the Middle East (it had been 20,000 only five years before), the rest from a wide range of other markets. In terms of percentages, about 23 per cent are Japanese, 10 per cent South-East Asian, 11 per cent American, 19 per cent European (Teh, 2007: 3). Medical tourism is growing annually at a trend rate of 25 per cent to 30 per cent. In 2006 it earned the country about US$1.15 billion.

Thailand is the principal exporter of health care services in the whole of Asia. Proximity helps: in 2007 it received 36,000 patients from Myanmar, plus large numbers from Laos, Cambodia, Bangladesh and other less-developed countries in the region. There is considerable traffic from Europe and America. Care in Thailand costs less despite the airfares and the weak US dollar.

Of 471 hospitals in Thailand about 33, all private, are actively involved in international business. Cosmetic surgery and dentistry are major attractions. Sex-change surgery is one of the top ten most popular procedures among foreigners (Demicco and Cetron, 2006: 529). The most prominent hospitals are Bangkok Hospital Medical Center, Samitivej Sukumvit Hospital and Bumrungrad International Hospital. All three are accredited by the JCI: this is required by third-party payers in the USA. Effectively, all doctors are Thai. The professional examination is conducted only in Thai. No more than seven foreigners have passed in the last quarter-century. That is more than all the foreign doctors in practice in Japan, where only citizens can obtain a licence.

The policy is a mixed blessing. While doctors who speak Thai will be able to communicate with the local population, international patients might prefer to be seen by doctors who are fluent in the client's own language and can pick up the cultural cues. Virtually all Thai doctors speak good English. Not all, however, are equally fluent in Arabic, Korean or Spanish. It is also the case that, because the inflow of doctors is negligible, the country is only able to tap into foreign knowledge and expertise where its own nationals have gone abroad for further training.

Inward investment is limited. While some hospitals in Thailand have had an infusion of foreign capital, the beneficiaries are almost entirely in Bangkok and the amounts involved are not very large. Foreign ownership by law cannot exceed 49 per cent. Citizens are expected to retain the controlling interest. The largest investors are from Japan and Singapore. Foreign direct investment accounts for less than 3 per cent of total direct investment in the Thai private hospital sector (Arunanondchai and Fink, 2007: 13).

Private hospitals are disproportionately represented in Bangkok, where 43.3 per cent of Thailand's bedstock is situated. Such concentration is bound to mean tough competition and also some excess capacity. Market saturation will lead to devolution as an economic alternative to thinning out. As well as the push there will be the pull. Profit-seeking hospitals will recognise the commercial potential of under-supplied regions. Examples of such regions would be the highly industrialised Eastern Seaboard from Chonburi to Rayong, tourist and retirement destinations such as Hua Hin and border areas such as Mukhdahan which have easy access to the rapidly-growing economies of Indochina.

Bangkok Hospital Medical Center is part of Bangkok Dusit Medical

Services PCL. Dusit is the largest hospital chain in Thailand. Bangkok Hospital has 600 beds in four institutions. About 40 per cent of its patients are foreigners. In 2007 the Centre treated 139,000 foreign patients from 134 countries. It earned about US$53 million in revenue (Velasco, 2008: 15). Expansion is rapid. In some years the volume of international business has increased by 50 per cent.

Many of the patients come from the Middle East, especially the Gulf. The group has a Japanese clinic. It is staffed by Japanese-speaking Thais with personal experience in Japan. Bangkok Hospital was the first hospital in Thailand to offer Gamma Knife treatment for neurological diseases. It operates an emergency helicopter service covering the whole of Thailand, Laos and Cambodia. The helicopter is fully equipped. Crew members have skills in areas such as cardiac arrest, burns and neo-natal care.

Within Thailand the Bangkok Hospital Group has targeted the health *tourism* market through hospitals in beach resorts at Pattaya, Phuket, Koh Chang and Koh Samui. Outside Thailand it has been aggressive in developing a new client base. In Nepal it has set up a referral centre: patients might have gone to India if the Bangkok Hospital had not been proactive in arranging appointments. In Cambodia it has entered into a joint venture with the Royal Phnom Penh Hospital: a top-end clinic allows wealthy Cambodians to obtain Thai-standard care without going abroad. Bangkok Dusit (supported by Bangkok Airways which is in the same group) has itself made a similar arrangement with the Royal Ratanak Hospital.

The Samitivej Group has a number of hospitals in the Bangkok area. About 40 per cent of patients seen are foreigners (Deloitte Center for Health Solutions, 2009: 1). Samitivej Sukhumvit has considerable experience with international patients. It has 270 beds, 87 examination suites and over 400 specialists. The Group also has hospitals at Srinakarin, near the airport, and Sriracha, near the Laem Chabang Port. The Samitivej Group operates the specialist Samitivej Srinakarin Children's Hospital. It is the first and only dedicated private hospital for children in Thailand. Most hospitals in Thailand are general.

Bumrungrad International Hospital in Bangkok is the largest private hospital in South-East Asia. It was the first hospital in Asia (in 2002) to become JCI-accredited. It has 554 inpatient beds and 1 million square feet of floor space (www.bumrungrad.com). There are 1000 doctors on the Bumrungrad panel. Many have trained or worked in the United States, Japan or other foreign countries. A fifth are Board-certified in the United States.

Only the medical executives and a small number of doctors (in the hospital's International Medical Coordination Office) are directly employed.

They are salaried and full-time. A further 200 are full-time at Bumrungrad but earn their income from professional fees. The other doctors at Bumrungrad split their time between the hospital and other institutions. They see patients on a fee-for-service basis. It is normally the hospital and not the doctor that markets itself on the strength of its reputation. Patients select their hospital first. Only then will they choose a doctor whom the hospital trusts sufficiently to put on its list.

In 2007 a total of 1.2 million patients were treated at Bumrungrad. Of that 1.2 million, 430,000 were foreigners and 60,000 were Americans. About half of the Americans were expatriates. Of the other half, about half (25 per cent of the total) were intentional medical travellers who had come to Thailand specifically for medical care. The remainder were tourists who needed unplanned medical attention while in the country. Americans, Japanese and Emiratis were the three largest groups of foreign patients. Nationals of 190 countries have received treatment at the hospital. The census of foreign patients is high. Bumrungrad treats more foreign patients than all of the hospitals in Singapore combined. It also treats some Singaporeans who have been attracted to it by the price.

Bumrungrad in 2007 earned over US$110 million from its non-resident business. Foreigners generate about half of the hospital's revenues. About 75 per cent of its patients are self-funding. Only about 25 per cent of its income is derived from insurance companies or corporate contracts. One consequence is that bad debt is not a problem. Most patients pay cash or by credit card when they check out.

Bumrungrad is owned locally and operated for profit. It is listed on the Stock Exchange of Thailand. The majority shareholders are the Bangkok Bank PLC and the Sophonpanich family. The management team is, however, international: American, British, Australian and Singaporean as well as Thai. Half of the executives are doctors. Most of the others are experienced health care administrators. Coming from a medical background but with an interest in business, they understand about competition and consumer satisfaction.

Bumrungrad is strong on comfort. There is a McDonalds, a Starbucks and a sushi restaurant on the premises. They will deliver to the patient's room. Marble floors, fountains and liveried attendants give Bumrungrad the feel of a high-end hotel. Elephant riding, temple tours, cookery classes and convalescence on the beach can be booked with a travel agent in the lobby. Fully-serviced flats are available for relatives. There is high-speed Internet connectivity. As with all leading hospitals in Thailand, there are interpreters on call. There is an immigration centre. It can secure visa extensions for patients who are too ill to travel.

Bumrungrad opened in 1980 to service a middle-class Thai clientele. It continues to benefit from rising incomes in a rapidly-growing economy. When the Thai baht collapsed in 1997 in the 'Asian economic crisis', some hospitals went into liquidation and Bumrungrad was forced to fight for a client base. Unable to depend on local demand, it decided to take advantage of devaluation to promote itself as a cost-effective international option. Thailand was already a popular tourist destination. After 2001, when terrorism made it more difficult for patients from the Middle East to travel to the traditional centres of excellence in America and Europe, Bumrungrad positioned itself as a good alternative.

Bumrungrad continues to market aggressively. It has 23 offices abroad: the list goes from Australia and Cambodia to Ukraine and Yemen. Its representatives are able to answer questions and book appointments. Tie-ins exist. Thai Airways through its subsidiary, Royal Orchid Holidays, offers 'check-in-and-check-up' packages that include medical examinations.

As with the Singapore hospital groups, Bumrungrad has invested in hospitals and clinics abroad. It owns a 40 per cent stake (the largest single holding) in the Asian Hospital and Medical Center, Manila, where it is involved in management. Bumrungrad also has the management contract for the Al Mafraq Hospital in Abu Dhabi. It has expressed an interest in setting up a Bumrungrad Dubai: it would hold 49 per cent of the equity and undertake the management. Networks such as these send referrals up to Bangkok. Other Thai hospitals have used the same business plan. Piyavate Hospital, for example, has been able to attract international clients through its clinic in Oman.

Bumrungrad is successful in no small measure because it is price-competitive. It costs $90,000 to repair a herniated neck in the United States. It costs only US$10,000 to restore the same disk at Bumrungrad. Room charges and medical fees are lower than equivalent charges not just in America but in Singapore as well. Prospective patients can use an online service to find out the approximate cost of their treatment. The screen shows what patients actually paid (in 45 different currencies) for the 40 procedures performed at the hospital in the course of the previous year. In each case a high, a low and a medium estimate is given. The precise bill cannot be known until the treatment has been completed and the patient is discharged.

Pricing is competitive. One reason is internal efficiency. Administration is electronic: only 13 per cent of US hospitals have computerised their record-keeping. Wireless infrastructure (wifi) is general: hospital staff can access personal data and medical histories anywhere in the building. Satellite can be used to obtain patient records from overseas.

Supplies are barcoded to simplify reordering. Computers ensure that misdispensed pharmaceuticals will not necessitate additional treatments. Specialists are on duty 12 hours a day: a referral from a general practitioner is not required. There are 150 consulting rooms. They are in use 16 hours a day. CAT scanners are in use 12 hours a day. ECG machines are in use 100 times a day. Bumrungrad has the largest outpatient capacity in the world. It is able to see 6000 patients a day.

There is slack. It works to the advantage of the patient. Knowing that they will not have to wait, 50 per cent of patients arrive without an appointment. A bed can always be found: the occupancy rate is only 70 per cent. Idle capacity is consumer-friendly. Throughput is nonetheless sufficient for the economies of scale that keep the average cost down.

10.5   THE WORLD IS FLAT

There is a final thought. China is less than a decade away from being a medical tourism destination on its own. The Renai International Patient Center at Renai Hospital in Shanghai (established in 2001) is already performing cosmetic surgery on 4000 foreign patients a year. Many of them are from Europe and America. The cost of a facelift is a quarter of what it would be in the West. Quality is ensured through a link with the Massachusetts Institute of Technology. The RIPC offers ten different medical specialities, schedules consultations round the clock, and musters expatriate as well as Chinese doctors.

China is able to supply a range of medical and dental services. Also, precisely because it is growing so rapidly, it is generating a local consumer base with high discretionary incomes and a local supply of savings which can be converted into plant. State-of-the-art new hospitals are bound to move in to capture this large and dynamic market. Good quality education has expanded the pool of professionals. Singapore will have to move fast to seal in its head start. It will have to exploit first-mover advantage to build up brand loyalty among its Chinese patients. The window of opportunity will one day close.

Indonesia, similarly, knows that it is behind in hospitals and needs to catch up. Here a lesson may be learned from the Kenyan experience. Middle-class Kenyans with heart problems used to go to South Africa for treatment. Now they can receive treatment of the same standard at the Kenyatta National Hospital, Nairobi. The next step will be for Kenya to become a medical tourism hub for the less-developed countries in its region. Import substitution is taking place. As with Kenya, so with Indonesia. Indonesia may not be sending its patients to Singapore forever.

The world is flat and the flights are short. Singapore, in sizing up the opposition, is obliged to take into account the plethora of treatment options that are meshing the disparate into a single globe. New Zealand is cheaper than Singapore although more expensive than India: it is already playing host to Americans despite the 7000-mile flight. Macao is capitalising on its casinos: its integrated resorts are an obvious location for executive check-ups, dental care and outpatient interventions. Ho Chi Minh City has the 220-bed Franco-Vietnamese Hospital. Accredited by the French HAS and half as expensive as Bumrungrad, it is drawing visitors not just from Laos and Cambodia but from Australia and further afield.

Iran, currently attracting only 7000 medical tourists a year, wants to be a regional hub for Arabs and Farsi-speakers, Middle Eastern and uprooted. Care in Iran is less expensive than in Jordan or Egypt. Jamaica, although lacking managerial and medical expertise, is considering tax-free enterprise zones and partnerships with multinational investors to compensate for the collapse in its bauxite. Montego Bay and Ocho Rios are iconic locations for the medical trade. Ghana wants to upgrade its Central Regional Hospital at Cape Coast into a regional hub. Cuba, despite the American boycott, was able annually to draw in 20,000 medical tourists. They came from 38 countries. Cuba's success in attracting foreigners is showing new players like Jamaica that it can done.

South Africa and Kenya are offering cardiovascular care. Barbados is bringing in cosmetic surgeons from California. Turkey is marketing laser eye surgery at a third of the price in the European Union. Bulgaria is keen to attract more Germans. Bonn, which lost much of its income when the Government and the embassies transferred to Berlin, is moving into the health care field. One in every ten jobs in Bonn is already health-related. The potential is there. Singapore is not alone in wanting to tap into the seam.

Bibliography

Adams, J., B.A. Archbold, E.L. Mounib and D. New (2007), *Healthcare 2015 and US Health Plans: New Roles, New Competencies*, Somers, New York: IBM Institute for Business Values.

Adlung, R. and A. Carzaniga (2001), 'Health services under the General Agreement on Trade in Services', *Bulletin of the World Health Organization*, **79**, 352–64.

American College of Surgeons (2009), Statement on medical and surgical tourism, ST-65, www.facs.org/fellows_info, accessed on 30 June 2009.

Apollo Hospitals Group (2008), *Annual Report*, Chennai: Apollo Hospitals Enterprise Ltd.

Arunanondchai, J. and C. Fink (2007), 'Trade in health services in the ASEAN Region', Policy Research Working Paper 4147, Washington, DC: World Bank.

Balch, O. (2006), 'Buenos Aires or bust', *Guardian*, 24 October, www.guardian.co.uk/business/2006/0ct/24/argentina.travelnews, accessed on 6 November 2008.

Barrett, S. (2007), *Why Cooperate? The Incentive to Supply Global Public Goods*, Oxford: Oxford University Press.

Bhagwati, J.N. (1998), *A Stream of Windows: Unsettling Reflections on Trade, Immigration, and Democracy*, Cambridge, MA: MIT Press.

Bies, W. and L. Zacharia (2007), 'Medical tourism: outsourcing surgery', *Mathematical and Computer Modelling*, **46**, 1144–59.

Bina, M. (2007), 'Unaffordability Ebola', *Medical Tourism*, No. 1, 48–9.

Blinder, A.S. (2006), 'Offshoring: the next industrial revolution?', *Foreign Affairs*, **85**, 113–28, reprinted in http://proquest.umi.com.ezlibproxy1, accessed on 15 January 2009.

Blouin, C. (2006), 'Economic dimensions and impact assessment of GATS to promote and protect health', in C. Blouin, N. Drager and R. Smith (eds), *International Trade in Health Services and the GATS*, Washington, DC: World Bank, pp. 169–202.

Bookman, M.Z. and K.R. Bookman (2008), *Medical Tourism in Developing Countries*, New York and Basingstoke: Palgrave Macmillan.

Bramstedt, K.A. and J. Xu (2007), 'Checklist: passport, plane ticket, organ transplant', *American Journal of Transplantation*, **7**, 1698–701.

Brown, H.S. (2008), 'Do Mexican immigrants substitute health care in

Mexico for health insurance in the United States? The role of distance', *Social Science & Medicine*, **67**, 2036–42.

Bureau of Labor Statistics (USA) (2009), *International Comparisons of Hourly Compensation Costs in Manufacturing, 2007*, www.bls.gov, accessed on 16 April 2009.

Bustamante, A.V., G. Ojeda and X. Castañeda (2008), 'Willingness to pay for cross-border health insurance between the United States and Mexico', *Health Affairs*, **27**, 169–78.

Chan, A. and M.T. Yap (2009), *Baby-Boomers Survey*, Singapore: Ministry of Community Development, Youth and Sports.

Chanda, R. (2002), 'Trade in health services', in N. Drager and C. Vieira (eds), *Trade in Health Services: Global, Regional and Country Perspectives*, Washington, DC: Pan American Health Organization, pp. 35–44.

Chee, H.L. (2007), 'Medical tourism in Malaysia: international movement of healthcare consumers and the commodification of healthcare', Asia Research Institute, National University of Singapore, Working Paper No. 83.

Chee, H.L. (2008), 'Ownership, control and contention: challenges for the future of healthcare in Malaysia', *Social Science and Medicine*, **66**, 2145–56.

Chinai, R. and R. Goswami (2007), 'Medical visas mark growth of Indian medical tourism', *Bulletin of the World Health Organization*, **85**, www.scielosp.org/scielo.php?pid=S0042-968620070000300004&script=sci.artex, accessed on 10 November 2008.

Cohen, J. (2006), 'The new world of global health', *Science*, **311**, 162–7.

Comarow, A. (2008), 'Saving on surgery by going abroad', *U.S. News and World Report*, 1 May, http://health.usnews.com, accessed on 9 April 2009.

Competition Authority (Ireland) (2005), *Competition in Professional Services – Dentists*, Dublin: Competition Authority.

Connell, J. (2006), 'Medical tourism: sea, sun, sand and . . . surgery', *Tourism Management*, **27**, 1093–100.

Credit Suisse (2008), *Singapore Healthcare Sector*, Hong Kong: Credit Suisse.

Deloitte Center for Health Solutions (2008), *Medical Tourism: Consumers in Search of Value*, www.deloitte.com/dtt/article, accessed on 25 November 2008.

Deloitte Center for Health Solutions (2009), *Medical Tourism: The Asian Chapter*, www.deloitte.com/dtt/article, accessed on 23 June 2009.

Demicco, F.J. and M. Cetron (2006), 'Club Medic', *Asia Pacific Biotech News*, **10**, 527–31.

Dentale (2008), 'Britons can't afford dental care', www.dentale.co.uk, accessed on 9 December 2008.

Department of Statistics (Singapore) (2009), *Singapore's International Trade in Services 2007*.

DiMaggio, P. and H. Louch (1998), 'Socially embedded consumer transactions: for what kinds of purchases do people most often use networks?', *American Sociological Review*, **63**, 619–37.

Duggal, R. (2003), 'Should public hospitals participate in medical tourism?', *Healthcare Management*, 15–30 December, www.expresshealthcaremgmt.com.

Eastwood, J.B., R.E. Conroy, S. Naicker, P.A. West, R.C. Tutt and J. Plange-Rhule (2005), 'Loss of health professionals from sub-Saharan Africa: the pivotal role of the UK', *The Lancet*, **365**, 1893–900.

Economic Development Board (Singapore) (2009), *Biomedical Sciences: Factsheet 2009*.

Economist (2008), 'Globalisation and health care: operating profit', 14 August, www.economist.com/business/displaystory.cfm?story_id=11919622, accessed on 10 November 2008.

Edelheit, J. (2008), 'American healthcare and the economic crisis', *Medical Tourism Magazine*, No. 7, 21–2.

Ehrbeck, T., C. Guevara and P.D. Mango (2008), 'Mapping the market for medical travel', *McKinsey Quarterly*, www.mckinseyquarterly.com, accessed on 11 February 2009.

Einhorn, B. (2008), 'Checking into Bumrungrad Hospital', *Business Week*, 17 March, www.businessweek.com, accessed on 30 January 2009.

Eturbonews (2008), 'Is medical tourism worth the risk?', www.eturbonews.com, accessed on 8 January 2009.

Friedman, M. (1962), *Capitalism and Freedom*, Chicago: University of Chicago Press.

Friedman, T.L. (2007), *The World is Flat: A Brief History of the Twenty-first Century*, expanded edition, New York: Farrar, Straus and Giroux.

Gallup Organization (2007), *Cross-border Health Services in the EU: Analytical Report*, Flash Eurobarometer 210, Budapest: Gallup Organization for the European Commission.

Ghosh, J. (2003), 'Medical knowledge', in R.D. Smith, R. Beaglehole, D. Woodward and N. Drager (eds), *Global Public Goods for Health: Health Economics and Public Health Perspectives*, Oxford: Oxford University Press, pp. 119–36.

Grail Research (2009), *The Rise of Medical Tourism*, www.grailresearch.com, accessed on 6 November 2009.

Gupta, A.S. (2004) 'Medical tourism and public health', *People's Democracy*, 9 May, www.cpim.org.

Gupta, I., B. Goldar and A. Mitra (1998), 'The case of India', in S. Zarrilli and C. Kinnon (eds), *International Trade in Health Services: A Development Perspective*, UNCTAD-WHO Joint Publication, Geneva: United Nations, pp. 213–36.

Health Affairs (2008), 'New international survey: more than half of US chronically ill adults skip needed care due to costs', 13 November, www. healthaffairs.org, accessed on 31 July 2009.

Healthcare Commission (UK) (2008), *State of Healthcare 2008*, Norwich: Stationery Office.

Hedrick-Wong, Y.W. (2007), *The Glittering Silver Market: The Rise of Elderly Consumers in Asia*, Singapore: Wiley (Asia).

Held, D. and A. McGrew (2003), 'Political globalization: trends and choices', in I. Kaul, P. Conçeicão, K. Le Goulven and R.U. Mendoza (eds), *Providing Global Public Goods: Managing Globalization*, Oxford: Oxford University Press, pp. 185–99.

Henderson, J.C. (2004), 'Paradigm shifts: national tourism organisations and education and healthcare tourism. The case of Singapore', *Tourism and Hospitality Research*, **5**, pp. 170–80.

Herrick, D.M. (2007), *Medical Tourism: Global Competition in Health Care*, National Center for Policy Analysis, NCPA Policy Report No. 304, www.ncpa.org/pub/st/st304, accessed on 6 November 2008.

Herrick, D.M. (2008), *Health Care Entrepreneurs: The Changing Nature of Providers*, National Center for Policy Analysis, NCPA Policy Report No. 318, www.ncpa.org/pub/st/st304, accessed on 9 April 2009.

Himmelstein, D.U., E. Warren, D. Thorne and S. Woolhandler (2005), 'Illness and injury as contributors to bankruptcy', *Health Affairs*, **24**, http://proquest.umi.com.ezlibproxy1, accessed on 22 July 2009.

Hotel Marketing Newsletter (2006), 'Medical tourism, Asia's growth industry', www.hotelmarketing.com, accessed on 31 July 2009.

House of Lords (UK), European Union Committee (2009), *Healthcare Across EU Borders: A Safe Framework*, London: The Stationery Office.

Hunter-Jones, P. (2003), 'The perceived effects of holiday-taking upon the health and wellbeing of patients treated for cancer', *International Journal of Tourism Research*, **5**(3), 183–96.

Ihekweazu, C., I. Anya and E. Anosike (2005), 'Nigerian medical graduates: where are they now?', *The Lancet*, **365**, 1847–8.

Institute of Medicine (2000), *To Err is Human: Building a Safer Health System*, Washington, DC: National Academies Press.

International Medical Travel Journal (2008a), 'Dubai Healthcare City faces challenge', www.imtjonline.com/news, accessed on 25 November 2008.

International Medical Travel Journal (2008b), 'United States: focus shifts to domestic travel', www.imtjonline.com/news, accessed on 25 November 2008.

International Medical Travel Journal (2008c), 'United States: Americans' awareness of medical travel increases', www.imtjonline.com/news, accessed on 3 December 2008.

International Medical Travel Journal (2008d), 'Industry: report on Asia's medical tourism market', www.imtjonline.com/news, accessed on 5 December 2008.

International Medical Travel Journal (2008e), 'USA: greater transparency allows consumers to understand domestic quality of care issues', www.imtjonline.com/news, accessed on 14 January 2009.

Janjaroen, W.S. and S. Supakankunti (2002), 'International trade in health services in the millennium: the case of Thailand', in N. Drager and C. Vieira (eds), *Trade in Health Services: Global, Regional and Country Perspectives*, Washington, DC: Pan American Health Organization, pp. 87–106.

Jensen, J.B. and L.G. Kletzer (2005), 'Tradable services: understanding the scope and impact of services outsourcing', Working Paper 05-9, Washington, DC: Institute for International Economics.

Kaul, I., P. Conçeicão, K. Le Goulven and R.U. Mendoza (2003), 'Why do global public goods matter today?', in I. Kaul, P. Conçeicão, K. Le Goulven and R.U. Mendoza (eds), *Providing Global Public Goods: Managing Globalization*, Oxford: Oxford University Press, pp. 2–20.

Khaw, B.W. (2009), 'Statement on medical tourism', Singapore Parliament, *Singapore Parliament Reports*, 14 October, www.parliament.gov.sg, accessed on 6 November 2009.

Kher, U. (2006), 'Outsourcing your heart', *Time*, 21 May, www.time.com, accessed on 5 November 2008.

Khoo, L. (2003), 'Trends in foreign patient admission in Singapore', Information Paper 2003/01, Singapore: Ministry of Health.

Khoury, C. (2009), 'Americans consider crossing borders for medical care', www.gallup.com/poll, accessed on 16 June 2009.

Kierzkowski, H. (2002), 'Trade and public health in an open economy: a framework for analysis', in N. Drager and C. Vieira (eds), *Trade in Health Services: Global, Regional and Country Perspectives*, Washington, DC: Pan American Health Organization, pp. 47–52.

Krugman, P.R. and M. Obstfeld (2009), *International Economics: Theory and Policy*, 8th edn, Boston: Pearson Addison Wesley.

Lautier, M. (2008), 'Export of health services from developing countries: the case of Tunisia', *Social Science & Medicine*, **67**, 101–10.

Leach, B. (2009), 'Number of IVF blunders "to rise for fifth consecutive year"', *Telegraph*, 15 June, www.telegraph.co.uk, accessed on 1 July 2009.

Lee, T.H. (2009), 'Is medical tourism gold mine or time bomb?', *Korea Times*, 24 June, www.koreatimes.co.kr, accessed 14 August 2009.

Lee, W.L. (2008), 'Medical care is not a commodity', *Straits Times*, 15 October, A23.

Lloyd, G.E.R. (ed.) (1978), *Hippocratic Writings*, Harmondsworth: Penguin Books.

Margolis, M. (2009), 'Crisis: redrawing the world migration map', *Newsweek*, 23 March, 14–15.

Marshall, A. and M.P. Marshall (1881 [1879]), *The Economics of Industry*, 2nd edn, London: Macmillan.

Mattoo, A. and R. Rathindran (2006), 'How health insurance inhibits trade in health care', *Health Affairs*, **25**(2), 358–68.

McIndoe, A. (2009), '"Transplant tourists" not welcome', *Straits Times*, 22 July 2009, A10.

Medical News Today (2009), 'Biomedical sciences companies expanding in Asia invested more than US$500 million in Singapore', 20 May, www.medicalnewstoday.com, accessed 9 June 2009.

Medical Tourism Association (2009), 'MTA releases first patient surveys on medical tourism', *Medical Tourism Magazine*, No. 10, 34–6.

Milstein, A. (2006), 'American surgical emigration is a treatable symptom', testimony to the United States Senate Special Committee on Aging, 27 June, http://aging.senate.gov/hearing_detail.cfm?id=270728&, accessed on 10 April 2009.

Milstein, A. and M. Smith (2007), 'Will the surgical world become flat?', *Health Affairs*, **26**(1), 137–41.

Ministry of Health (Singapore) (2009a), 'Medical travellers update', 22 January, www.moh.gov.sg, accessed on 29 July 2009.

Ministry of Health (Singapore) (2009b), 'Health facts Singapore: health facilities', www.moh.gov.sg, accessed on 29 July 2009.

Ministry of Health (Singapore) (2009c), 'Further Medisave liberalisation', Press Release, 29 March.

Ministry of Manpower (Singapore) (2008), *Singapore Yearbook of Manpower Statistics 2007.*

Ministry of Trade and Industry (Singapore) (2003), 'Developing Singapore as the healthcare services hub in Asia', *Report of the Healthcare Services Working Group, Sub-Committee on Service Industries of the Economic Review Committee*, http://www.mti.gov.sg, accessed 12 November 2008.

Ministry of Trade and Industry (Singapore) (2008), *Economic Survey of Singapore 2007.*

Mitra, S. (2007), 'Medical tourism: the way to go', Frost and Sullivan Research Paper, www.frost.com, accessed on 30 July 2009.

Mullan, F. (2005), 'The metrics of the physician brain drain', *New England Journal of Medicine*, **353**, 1810–18, http://.content.nejm.org, accessed on 10 June 2009.

Mutchnick, I.S., D.T. Stern and C.A. Moyer (2005), 'Trading health services across borders: GATS, markets and caveats', *Health Affairs*, 25 January, 42–51.

Newman, B.Y. (2006), 'Medical tourism', *Optometry*, **77**, 581.

Olson, M. (1965), *The Logic of Collective Action*, Boston: Harvard University Press.

Oxfam International (2003), 'Robbing the poor to pay the rich? How the United States keeps medicines from the world's poorest', Oxfam Briefing Paper No. 56.

Patients Association (UK) (2009), *Patients . . . not Numbers, People . . . not Statistics*, Harrow: Patients Association.

Pigou, A.C. (1932[1920]), *The Economics of Welfare*, 4th edn, London: Macmillan.

Pollock, A.M. and D. Price (2000), 'Rewriting the regulations: how the World Trade Organization could accelerate privatisation in health-care systems', *The Lancet*, **356**, 1995–2000.

Rai, S. (2008), 'Senior moment', *Forbes Asia*, 15 September, 64–8.

Reisman, D.A. (2007), *Health Care and Public Policy*, Cheltenham, UK and Northampton, MA, USA: Edward Elgar.

Reisman, D.A. (2009), *Social Policy in an Ageing Society: Age and Health in Singapore*, Cheltenham, UK and Northampton, MA, USA: Edward Elgar.

RevaHealth.com (2008), 'The first comprehensive dental tourism survey by RevaHealth.com reveals large savings and high levels of satisfaction', www.revahealth.com, accessed on 9 December 2008.

Rhea, S. (2008), 'Medical migration', *Modern Healthcare*, **38**, 5 May, http://proquest.umi.com.ezlibproxy1, accessed on 10 November 2008.

Ricardo, D. (1951[1817]), *Principles of Political Economy and Taxation*, ed. by P. Sraffa, Cambridge: Cambridge University Press.

Santos, E.M. (2008), 'Taking excellence to heart', *Medical Tourism Magazine*, No. 5, 24–6.

Sarnsamak, P. (2008), 'Medical errors law will compensate victims of malpractice', *The Nation* (Bangkok), 13 August, www.nationmultimedia.com, accessed on 1 July 2009.

Singapore Tourism Board (2008), *Annual Report on Tourism Statistics, 2007*.

Skerritt, D. and T. Huybers (2005), 'The effect of international tourism on economic development: an empirical analysis', *Asia Pacific Journal of Tourism Research*, **10**, 23–43.

Smith, A. (1961[1776]), *The Wealth of Nations*, ed. by E. Cannan, London: Methuen.

Smith, R.D. (2004), 'Foreign direct investment and trade in health services: a review of the literature', *Social Science & Medicine*, **59**, 2313–23.

Smith, R.D. (2006), 'Trade in health services: current challenges and future prospects of globalisation', in A.M. Jones (ed.), *The Elgar Companion to Health Economics*, Cheltenham, UK and Northampton, MA, USA: Edward Elgar, pp. 164–75.

Smith, R.D. and D. Woodward (2003), 'Global public goods for health: use and limitations', in R.D. Smith, R. Beaglehole, D. Woodward and N. Drager (eds), *Global Public Goods for Health: Health Economics and Public Health Perspectives*, Oxford: Oxford University Press, pp. 246–65.

Smith, R.D., R. Chanda and V. Tangcharoensathien (2009), 'Trade in health-related services', *The Lancet*, **373**, 593–601.

Stiglitz, J.E. (2009), 'Trade agreements and health in developing countries', *The Lancet*, **373**, 363–5.

Teh, I. (2007), *Healthcare Tourism in Thailand: Pain Ahead?*, Singapore: Clearstate.

Timmons, K. (2008), 'JCI standards address physician competencies', *Medical Tourism Magazine*, No. 5, 12.

Titmuss, R.M. (1968), *Commitment to Welfare*, London: George Allen & Unwin.

Titmuss, R.M. (1970), *The Gift Relationship*, London: George Allen & Unwin.

Treatment Abroad (2008), 'Medical tourist survey: 2008 report', www.treatmentabroad.net, accessed on 12 January 2009.

United Nations Population Division (2009), *World Population Prospects: The 2008 Revision*, http://data.un.org, accessed on 23 June 2009.

USA Today (2006), 'Asian medical tourism to become multi-billion-dollar industry', 4 October, www.usatoday.com, accessed on 21 August 2009.

Velasco, N.A.O. (2008), 'Healthcare in paradise', *Asianews*, 24–30 October, 13–15.

Warner, D.C. (1998), 'The globalization of medical care', in S. Zarrilli and C. Kinnon (eds), *International Trade in Health Services: A Development Perspective*, UNCTAD-WHO Joint Publication, Geneva: United Nations, pp. 71–8.

Weekly Telegraph (2008), 'Tooth tourism fills the gaps in "flawed" NHS dental care', 17–23 September, 37.

Wolff, J. (2007), 'Passport to cheaper health care?', *Good Housekeeping*, October, www.goodhousekeeping.com, accessed 21 August 2009.

Woodman, J. (2007), *Patients Beyond Borders (Singapore Edition): Everybody's Guide to Affordable, World-Class Medical Tourism*, Chapel Hill, NC: Healthy Travel Media.

World Health Organization (1962 [1946]), *Constitution of the World Health Organization*, in WHO, *Basic Documents*, Geneva: WHO, pp. 1–18.

World Health Organization (2009), *World Health Statistics 2009*, Geneva: WHO.

World Trade Organization (1995), *General Agreement on Trade in Services*, in *WTO: Legal Texts*, Geneva: WTO, pp. 283–317.

World Trade Organization (2001), *Declaration on the TRIPS Agreement and Public Health*, http://www.wto.org, accessed 9 April 2009.

Yeoman, I. (2008), *Tomorrow's Tourist: Scenarios and Trends*, Amsterdam: Elsevier.

Yeoman, I. (2009), 'How many American medical tourists are there?', *International Medical Travel Journal*, www.imtjonline.com/news, accessed on 16 June 2009.

Yoopetch, C. (2006), 'Medical tourism: the case of private hospitals in Thailand', in S.M. Lee, J. Lee and D. Chang (eds), *Strategic Innovation in the E-global Age*, Lincoln: Pan Pacific Business Association, pp. 307–9.

York, D. (2008), 'Medical tourism: the trend toward outsourcing medical procedures to foreign countries', *Journal of Continuing Education in the Health Professions*, **28**, 99–102.

Index